Theory, Text, Context

Theory, Text, Context

Issues in Greek Rhetoric and Oratory

Edited by
Christopher Lyle Johnstone

STATE UNIVERSITY OF NEW YORK PRESS

Production by Ruth Fisher
Marketing by Theresa Abad Swierzowski

Published by
State University of New York Press, Albany

For information, address the State University of New York Press,
State University Plaza, Albany, NY 12246

Library of Congress Cataloging-in-Publication Data
Theory, text, context : issues in Greek rhetoric and oratory / edited
   by Christopher Lyle Johnstone.
      p.   cm. — (SUNY series in speech communication)
   Includes index.
   ISBN 0-7914-3107-X (hardcover : alk. paper). — ISBN 0-7914-3108-8
(pbk. : alk. paper)
   1. Speeches, addresses, etc., Greek—History and criticism—
Theory, etc. 2. Rhetoric, Ancient. 3. Oratory, Ancient.
I. Johnstone, Christopher Lyle, 1947–   . II. Series.
PA3263.T48   1996
808'.0481—dc20   95-51406
                                                            CIP

10 9 8 7 6 5 4 3 2 1

CONTENTS

ACKNOWLEDGMENTS

Needless to say, a cooperative venture such as the present volume owes its existence to the contributions of a number of people. I want here to thank those whose efforts have enabled this project to come to fruition. First, and most obviously, I wish to thank my colleagues who have contributed their work to this volume, both for their scholarship and for their patience during what has been a long publication process. Second, because the contributed essays originated in a lecture series presented at Penn State from 1989–91, I would also like to express my gratitude to those at the university whose support made these lectures possible: the Institute for the Arts and Humanistic Studies, the Associate Dean for Undergraduate Education in the College of the Liberal Arts, and the departments of Classics, English, History, Philosophy and Speech Communication. I especially want to thank Dennis S. Gouran, Head of the Speech Communication Department, for his continued support and encouragement in the completion of this project; and I wish to thank Stephen H. Browne for his help in the early stages of the project and for his encouragement throughout.

For support of my own scholarship in connection with this volume, I wish to thank the Pennsylvania State University and the College of the Liberal Arts for granting me the 1986–87 sabbatical leave during which research was begun for both of my essays that appear here. I would also like to express my appreciation to the Department of Classics at Cambridge University, and specifically to the staff of the Classics Library, for their cooperation and assistance during my residence in Cambridge, and to the American School of Classical Studies in Athens for similar support during my residence in Greece. Finally, I wish to thank my students, both graduate and undergraduate, who have helped me explore the problems and ideas I address later in this volume—most particularly the members of the Penn

State Education Abroad Program's 1991 spring semester in Athens, who assisted me in "acoustical field tests" at numerous speaking sites throughout Greece.

Portions of John Poulakos' essay in this volume appeared previously in his book, *Sophistical Rhetoric in Classical Greece* (1995), and are published here with the permission of the University of South Carolina Press.

Introduction: The Origins of the
Rhetorical in Archiac Greece

Christopher Lyle Johnstone

Continued scholarly interest in the origins, development, and early practice of rhetoric is attested by the recent appearance of books and articles that have these subjects as their focus. During the past five years, a number of studies have examined the emergence of rhetoric in ancient Greece and its theory and practice during the fifth and fourth centuries.[1] Indeed, the study of speech in our own time has been rooted in an appreciation of Greek rhetoric and an application of its precepts. From the pioneering work of Bromley Smith early in the present century, to the later inquiries of Hunt, Parrish, Bitzer, Kennedy, and others, classical rhetoric has been central in theorizing about, teaching, and criticizing pragmatic speech.[2]

---

1. For instance, see Thomas Cole, *The Origins of Rhetoric in Ancient Greece* (Baltimore and London: Johns Hopkins University Press, 1991); Edward Schiappa, *Protagoras and Logos: A Study in Greek Philosophy and Rhetoric* (Columbia: University of South Carolina Press, 1991); Susan C. Jarratt, *Rereading the Sophists: Classical Rhetoric Refigured* (Carbondale: Southern Illinois University Press, 1991); George A. Kennedy, *Aristotle, On Rhetoric: A Theory of Civic Discourse* (New York: Oxford University Press, 1991); Richard Leo Enos, *Greek Rhetoric Before Aristotle* (Prospect Heights, Ill.: Waveland, 1993); John Poulakos, *Sophistical Rhetoric in Classical Greece* (Columbia: University of South Carolina Press, 1995); W. M. A. Grimaldi, S. J., *Aristotle, RHETORIC II: A Commentary* (New York: Fordham University Press, 1988); Barbara Warnick, "Judgment, Probability, and Aristotle's Rhetoric," *The Quarterly Journal of Speech* 75 (August 1989): 299–311; Susan C. Jarratt, "The Role of the Sophists in Histories of Consciousness," *Philosophy and Rhetoric* 23 (1990): 85–95; and the exchange between Edward Schiappa and John Poulakos regarding the Sophists in *Philosophy and Rhetoric* 23 (1990).

2. See, for example, the series of early studies by Bromley Smith in the *Quarterly Journal of Speech (QJS)*, including "The Father of Debate: Protagoras of Abdera," *QJS* 4 (1918): 196–215; "Prodicus of Ceos: The Sire of Synonymy," *QJS* 6 (1920): 51–68; "Corax and Probability," *QJS* 7 (1921): 13–42; and "Gorgias: A

The present volume was undertaken in an effort to contribute to this enterprise by having a number of contemporary scholars examine some of the important issues that persist in the study of Greek rhetoric and oratory. Historical, theoretical, critical, and contextual problems in our understanding of ancient rhetoric are illuminated and addressed in a series of essays that consider the early development and practice of the art of oratory. Out of these essays emerges a clearer portrait of Greek rhetoric as it unfolded during the fifth and fourth centuries B.C.E. and thus of the early study and exercise of suasory speech.

The aim of this introductory discussion, in addition to previewing the essays to follow, is to set the context of these studies by surveying briefly the principal historical and intellectual conditions out of which Greek rhetoric

---

Study of Oratorical Style," *QJS* 7 (1921): 335–59. Other early articles include Everett Lee Hunt, "Plato on Rhetoric and Rhetoricians," *QJS* 6 (1920): 35–56; Paul Shorey, "What Teachers of Speech May Learn from the Theory and Practice of the Greeks," *QJS* 8 (1922): 105–31; Russell H. Sage, "The Rhetorical Theory of Isocrates," *QJS* 8 (1922): 322–37; and William E. Utterback, "Aristotle's Contribution to the Psychology of Argument," *QJS* 11 (1925): 218–25.

For later work in the same vein see, for example, Lester W. Thonssen, "A Functional Interpretation of Aristotle's Rhetoric," *QJS* 16 (1930): 297–310; Lane Cooper, "The Rhetoric of Aristotle," *QJS* 21 (1935): 10–19; James H. McBurney, "The Place of the Enthymeme in Rhetorical Theory," *Speech Monographs* 3 (1936): 49–74; George P. Rice Jr., "Aristotle's *Rhetoric* and Introductory Public Address," *Western Speech* 7 (1943): 2–5; Wayland M. Parrish, "The Tradition of Rhetoric," *QJS* 33 (1947): 464–67; Thomas H. Marsh, "Aristotle Versus Plato on Public Speaking," *Southern Speech Journal* 18 (1953): 163–66; Lawrence J. Flynn, S.J., "Aristotle: Art and Faculty of Rhetoric," *SSJ* 21 (1956): 244–54; Wilbur Samuel Howell, "Classical and European Traditions of Rhetoric and Speech Training," *SSJ* 23 (1957): 73–78; W. Scott Nobles, "The Paradox of Plato's Attitude Toward Rhetoric," *Western Speech* 21 (1957): 206–10; Edwin Black, "Plato's View of Rhetoric," *QJS* 44 (1958): 361–74; Ray Nadeau, "Hermogenes on 'Stock Issues' in Deliberative Speaking," *Speech Monographs* 25 (1958): 59–66; Lloyd F. Bitzer, "Aristotle's Enthymeme Revisited," *QJS* 45 (1959): 399–408; James G. Backes, "Aristotle's Theory of Stasis in Forensic and Deliberative Speech in the *Rhetoric*," *Central States Speech Journal* 12 (1960): 6–8; Paul D. Brandes, "Evidence in Aristotle's *Rhetoric*," *Speech Monographs* 28 (1961): 21–28; and Ralph Pomeroy, "Aristotle and Cicero: Rhetorical Style," *Western Speech* 25 (1961): 25–32.

The publication in 1963 of George Kennedy's *The Art of Persuasion in Greece* (Princeton: Princeton University Press) marks the beginning of a three-decade proliferation of scholarly research in Greek rhetoric to which the authors included in this volume have contributed significantly.

emerged. Much of this ground has been covered elsewhere, so this consideration is more synthetic than original. Nonetheless, since the studies of Greek rhetorical theory and practice included here take as their point of departure the appearance of teachers of argument in Sicily during the early fifth century, it would be useful and appropriate to review current thinking concerning the precursors of the art in which these men provided instruction.

I find compelling the contention of such scholars as Cole and Schiappa that *rhetoric* as a concept and as a systematic way of thinking about speech is an invention of the Classical Period, indeed of the fourth century. Cole argues that rhetoric, viewed as "a speaker's or writer's self-conscious manipulation of his medium with a view to ensuring his message as favorable a reception as possible on the part of the particular audience being addressed," is a "typically fourth-century phenomenon."[3] Schiappa (like Cole) contends that the term *rhêtorikê*, used to designate an intellectual discipline concerned with the art or skill of the *rhêtôr*, was coined by Plato in the course of composing the *Gorgias*.[4] Even so, the use of *rhêtôr* (or an earlier form, *rhêtêr*) to designate a public speaker or pleader occurs prior to the fifth century.[5]

Clearly, the art of rhetoric outlined by Plato in the *Phaedrus*, developed systematically by Aristotle, and practiced self-consciously by Demosthenes, Aeschines, and others, did not appear ex nihilo. Pericles was renowned a century before Aristotle's zenith as a skilled and persuasive orator. Protagoras, Gorgias, and other fifth-century Sophists taught techniques of argument. And what before them? What made argument about practical, political matters—

---

3. Cole, *The Origins of Rhetoric*, pp. ix–x. Cole's thesis, elaborated and argued for throughout his book, incorporates a conception of "ancient rhetoric's two fundamental assumptions—separability of matter from method and the existence of a number of equally adequate methods for transmitting any given piece of subject matter" (p. 19).

4. Schiappa, "The 'Invention' of Rhetoric," in *Protagoras and Logos*, pp. 39–63. This chapter is an elaboration of his earlier essay, "Did Plato Coin *Rhêtorikê?*" *American Journal of Philology* 111 (1990): 460–73. The central proposition in this article is also featured in his "*Rhêtorikê*: What's in a Name? Toward a Revised History of Early Greek Rhetorical Theory," *Quarterly Journal of Speech* 78 (1992): 1–15.

5. *Rhêtêr* is found in the *Iliad* (9.443), a work that includes numerous examples of speakers seeking to influence others' actions through exhortation and the invocation of divine will. Schiappa's search of the *Inscriptiones Graecae* revealed that "the earliest surviving use of *rhêtor* is in the Brea Decree, ca. 445 B.C.E." (*Protagoras and Logos*, p. 41 and p. 59 n. 2).

and subsequently an art of rhetoric—possible? Although a comprehensive answer to this question requires a rather more detailed examination of the history and culture of Archaic Greece than is feasible here, a summary of the most salient factors involved in the appearance of rhetoric during the fourth century emphasizes the following: (1) the oral tradition in Greece and the transition from orality to literacy, (2) the emergence of the *polis*, and (3) the shift from *mythos* to a naturalistic cosmology, with its consequent development of a scientific, rational worldview and a philosophical terminology and syntax.

The rhetorical impulse—that is, the disposition to incite to decision and action through eloquence of expression—was inherent in the language and culture of the Greeks. The numerous speeches in books 2 and 9 of the *Iliad*, the bardic songs of the *Odyssey*, and the lyrical flights of the archaic poets, even the oratorical *epideixis* of the Sophists, the somber verse of the tragedians, the linguistic wit of the comic playwrights: all bespeak an infatuation with the sounds and potencies of human speech that is characteristically Greek.

One important feature of the society that would give birth to rhetoric is that, as Havelock has noted, "in its formative and creative stages, it was wholly nonliterate. . . . [The Archaic Greeks possessed] an astonishingly sophisticated but unwritten language."[6] During the period after the decline and disappearance of the Mycenaean civilization (ca. 1100 B.C.E.) until the advent of the phonetic alphabet in the middle of the eighth century, Greece was a wholly oral culture. Even following the reinvention of writing in the Greek world, communication was largely the product of an oral consciousness for several centuries at least.[7] This consciousness shaped not only the process of

---

6. Eric A. Havelock, "The Linguistic Task of the Presocratics," in Kevin Robb, ed. *Language and Thought in Early Greek Philosophy* (LaSalle, Ill.: Monist Library of Philosophy, 1983), p. 7. See also Walter J. Ong, S.J., *Orality and Literacy: The Technologizing of the Word* (London and New York: Methuen, 1982) and Tony M. Lentz, *Orality and Literacy in Hellenic Greece* (Carbondale: Southern Illinois University Press, 1989).

7. See Havelock, "The Linguistic Task," especially pp. 7–15. See also his discussion of the transition from orality to literacy in *Preface to Plato* (Cambridge, Mass. and London: Belknap Press of Harvard University Press, 1963), particularly ch. 7 ("The Oral Sources of the Hellenic Intelligence") and ch. 8 ("The Homeric State of Mind"). See also Ong, *Orality and Literacy*, especially ch. 1 ("The Orality of Language.")

It should be noted that Havelock is not without his critics, and it seems possible that his central theories about the effects of orality and literacy on consciousness

composition, but also the activities of listening and thinking. When, in the *Encomium of Helen*, Gorgias likened the effect of speech on the soul to the power of drugs over the body, he expressed a cultural truth: "Speech is a powerful lord." Oral eloquence, first in poetry and later in prose, was a conspicuous presence in public life, and those who experienced it were moved by and took pleasure in it. They became sophisticated consumers of speech. The eloquence of the proto-rhetorical age created the communicative habits and tastes that eventually made possible the rhetorical culture of the Classical Period, for it shaped the audience upon which the art could be practiced.

A second formative factor in the antecedents of rhetoric was the reinvention of writing.[8] Though it would be several centuries before literacy would replace orality as a mode of popular consciousness, nonetheless the advent of writing brought about an objectification of speech that eventually made possible an *art* of oral persuasion that could be studied and taught. If we take as essential to rhetoric, following Cole, the conscious manipulation of language with a view to producing desired effects in hearers, then the objectification of speech through writing is a prerequisite.[9] It allows the deliberate manipulation of the medium of expression. A written text takes on a

----

are somewhat overstated. In this connection, see Friedrich Solmsen's review of *Preface to Plato* in the *American Journal of Philology* 87 (1966): 99–105; also John Halverson, "Havelock on Greek Orality and Literacy," *Journal of the History of Ideas* 53 (1992): 148–63. Nonetheless, Havelock has, I think, rightly understood that the transition from orality to literacy was a key factor in the development of Greek thought, and that this transition included the emergence of new ways of using the language that previously had given expression to a mythopoeic worldview.

8. I say "reinvention" because, however limited in function and despite being syllabic rather than phonetic in structure, the Linear A and B scripts of the late Minoan and the Mycenaean periods were forms of recorded speech. Linear B has been deciphered by Michael Ventris and is recognized by most scholars as an early form of Greek. The story of the decipherment can be found in John Chadwick, *The Decipherment of Linear B*, 2nd ed. (Cambridge: Cambridge University Press, 1967). Many of the texts are reproduced in Michael Ventris and John Chadwick, *Documents in Mycenaean Greek*, 2nd ed. (Cambridge: Cambridge University Press, 1973). A historical interpretation of the texts appears in Chadwick's *The Mycenaean World* (Cambridge: Cambridge University Press, 1976).

9. I should note here that my analysis of the precursors to rhetoric is somewhat at odds with Cole's. He contends, contrary to "the unanimous tradition derived from aniquity, that rhetoric . . . [is not] a system that emerged gradually out of attitudes toward speech and poetry well attested in Greece at a much earlier date. It is,

life of its own, and in doing so it makes itself available for study, criticism, and revision. Thus does mere expression become a message, and thus ultimately can one view alternative forms of expression as tactical options in seeking to communicate effectively.

Just as it did not arise out of a cultural vacuum, so was the emergence of an art of rhetoric in the fourth century a consequence of the political developments and activities of the Archaic Period, and perhaps of a still earlier era. When he had Gorgias identify the subject of his expertise as "the speaker's art" *(hê rhêtorikê technê)*, Plato identified as the product of craftsmanship a mode of activity that had been practiced in the Greek world for at least the previous two centuries. Indeed, some scholars find the roots of rhetoric in the Dark Age chiefdoms that followed the Bronze Age (ca. 1100–750 B.C.E.).[10] In any case, constitutional and legal developments in Athens and elsewhere during the seventh and sixth centuries fostered circumstances in which the ability to address audiences convincingly about public issues was prized.

The case of Athens is illustrative. The transition from the local kingships of the Dark Age to the democratic *poleis* of the Classical Era was marked politically by growth in the sphere of public decision making. Greek communities as they emerged from the Dark Ages in the eighth century had the most

---

rather, a typically fourth-century phenomenon" (*The Origins of Rhetoric in Ancient Greece*, p. x). The position I am advancing here is that, though the art as Cole has described it is, indeed, a Classical invention, it necessarily arose out of earlier intellectual, political, and cultural conditions in the absence of which it could not have developed. These conditions provided the milieu in which the theory and *technai* of persuasive speech were born and nourished.

10. In an unpublished paper, classicist Walter Donlan contends that "speaking persuasively was a necessary skill for political leaders at least as early as the ninth century B.C.E., and most likely a good deal earlier." Donlan, whose research has concentrated on the origins of the *polis*, observes that because Dark Age chiefs *(basileis)* could not easily coerce the loyalty of the small farmers who constituted their fighting forces, "the leader-people arrangement worked by persuasion and argument." Moreover, he continues, "the occasions of public discourse were the same in the pre-state chiefdom as in the *polis*. The full assembly of all adult males (*agorê* in Homer) and the smaller council of the leading men *(boulê)* passed on into the city-state." In contrast to Cole, Donlan even suggests that "what one must call a self-conscious art of oratory was well established in the later Dark Age. Nor is there any reason, social or aesthetic, to believe otherwise" (Walter Donlan, "The Dark Age Chiefdoms and the Emergence of Public Argument," presented at the Speech Communication Association convention, New Orleans, 5 November 1988).

simple form of political organization. Local aristocratic lords (the *basileis*) were jealous of their autonomy, acknowledging only reluctantly any form of central control. Loyalty to family, clan, and followers came first. The *basileus* was advised by a "council of elders," a group most likely made up of the heads of the noble families. In Athens, this group was known as the Council of the Areopagos, named for the rocky "Hill of Ares" overlooking the *agora*, where it originally convened.[11]

How long the monarchy lasted in Athens is uncertain. Even the name of the last genuine king remains undecided, although among ancient writers the popular choice was Codrus. All accounts agree, however, that because of changes that occurred before the seventh century, the kingship was no longer what it once was. While the title *basileus* remained attached to an office onto which devolved sacred duties connected with religious observance, the real power passed to the nobility, who substituted their own privileged rule for that of the monarch. It is not clear whether the usurpation was carried out by the whole aristocracy acting in concert or by a single, powerful clan. By whatever means, the reduction of the kingship took place gradually.[12]

It seems clear that some sort of deliberation took place within the Council. It was a decision-making body that ruled on questions of policy and law. The assembly of the Athenian people (the *ekklêsia*) existed more in principle than in fact in earliest times. Consistent with the pattern common in other Indo-European societies, the *dêmos* was asked to voice its formal support in times of danger, but under the monarchy this earliest Assembly was more akin to a rally of roused tribesmen than to a meeting of informed citizens prepared to vote.

Solon came into this situation at the beginning of the sixth century. An aristocrat and merchant, Solon was chosen by the Athenians to serve as mediator and law-giver. As Plutarch and Aristotle describe in some detail, he responded by crafting his constitutional reforms of 594 B.C.E., which created

---

11. The history of the *agora* and the Areopagos during the Archaic period, as revealed in the archaeological and epigraphical record, is presented well in John M. Camp, *The Athenian Agora* (London: Thames and Hudson, 1986), especially ch. 3; and in R. E. Wycherley, *The Stones of Athens* (Princeton: Princeton University Press, 1978).

12. For a more detailed consideration of this period in Athenian history, see Finley Hooper, *Greek Realities: Life and Thought in Ancient Greece* (Detroit: Wayne State University Press, 1967), especially ch. 6; and the Joint Association of Classical Teachers, *The World of Athens* (Cambridge: Cambridge University Press, 1984).

a system of political classes among Athenian citizens based on wealth and which reorganized the political structure such that the powers of the former monarch were distributed among magistrates (the *archons*) elected from among the wealthiest class. Moreover, the folk gathering comprising the earliest *ekklêsia* was replaced by a regularly-constituted body that may have been given some voice in the election of magistrates, and that had principal responsibility for passing judgment on proposed legislation. Participation in this assembly was limited to men with some amount of property, and election to office was open only to those of noble birth.

Although the traditional Council of the Areopagos retained its responsibility for adjudicating religious disputes and for trying cases of murder, Solon instituted a second body, the Council (*Boulê*) of Four Hundred. Composed of members of the four Athenian "tribes" (also created by Solon), the *Boulê* discussed all policy questions and proposed laws, and it decided which matters were to be brought to the *Ekklêsia* for a vote. As such it took over the prerogative that the Areopagos had had during the time of aristocratic domination. Under Solon, then, constitutional arrangements were established that extended the sphere of public participation in the political process. Moreover, this participation took a form that became the dominant mode of political activity during the Classical Period: oratory in a public setting.

The reforms instituted by Solon were preserved during the tyranny of the Peisistratids,[13] and they were augmented at the end of the sixth century by Kleisthenes. Almost nothing is known personally about this man and yet he, if anybody, was the founder of the Athenian democracy. Solon and Peisistratos may have indirectly prepared the way for democracy, but it was the reforms of Kleisthenes between 510 and 507 B.C.E. that actually put the power in the hands of the *dêmos*. He abolished wealth as a criterion of political participation and replaced it with parentage and residence: citizenship and franchise depended on living in the Athenian *polis* as a free-born male of an Athenian father (after Pericles' citizenship law of 451 only men who had full Athenian parentage qualified as citizens). Kleisthenes replaced the four tribes of Solon with ten tribes *(phylai)*, each of which contained a

---

13. The tyrant Peisistratos seized power in the 560s and was ousted twice before establishing himself in 545. Upon his death in 527 B.C.E., he was succeeded by his sons Hippias and Hipparchos. Though he took power unconstitutionally, there is evidence that the reign of Peisistratos was not unduly oppressive. Aristotle specifically states (*Athênaiôn Politeia* 14.3 and 16.2) that for the most part he governed according to the existing constitution, though with his own men in the principal offices and magistracies.

cross-section of the whole population of Attica. He abolished the Council of Four Hundred, drawn from members of the top three classes, and replaced it with a Council of Five Hundred—fifty men drawn from each of the ten tribes.

Though the objective of Kleisthenes' reforms was to retain the freedom of the aristocratic families to compete with each other politically, the eventual effect was to open the political system to all Athenian (male) citizens (though representation of rural and agrarian interests was inhibited by practical constraints). This was the system that was in operation at the beginning of the fifth century, the century that would see the flourishing of Athenian democracy, the rise of Pericles, the emergence of the Athenian empire, and (not coincidentally) the initial systematization of the principles of effective public oratory into a *technê* that could be taught.

The point to be taken from all this is that the political and social conditions that gave rise to public speaking as a mode of political activity preceded the Classical Era by a century, if not more. If public argument flourished during the Classical Era as a result of the requirements of popular government, it had been an important practice during the Archaic Period in which the foundations were laid for such a political system. The art of rhetoric that emerged during the fourth century, like the practice of public persuasion that dominated Athenian life during the fifth, can only be understood against the background of the political developments of the preceding period. In the Archaic *ekklêsia* and *boulê* we find the institutions in which the *logoi* of the Sophists were first crafted and employed as instruments of political influence.

The last point to be considered here concerns the role in the development of rhetoric of the transition from *mythos* to *logos* (i.e., from a mythopoeic theogony to a naturalistic cosmology) as ways of understanding the world. Rhetoric, as both an art of public argument and a theory of civic discourse, was made possible in the fourth century by the development during the Archaic Era of rational rather than mythopoeic uses of language. Essential to the theory and technique of rhetoric as these were conceived by Aristotle (whose treatise on the art is the first systematic account and the fullest expression of its Classical theory) are argument, proof, and probability. These linguistic resources were generated and conditioned by the inquiries and speculations of the first Greek "proto-philosophers" who invented a rational worldview and developed an abstract, analytical syntax and vocabulary.

The shift from myth and poetry to cosmology and analytic prose marks one of the most profound changes in the intellectual history of the human race. Although it provides an account of the origins and workings of the natural world, myth does so in terms of supernatural beings whose personal wills, not bound by any absolute law, can affect natural and human events.[14] The original forms of this account—the epic verse of Homer and Hesiod, itself a reformulation and record of oral tales about the Heroic Age—was a medium of preservation and inspiration, not of definition and justification.[15] The mythopoeic consciousness—which finds perhaps its fullest Greek expression in Hesiod's *Theogony*—sees in the world the work of divine personalities whose caprices, contests, and couplings have created the history in which human beings are swept up. It is a world where events are to a large extent unpredictable, and in which the observed regularities of experience are liable to be upset by the actions of beings who can keep the sun from rising, keep spring from coming, and cause people to take nonhuman forms.

Reasoned discourse, in contrast to the tale-telling and narrative structure of myth, is marked by the use of the impersonal noun and of verbs of attribution rather than of action; moreover, it articulates a worldview in which events are ordered according to an in-dwelling, singular, self-consistent (in sum, rational) principle. The *kosmos* is ordered by a *logos*. The language of

---

14. Guthrie notes that the transition in Greek intellectual life from a mythopoeic to a cosmological view of the world is marked in the first instance by the shift from seeing world events in terms of "a clash of living, personal wills" to understanding them as manifestations of "impersonal forces": "Myth seeks an individual cause [for an event]—the wrath of a god, the jealousy of a goddess— whereas reason is only satisfied when it can explain in terms of a general law." See W. K. C. Guthrie, *Myth and Reason* (London: London School of Economics and Political Science, 1953), p. 5. This point is also made by Bruno Snell in *The Discovery of the Mind in Greek Philosophy and Literature* (New York: Dover, 1982), especially in ch. 9, "From Myth to Logic"

15. Havelock, among others, notes the first feature. "All cultures," he writes, "preserve their identity in their language, not only as it is casually spoken, but particularly as it is preserved, providing a storehouse of cultural information which can be reused. . . . [How] is such information preserved in an oral culture? It can subsist only in the individual memories of persons, and to achieve this the language employed—what I may call the storage language—must meet two basic requirements, both of which are mnemonic. It must be rhythmic, to allow the cadence of the words to assist the task of memorization; and it must tell stories rather than relate facts: it must prefer mythos to logos. For the oral memory accommodates language which describes the acts of persons and the happening of events, but is unfriendly to abstracted and conceptual speech" ("The Linguistic Task," p. 13).

Epic poetry, in addition to being a medium of preservation, is also a means of evocation and inspiration. Its language is rich in simile and other vivid description, and its themes—heroism, pride, betrayal, conquest, loyalty—portray ideals to which we are invited to aspire. It is no accident that the moral education of Greeks throughout the Archaic and Classical Eras consisted in reciting and memorizing Homer.

theory and argument is not that of genealogy and description, but rather of abstraction, definition, and deductive inference. And this kind of language was not waiting ready-made for Plato and Aristotle, or even for the Sophists before them; it had to be invented.[16] The invention of the idiom of theoretical explanation, as of the intellectual architecture of probabilistic argument, was one accomplishment of the presocratic thinkers.

One facet of this achievement—the creation of a naturalistic worldview—is implicit in the earliest writings of the Ionian thinkers, and it becomes explicit in the work of Heraclitus. The chief contribution of Thales to the development of such a view was not his contention that the world is in its origin and nature water, but that it was constituted from a single, material substance. This idea made possible the more abstract and sophisticated theses of Anaximander and later thinkers concerning the operation in nature of a universal, impersonal, divine, and finally rational (that is, regular, measured, consistent, predictable) *archê*: an originating element or causative principle. It is the existence of such an *archê* that gives order to the world, thus making it a *kosmos*. The speculative task of the Ionian cosmologists, as of later philosophers of nature, was to identify and explain the operation of this ordering principle—whether it be "some . . . boundless *[apeiron]* nature from which all the heavens arise and the *kosmoi* within them . . . according to what must needs be,"[17] or the

---

16. Jean-Pierre Vernant, for instance, observes that "the birth of philosophy . . . seems connected with two major transformations of thought. The first is the emergence of positivist thought that excluded all forms of the supernatural and rejects the implicit assimilation, in myth, of physical phenomena with divine agents; the second is the development of abstract thought that strips reality of the power of change that myth ascribed to it, and rejects the ancient image of the union of opposites, in favor of a categorical formulation of the principle of identity" (*Myth and Thought Among the Greeks* [London: Routledge and Kegan Paul, 1983], p. 351). He writes elsewhere that "philosophy had little by little to invent a language, elaborate its concepts, erect a logic, construct its own rationality" (*The Origins of Greek Thought* [Ithaca: Cornell University Press, 1982], p. 132). The same point is made by Havelock in "The Linguistic Task of the Presocratics."

17. This is Kahn's translation of Anaximander's extant fragment. See Charles H. Kahn, *Anaximander and the Origins of Greek Cosmology* (New York: Columbia University Press, 1960), especially ch. 3, "Anaximander's Fragment: The Universe Governed by Law." Kirk and Raven tell us of "some . . . *apeiron* [unbounded] nature, from which come into being all the heavens and the worlds *[kosmoi]* within them . . . 'according to necessity.' " See G. S. Kirk, J. E. Raven, and M. Schofield, *The Presocratic Philosophers*, 2nd ed. (Cambridge: Cambridge University Press, 1983), p. 118.

condensation and rarefaction of *aêr*,[18] or the *logos* in accordance with which "all things come to pass."[19]

The idea of probability owes its inception to such a worldview. In order for a thing to be probable, the world must behave in a relatively regular, consistent way. If natural events are merely manifestations of the actions and preferences of anthropomorphized divinities, and if such beings are capable of acting and preferring in irregular and inconsistent ways (which they clearly were, for the Greeks), then one cannot surmise that the potential occurrence of one thing is more or less probable than that of another on the basis of past regularities. The fact that there is no evidence of probabilistic reasoning prior to the sixth century suggests that this form of thinking and of persuading required a worldview that only came into being during that century.[20]

In addition to a worldview that postulates unity and regularity in events, the development of rhetoric as both a theory and a technique of public argument necessitates certain enrichments in language itself that were also accomplishments of the presocratic thinkers. In Aristotle's account of the *pisteis*

-----

18. This refers, of course, to the view of Anaximenes that *aêr* is the material principle (*archê*) of things. See Kirk, Raven, and Schofield, pp. 144 ff., and W. K. C. Guthrie, *A History of Greek Philosophy*, vol. 1 (Cambridge: Cambridge University Press, 1962), pp. 115 ff.

19. This is Kahn's translation of Heraclitus, fragment DK 1. See Charles H. Kahn, *The Art and Thought of Heraclitus* (Cambridge: Cambridge University Press, 1979), p. 29.

20. Plato attributes the invention of argument from probability to Tisias and Gorgias (*Phaedrus*, 267a). What examples of persuasive oratory we have from before the fifth century are found almost exclusively in Homer, and they exhibit not so much argumentative technique as they do exhortation. Moreover, the ground of such exhortation is not in any sense probabilistic; rather, speakers appeal to divine signs and portents, to omens and the will of Zeus, and to the pursuit of honor and avoidance of disgrace. The Homeric speaker might have employed a sort of primitive rhetoric, but he did not employ reasoning from probabilities. In his account of Homeric speech, Kennedy notes that "in all early invention the most important fact is the absence of what was to be the greatest weapon of Attic oratory, argument from probability. The speakers in Homer are not even conscious that the subject of their talk is limited to probable truth" (*The Art of Persuasion in Greece*, p. 39).

The one exception to this observation, noted by Kennedy (p. 40), is the (probably late-sixth-century) *Hymn to Hermes*, where the day-old Hermes, accused by Apollo of stealing his cattle, argues that it is unlikely that a newborn in swaddling clothes could have done such a deed. Of course, one might ask how likely it is that a day-old infant could articulate such a sophisticated argument.

of rhetoric, in particular, we find evidence of the Presocratics' legacy. The proofs of rhetoric, by means of which the orator seeks to secure the auditor's assent, function as "a sort of demonstration."[21] The form taken by this demonstration, of course, is the enthyeme, a deductive argument. When Aristotle describes argument—the "proof, or apparent proof, provided by the words of the speech itself" (1356a3–4)—he characterizes a use of language in which ideas are structured and expressed in such a way that other ideas follow logically from these.[22] Rhetorical argument, then, embodies principles of deductive logic that inhere in the very nature of language itself—principles that were first identified and employed by Parmenides and Empedocles a century and a half before Aristotle set out to systematize the elements of the rhetorical art.

Analytic thinking and deductive reasoning—both essential aspects of rhetorical demonstration—require a syntax in which mythopoeic verbs of action are replaced by the verb of analysis: to be *(einai)*.[23] In the "was and is and will be"[24] of the rationally ordered *kosmos*, verbs of becoming and dying away, of doing and acting and happening must be replaced by the timeless present of the verb to be: "The angles *are* equal to two right angles. They are not born that way or become or are made so."[25]

---

21. Aristotle, *Rhetoric*, 1355a5–7: "...*pistis apodeixis tis....*" *Apodeixis* has the sense of scientific proof, such as the dialectician employs. Rhetorical proof, of course, is in some sense an *antistrophos* of dialectical demonstration. Subsequent citations from the *Rhetoric* will appear in the text.

22. See, for example, *Rhetoric*, 1156b15–17: "When it is shown that, certain propositions being true, a further and quite distinct proposition must also be true in consequence, whether invariable or usually, this is called syllogism in dialectic, enthymeme in rhetoric."

23. In his account of the emergence of a "new language of philosophy" in the work of the Presocratics, Havelock observes that construction of a "single, comprehensive statement" that would reduce all worldly events to a single whole—"a cosmos, a system, a one and an all"—would require the replacement of "verbs of action and happening which crowded themselves into the oral mythos by a syntax which somehow states a situation or set of situations which were permanent, so that an account could be given of the environment which treated it as a constant. The verb called upon to perform this duty was *einai*, the verb to be." See "The Linguistic Task of the Presocratics," p. 21. Vernant makes the same point in *The Origins of Greek Thought*, especially in ch. 8, "The New Image of the World."

24. The allusion is to Heraclitus, fragment DK 30: "The order *[kosmon]*, the same for all, no god nor man had made, but it was always and is and will be fire everliving, kindled in measures and in measures going out."

25. Havelock, "The Linguistic Task," p. 14.

If the development of deductive reasoning—and thus of enthymematic argument—required the invention of an analytical syntax and a rational worldview, the capacity to theorize about argument required the invention of a philosophical vocabulary. In order to speculate about and describe the structure and functions of thought and speech, one requires a set of conceptual categories—and thus an abstract vocabulary—in terms of which to speculate and describe. In the case of Aristotle's theory of rhetorical argument, what was required was a conceptual system and terminology that would allow him to grasp and articulate the theoretical principles that explain rhetoric. These include such ideas as "first principle" *(archê)*, "probabilities" *(eikota)*, and "the universal" *(to katholou)*. The development of such an abstract vocabulary, and so of the concepts they express, was another contribution of the presocratic thinkers.[26]

The fashioning of a conceptual terminology—such as is reflected in Aristotle's discussion of the Enthymeme, with its emphasis on "the particular" *(to kata meros)*, "the probable," and "the universal"—is the result of two modifications to the language made by the earliest Greek thinkers: the employment of the neuter article *to* in connection with certain nouns and the metaphorical use of these and other nouns to effect a "stretching" of terminology that made possible their use in expressing abstract concepts.

In myth, the things of the world around us—sun, moon, earth, sea, sky, wind—are personified as masculine or feminine beings who hold sway over certain important spheres of human experience and activity: hence, *ho hêlios* (sun, masculine), *hê selênê* (moon, feminine), *hê gaia* (earth, feminine), etc. In moving from masculine/feminine to the neuter, Greek was augmented in its capacity for expressing the abstract concepts upon which philosophy draws in its effort to provide a rational account of the world, and upon which

---

26. "From the standpoint of a sophisticated philosophical language," Havelock writes ("The Linguistic Task," p. 14), "such as was available to Aristotle, what was lacking [for the Presocratics] was a set of commonplace but abstract terms which by their interrelations could describe the physical world conceptually; terms such as space, void, matter, body, element, motion, immobility, change, permanence, substratum, quantity, quality, dimension, unit, and the like. . . . The history of early philosophy is usually written under the assumption that this kind of vocabulary was already available to the first Greek thinkers. The evidence of their own language is that it was not. They had to initiate the process of inventing it."

Aristotle drew in his effort to conceive and articulate the idea of rhetorical argument or proof.[27]

The second pertinent contribution of the Presocractics to the development of a speculative terminology lies in their metaphorical expansion of the language of myth. In their effort to grasp that "all things are one" and to find the "hidden attunement" in the cosmos,[28] these earliest explorers of the rational universe had no adequate terminology through which to articulate their emerging apprehensions of the cosmic order. They were inheritors, however, of the epic vocabulary of myth, and this they employed in a novel fashion by "stretching" (as Havelock puts it) the meanings of terms taken from what Aristotle calls "the ancient tongue" (*Rhetoric*, 1357b10) so they could be used to express new conceptions.[29] The presocratic task of stretching the language is performed by using figuratively such mythopoeic terms as *genesis*, *logos*, *kosmos*, and *archê* to give expression to radically new ways of

---

27. As Kahn points out (*Anaximander and the Origins of Greek Cosmology*, p. 193), "in the historical experience of Greece, Nature became permeable to human intelligence only when the inscrutable personalities of mythic religion were replaced by well-defined and regular powers. The linguistic stamp of the new mentality is a preference for neuter forms, in place of the 'animate' masculines and feminines which are the stuff of myth. The Olympians have given way before *to apeiron* [the unbounded], *to chreon* [necessity], *to periechon* [the environment], *to thermon* [heat], *ta enantia* [opposites]. The strife of elemental forces is henceforth no unpredictable quarrel between capricious agents, but an orderly scheme in which defeat must follow aggression as inevitably as the night [follows] the day."

28. Heraclitus, fragments DK 50 and 54.

29. One example of such "linguistic experimentation" offered by Havelock involves the word *kosmos*: "It was doubtfully put forth by the Milesians, but his [that is, in Heraclitus, fragment DK 30] is the first fully attested entry of the term into philosophical language. It has been borrowed from the epic vocabulary, in particular from previous application to the orderly array of an army controlled by its 'orderer' (*kosmêtôr*); but it is now 'stretched,' so to speak, just as the neuter of the numeral *one* is being stretched, to cover a whole world or universe or physical system, and to identify it as such" ("The Linguistic Task," p. 24). Kahn (in *Anaximander*, p. 193) makes the same point when he observes that "all philosophic terms have necessarily begun in this way, from a simpler, concrete usage with a human reference point. For example, the concept of a 'cause,' *aitios*, is clearly a development from the idea of the 'guilty one, he who is to blame,' *aitios*. Language is older than science, and the new wine must be served in whatever bottles are on hand."

perceiving the causes of events and the relations between them. In this sense, much of theoretical language even now is metaphorical, and we understand that language and its implications fully only when we see in it its archaic significance—only, for instance, insofar as we read into the term *generate* the wholly organic process of procreation and birth. The linguistic accomplishment of the Presocratics was to give a metaphorical dimension to terminology that had been in use orally in service of myth, and to have employed this terminology to provide for things an explanation that was capable of rational examination.

Aristotle is the beneficiary of this linguistic accomplishment. It is precisely the existence of such terms as *logos* (as rational principle and as reasoned discourse or argument), *eikos* (as probability, from *eoika*, to be like, to seem likely), and *katholou* (as universal, from *kath' holou*, on the whole, in general) that makes possible his conceptualization of rhetorical argument as demonstration from probable premises. Had such terminology not existed, Aristotle himself would have had to invent it before this construction of "rhetorical proof" could have been conceived.

The foregoing survey of Archaic antecendents to the fourth-century emergence of rhetoric as *technê* and *praxis* illuminates some of the cultural, political, and intellectual conditions that made this emergence possible. Classical rhetoric may have been an invention of the fourth century, but it was invented using tools and materials that had been crafted during the preceding two hundred and fifty years. The rhetoric of Isocrates and Aristotle, of Lysias and Demosthenes was a product, it is true, of a distinctively Classical consciousness, but this consciousness itself was a product of ways of thinking, of using language, and of doing politics that emerged during the Archaic Era. Only with this in mind can we understand and appreciate fully the essays that follow.

These essays survey the full range of Classical Greek rhetoric, from its origins with Corax and Tisias at Syracuse in the early fifth century, through the zenith of the Older Sophists and the oratory of Periclean Athens later in the same century, to the fourth-century apogee of Classical theory and practice in Aristotle and Demosthenes. Moreover, the discussions of Greek oratory during this period consider both the theory and practice of the art and the physical circumstances in which speech took place. The late Father William Grimaldi, in one of his last writings, traces a progression in thought and methodology from the earliest teachers of rhetoric to Aristotle's sophisticated analysis of the art. He seeks to identify the sources in sophistic thought and Eleatic philosophy of the rhetorical precepts advanced by Plato, Isocrates, and Aristotle. His accomplishment has been to provide a comprehensive, detailed account of the evolution of these precepts from their roots. John Poulakos augments this effort in his examination of Aristotle's account of and response to the Sophists. He begins by noting that those wishing to study the ideas and rhetorical practices of the Sophists generally turn to Plato for insight, ignoring Aristotle's account owing to the belief that he mainly reflected the views of his teacher. As Poulakos demonstrates, however, Aristotle's report of the Sophists both resembles and deviates from Plato's perception, and the former both preserves and corrects their rhetorical precepts. In correcting the Sophists' reasoning, Aristotle follows Plato, but in attempting to extend the rhetorical tradition they initiated, he makes his own path. Edward Schiappa also considers sophistic practice as it is revealed in Gorgias' *Encomium of Helen*. His analysis of this speech proceeds in the awareness that certain intellectual disciplines had, in the fifth century, not yet been formalized either in theory or in practice. This approach "problematizes" some of the conclusions drawn from more conventional readings, and he advances novel answers to three key questions: What is the speech's purpose? What are its contributions to fifth century discursive practices? And what are its contributions to fifth century theory? Pursuing these questions, Schiappa concludes that the *Helen* represents an earnest (and early) effort to illuminate the workings of *logos*, passion, and the mind.

The next three papers concentrate more extensively on certain pragmatic features of Classical oratory, though not to the exclusion of theoretical and historical interests. Michael Leff takes as his point of departure a distinction between Classical rhetoric, which emphasizes production and action, and contemporary rhetoric with its hermeneutic functions of interpretation and understanding. The central question he considers is whether the former, embodying as it does an "ideology of human agency," remains useful for hermeneutic inquiry. Through an examination of Thucydides' account of the Mytilene debate in Athens of 428 B.C.E., Leff argues that human agency is necessarily constrained by historical circumstances and that pragmatic discourse can be studied to explain the interaction between the ideology of agency and the demands of history. My study of Greek oratorical settings opens with the observation that one cannot understand nor appreciate fully the meanings of oratorical texts and events except by taking into account the physical settings in which texts were performed. Physical context can affect the style, delivery, and effectiveness of public speech and even our historical understanding of how rhetoric functioned in Greek public life. A survey of types of oratorical settings is followed by a detailed consideration of the acoustical deficiencies of the Pnyx (the meeting place of the Athenian civic assembly). The limitations of this site rendered public speaking problematic as a direct means of affecting judgment, and so we must re-examine our understanding of how oratory functioned in the Athenian deliberative arena. Donovan Ochs' analysis of Demosthenes' most famous speech, applying Kenneth Burke's conception of form as the creation and satisfaction of appetite, proposes that the efficacy of the speech can be productively understood in terms of an analogy with the athletic contest known as the *pankration*. He argues that the speech offered the auditor an opportunity to satisfy desires for vindication, aesthetic superiority, and the symbolic death of an opponent. After reviewing the current state of theory concerning *apologia* as a genre of discourse, Ochs accounts for the success of Demosthenes' speech of self-defense in terms of the *pankration*, an Olympic event in which two opponents employed techniques of both boxing and wrestling in what could be a battle to the death. Demosthenes' artistic domination of Aeschines and his verbal fisticuffs help to account for his rhetorical success.

The last two papers included here concentrate on Aristotle's theory of rhetoric. William Fortenbaugh, extending work he has done elsewhere, considers Aristotle's discussion of persuasion through character in two passages in the *Rhetoric*. Contending that Cicero has blurred Aristotle's distinction between persuasion through character and emotional appeal, Fortenbaugh finds that *êthos* provides grounds on which the audience can trust the orator rather than creating favor for the orator and his client, and he sees Aristotle distinguishing between judicial and deliberative applications of *êthos* as a means of persuasion. In his "reworking" of Aristotle's *Rhetoric*, George Kennedy reflects on his recent retranslation of the work and explores several related issues that arose in the course of the task. His approach here concentrates on Aristotle's use of metaphor in explaining the foundations and dynamics of rhetoric, and he considers particularly such images as sight, place, and gender in Aristotle's account of the art. Kennedy concludes by discussing the nature and functions of language itself as these pertain to understanding the *Rhetoric*, and by inviting the reader to continue the task he has undertaken.

One objective of seeking some balance in these essays between theory and practice, between origins and culminations, between text and context, between the traditional and the unconventional, has been to provide as comprehensive a consideration of Classical Greek rhetoric as is possible in a relatively brief volume. I will leave it to the reader to determine the extent to which this aim has been met.

One

How Do We Get from Corax-Tisias to Plato-Aristotle
in Greek Rhetorical Theory?

William M. A. Grimaldi, S.J.

T he problem presented here, I believe, is not something totally strange to the reader, but to my knowledge there has not been any presentation that has come to grips with it as such. My inclination now is to think that the resolution is more solidly grounded among those whose influence I acknowledge in my *Studies in the Philosophy of Aristotle's Rhetoric*: "when we turn to the men who are considered to be the exponents of practical rhetoric, the Sophists, we find sufficient evidence to challenge the view that their interest was confined to the superficial tricks of language expression in order to achieve one's practical aims."[1] I went on to illustrate this by citing the interest of these men in literary criticism, in correctness of diction and of language construction, and in the semantics of language, and by further stating: "very common techniques, to cite but two, from the teaching of the Sophists were probability argumentation and the use of antithesis [which] in the final analysis are logical methods to open up a question or a problem to all of its implications since both are in fact forms of critical analysis."[2]

---

1. W. M. A. Grimaldi, *Studies in the Philosophy of Aristotle's Rhetoric* (Wiesbaden: F. Steiner, 1972), p. 8.

2. Ibid., pp. 6–7. My understanding of the work of the Sophists in rhetoric is different from that of George Kennedy in "The Earliest Rhetorical Handbooks," *American Journal of Philology* 80 (1959): 169–78. What I wish to emphasize is the work of the Sophists, rhetoricians and philosophers both, as a bridge to the forms of rhetorical presentation that we find in a well-developed form in Aristotle, Plato, and Isocrates; cf. R. Bolgar, "The Training of Elites in Greek Education," in *Governing Elites*, ed. R. Wilkinson (Oxford: Oxford University Press, 1969), p. 38. I would like to show that the actual thinking and teaching of the Sophists in a

And so I would like to engage in what Montaigne called an "essay," namely, a tentative discussion, or a trial of ideas with a tentative conclusion—a conclusion that may turn out to be not so tentative.

What has puzzled me is the fact that there was obviously a progression in thought and methodology between the earliest teachers of rhetoric and the sophisticated analysis of an Aristotle. But there is no account or mention of it. As Aristotle remarks:

> In the case of all discoveries we have on the one hand material taken over from others which, when it has been worked upon first, has subsequently advanced by degrees at the hands of those who took it over, or else the discoveries are original. These latter usually make a contribution, small at first, but far more useful than what is later developed from them. For, as it is said, the beginning of anything is perhaps the greatest contribution, and so it is the most difficult (to discover). For as the beginning is the most powerful in its potential, so it is the smallest in size, and so most difficult to find. This, indeed, has happened with rhetorical discourse, and to all extents and purposes with all the other arts. Those who discovered the beginnings of rhetoric have assuredly advanced it to some extent. But the distinguished teachers of today receiving the art from a long line of predecessors, who in turn, as it were, gradually moved the art forward, have brought it to its present perfection.[3]

What can we reasonably point to in the fifth century as the source/sources that led to the rhetorical studies of the fourth? The evidence we have is both contemporary (and often biased, e.g., Plato) and later (to the second half of the second century C.E. or even later). The later testimony claims to cite fifth- and fourth-century B.C.E. sources or attests to an accepted tradition. In general I accept all of the evidence, not necessarily as true, but as manifesting a consistency of opinion on the development. Indeed, we must recognize that the formal beginnings of the art in the fifth century were puzzling even to the Greeks of the fourth. For example, Aristotle (*Rhet.* 02a) speaks

---

variety of disciplines formed a body of knowledge that was the foundation for the perceptive analysis of these three men. Kennedy would confine the Sophists' teaching, such as it was, to their handbooks or specimen speeches, a view more fully amplified in M. Ostwald, *From Popular Sovereignty to Sovereignty of Law* (Berkeley: University of California Press, 1986), pp. 236–47, 258–61.

3. *De Sophisticis Elenchis* 183b17–31.

of a *technê* of Corax that was concerned with probability. Plato (*Phaedrus*, 272d ff.), speaking of probability argumentation, mentions Tisias, but wonders (273c) whether Tisias or someone else discovered the argument.[4]

Corax and Tisias, generally accepted by the Greeks as the founders of rhetoric, are faced with the challenge of other claimants put forward by that same tradition. Aristotle in the *Sophist*[5] calls Empedocles the "discoverer of rhetoric." Quintilian (*Instit. Orat.* 3.1.8) more or less repeats this, as does Sextus Empiricus[6] (c. 175–200 C.E.) and the scholiast to Iamblichus' *Life of Pythagoras*.[7]

In the ordinary tradition Corax and Tisias are accepted as the founding fathers of rhetoric.[8] The typical account is found in Cicero, *Brutus* 12.46–48. As his authority Cicero cites Aristotle. Aristotle at *Sophisticis Elenchis* 183b31 ff., however, raises a doubt about this in giving his account. He calls attention to the fact that Tisias came after the first men engaged in rhetorical study, and was followed in his turn by Thrasymachus and Theodorus. When we compare this statement with Quintilian (3.18), some further doubt arises as to the truth of the traditional account. Quintilian speaks of Corax and Tisias as *scriptores antiquissimi*, which may well mean that they were the earliest authors of rhetorical *technai*. For example, Cicero (*De Inv.* 2.2.6), citing Aristotle as his source, writes: "Ac veteres scriptores artis usque a principe illo atque inventore Tisias repetitos unum in locum conduxit Aristoteles et nominatim cuiusque praecepta . . . diligenter exposuit."[9] These three observations throw some further dust on the real discoverers of rhetoric, for Aristotle states that work on rhetoric was in progress prior to Tisias. Quintilian implies that Corax and

----

4. See also Scholiast in Isocrates, *Against the Sophists* 19.

5. Frg. 65 cited by D. Laertius 7.57.

6. *Against the Schoolmasters* 7.6.

7. L. Radermacher, *Artium Scriptores* (Vienna: In Kommission, 1951), A. V. 5.

8. There were certainly good orators and good oratory prior to the early half of the fifth century, as can be seen in the epics of Homer. But to the best of our knowledge, just as there were no antecedents in other countries for the presence of the discipline of rhetoric as we find it in Greece, so there are no clearly known forerunners to the formal study of the discipline in Greece apart from Corax and Tisias. Any reading in the history of early rhetoric in Greece as to whether the first efforts were in dicanic exclusively or in dicanic and deliberative (e.g., Wilcox, Hinks, Kennedy, etc.) will find probable arguments for both: for dicanic, Strepsiades in Aristophanes, *Clouds*; for deliberative, Plato, *Phaedrus* 261b. See also Isocrates, *Against the Sophists* 19.

9. The reference is to Aristotele's lost *Synagôgê Technon*.

Tisias were the earliest in the tradition to give some structure to this work in their *technai*. Cicero seems to confirm this despite his "usque a principe illo atque inventore, Tisias." Such a remark could simply be a bow on Cicero's part to the traditional account as he knew it. Does any of the above dismiss the traditional account? No. But it does make us ask ourselves—or perhaps me ask myself—how valid is the account that fits in so nicely with the overthrow of tyranny and the introduction of democracy in Sicily, a democracy aided and abetted by the discovery of Corax and Tisias?

If we accept this tradition and move forward, we find that as the interest in rhetoric continued in fifth-century Athens several men enter the lists, according to later tradition. Gorgias is introduced by Quintilian as a disciple of Empedocles and as one of the earliest, along with Corax and Tisias, to compose a rhetorical *techné* on the rules of the art.[10] The scholiast to Isocrates' *Against the Sophists* 19 states the same. Cicero[11] mentions Protagoras, Gorgias, and Antiphon, while Quintilian[12] speaks of Thrasymachus of Chalcedon, Prodicus, Protagoras, Hippias of Elis, Alcidamas, and Antiphon. Cicero[13] calls Gorgias, Thrasymachus, Protagoras, Prodicus and Hippias *magistri dicendi*, and Plato[14] effectively says the same for Gorgias, Prodicus, and Hippias. All of the above are Sophists, whether their main interest was rhetoric or philosophy. In what follows I employ both groups.[15] For I am convinced that, despite the inadequacy of the evidence, what we do know of their teaching would (and some say did) influence the culture, the thinking on specific problems, in fact, the general education of the fifth century. In so doing it was propaideutic for the informed and perceptive work in rhetoric of Plato, Isocrates, and Aristotle.

This, then, is the story as we know it of the initial discovery and development of rhetoric. We know of no antecedent to it among the literate peoples of the ancient world. This is not to say (cf. n. 8) that it is unlikely that oratory, as we ordinarily think of it, was not in use among people prior to the fifth century—i.e., the ability to speak effectively and persuasively with attention to the feelings and attitudes of the auditors (see the introduction to the present volume). Antecedent literary remains inside and outside of Greece

---

10. Quintilian, *Institutio oratoria* 3.1.

11. *Brutus* 12.46–48.

12. *Instit. oratoria* 3.8–13.

13. *Brutus* 8.30.

14. *Apology* 19e.

15. See E. L. Harrison, "Was Gorgias a Sophist?" *Phoenix* 18 (1964): 183–92.

testify to this. But what fifth-century Greece introduced was an entirely new discipline: the formal study of what it was that made such speaking and writing successful—a τέχνη λόγων. It became a discipline that enjoyed from the fifth century B.C.E. to the seventeenth century of the present era a powerful cultural influence. It is still quite active and will be as long as we use language to communicate.

Among the people who fostered this study in the fifth and fourth centuries were the Sophists. Let us take a general view of the Sophists and what we know of their work. They represent an intellectual movement[16] that raised problems in critical areas: reality versus appearance (metaphysics); logic; epistemology (theory of knowledge); the nature of man (moral philosophy) and of society (sociology); the existence of gods (theology); political philosophy; law; the relations of language, thought, and reality (rhetoric); the nature of education; and finally literature, of which Kerferd (*The Sophistic Movement*, p. 78) remarks: "the theory of literature and rhetorical art was largely the creation of the Sophistic period." Much of this very likely resulted from the fact that the pre-Socratic philosophers were still active when the Sophists appeared.[17]

The world of the fifth-century Athens into which these Sophists came from various areas of Greece certainly contributed to their achievements. Without glamorizing it, Athens decidedly was not a cultural desert occupied by anthropoids.[18] Rather, confirmed in their sense of superiority by their successes in the Persian Wars, the Athenians entered the fifth century with confidence and enthusiasm. It affected their thinking and acting and readied

---

16. A reviewer in the *Times Literary Supplement* of Romilly's *Les grandes sophistes dans l'Athenes de Pericles* (Paris: Fallois 1988) describes what he calls Plato's view of them: "a group of harmful, pseudo-intellectuals." This is a rather strange judgment in light of the statement just made, which represents an accepted judgment of the problems they raised. It is fitting here to point to the opening words of Gorgias' *Helen*: "the proper adornment of speech is truth" (κοσμὸς . . . λόγῳ δὲ αλήθεια). We know of twenty-six Sophists by name from between 480–384 B.C.E., a number of whom are prominently cited in the history of Greek thought; cf. G. B. Kerferd, *The Sophistic Movement* (Cambridge: Cambridge University Press, 1981), ch. 5.

17. Xenophanes, Parmenides, Anaxagoras, Empedocles, Zeno, Melissus, Democritus, Leucippus, Diogenes of Apollonia.

18. As we shall shortly see. Recently J. Ober commented on this in *Mass and Elite in Democratic Athens: Rhetoric, Ideology, and Power of the People* (Princeton: Princeton University Press, 1989), p. 157. Also see Thucydides 3.38.2–9: Cleon speaking of Athenian interest in speeches *on various problems*.

them for making and accepting change. On the ostensible evidence, their society was mostly an oral culture with strong evidence of literacy: it possessed educators—certainly with the advent of the Sophists, and most likely before, as far back as the sixth century if not earlier.[19] Knowing what we know of the Sophists, they would be at home in Athenian society of the fifth century. In support of this, I find it of interest to note that in my readings I have yet to find mention of the Sophists in Sparta, the major city-state after Athens at this time.

Athens in the fifth century experienced significant changes[20] in the intellectual-cultural, political, social, and religious life of the people. In the first area we have the choral, lyric, and elegiac poetry of Corinna, Pindar, Bacchylides, Theognis, Timocreon, and others, some of whom were working very early in the century (e.g., from 490). There surely is no need to speak of the very active work in Greek tragedy and comedy, such as that of Aeschylus, Sophocles, Euripides, and Aristophanes (450–385). All of this work, particularly that in lyric and tragedy, called not merely for skilled, trained, and sophisticated poets, but also for an understanding and discriminating general audience to appreciate and enjoy this work. A knowledgeable audience is certainly necessary to savor the kind of literary parody we meet in Aristophanes. We must add to this evidence the extensive activity in philosophy under the Presocratics from the beginning of and throughout the fifth century: the Eleatic school of Parmenides,[21] Zeno, Melissus, Anaxagoras, the Ionian school, Leucippus, Democritus, and the Atomists.

---

19. For example, the historian Hellanicus (500–415 B.C.E.) of Mytilene is cited as the author under twenty-one listed book titles. A contemporary was Hecataeus of Miletus, historian, genealogist, and geographer as well as the author of a *Periegesis*, a journey around the world in two parts: Europe, Asia. Myths and fables were composed by prose writers and poets. As Socrates, referring to the jurors in his trial, says in his defense against the charges brought by Meletus: "do you so despise these men and think that they are so unacquainted with *written books* that they do not know that the books of Anaxagoras of Clazomene are filled with such statements?" (Plato, *Apol.* 26d–e). Furthermore, the actual practice of orators would confirm this: they cite older poets and historical events and readily assume that he auditors know what they are talking about. On education, see Bolgar, "The Training of Elites," pp. 25, 29.

20. W. K. C. Guthrie, *The Sophists* (Cambridge: Cambridge University Press, 1971), pp. 25 ff.

21. Cf. Plato, *Parmenides* 127a–c: the philosopher came to Athens early and met Socrates.

In the political sphere we have the constitutional reform of Kleisthenes at the end of the sixth century, a truly amazing achievement that called for the participation of the common people as well as the elite.[22] It was to be followed by constitutional reforms under Pericles. All of these were working toward an equalization of the citizens. This opened up the whole question of political rights and obligations[23] and extended them to a larger body of citizens. The consequence of this was to give more citizens a share in the political, civil, and financial responsibility of government administration. This called for education, and the ones who stepped in were the Sophists with their firm idea of man's ἀρετή (i.e., the excellence proper to the human being) as "skill in political matters": ἡ πολιτικη ἀρετή.[24]

To anyone aware of the architectural, sculptural, and ceramic achievements of the Athenians in the Golden Age of Greece, there can be really no question that the Sophists came into a mature, artistically gifted society in the fifth century. Athens was a cultural center like Vienna in the eighteenth and nineteenth centuries, Paris in the late nineteenth century, and New York in the early part of the twentieth century. To be part of such a society for the most part and for many people meant to be directly or indirectly affected by its interests and activities.

Historical writing (see n. 19) included chronicles of local city-states and accounts of circumnavigations of the known world, and work in history-

---

22. This is the manifest purpose of removing a number of judicial powers from the Areopagus and moving them to the Heliaea, the court of the people. This court was then broken down into individual courts called *dikastêria*. The purpose was to make the administration of justice more open and accessible to the people. This action was complemented by an increase in pay for jurymen—mostly commoners. Together with these actions, thirty circuit judges were established to assure that justice was open to all. Finally, there was a change in the law of citizenship limiting it to those whose parents were both Athenians.

23. See *Old Oligarch* 3.1–5 for the activities of both the Boule and Ecclesia in Athens.

24. S. Wilcox, "The Scope of Early Rhetorical Education," *Harvard Studies in Classical Philology* 53 (1942): 133. See the *Meno* 91a–b, and the *Sophist* 233d. This concern with the State has commonly been understood as a carry-over from Corax and Tisias at Syracuse. Could it not rather be seen as occasioned by the constitutional changes inaugurated in Athens under Kleisthenes? Further, if we say that the high fees of the Sophists kept the non-elite from an education, we must still ask where did these common people acquire it? For the writers of tragedy, comedy, history, and fable certainly assume, at a very minimum, a relatively educated audience.

geography climaxed in the writings two very well known historians: Herodotus with his panoramic view of Greece and the Near East, and Thucydides with his work on the disastrous struggle within Greece, the Peloponnesian War. The maturity of perspective of both writers conveys some idea of the character of Athenian thought.

This kind of thinking was further broadened by the continuing Greek colonization to the East (Ionia) and the West (Sicily, Italy).[25] Such an enlarged view would be encouraged and nourished by the appearance of written books and treatises[26] and their dissemination.[27]

Thus it was that the Sophists appeared in the fifth century as the new educators of Greece. "Sophist," of course, has been a much misunderstood and maligned name from the time of Plato[28] to the time of Clement of Alexandria and beyond. Clement spoke, and probably rightly, of the Sophists he

---

25. While Athens, to our knowledge, did not take an active part in this colonial effort of the eighth to the sixth centuries, her role as head of the Delian League enabled her to trade at will in either area. Apart from the extensive trading, this brought her into contact with peoples from other Greek city-states and in particular with the new Ionian and Eleatic philosophy, which became influential in fifth-century Athens.

26. In rhetoric the lectures are well attested, e.g., *Phaedrus* 261b, 266d, 271c; Thrasymachus and his (?) treatise on the emotions, *Eleoi*; Aristotle, *Rhetoric* 04a14–15, *Soph. Elenchis* 184a8–184b1; Isocrates, *Against the Sophists* 19; Aristotle, *Rhetoric* 54a12, 56a11, 00a4, 14b17.

27. Plato, *Apol.* 26d–e. G. Ryle, "Dialectic in the Academy," in *New Essays on Plato and Aristotle*, ed. R. Bambrough (London: Routledge and Kegan Paul, 1965), p. 39: "Between the time of Protagoras and that of Aristotle in his early teaching years, there had appeared a considerable number of *Arts of Rhetoric*."

28. Plato comments frequently on the Sophists, both directly and indirectly. In the former category see his *Sophist* 268c, or dialogues such as the *Protagoras, Gorgias,* and *Euthydemus*. Plato's major difficulty with them was that with his philosophic commitment there was one, absolute truth, *epistêmê*. He could not accept probable truth, to which the major effort of Sophists was directed. Probable truth is a very real fact of life and the source of most of people's decisions. To Plato probable truth was merely apparent truth and so was open to the charge of misrepresenting the real. Plato, however, does recognize a rhetoric that is genuine and authentic, e.g., *Phaedr.* 259e ff. He does not reject rhetoric as such, e.g., *Gorg.* 504c–e; *Politicus* 303e–304a, 304d–e; *Cratylus* 385b–c. Plato certainly does not hate rhetoric. B. Vickers, in his *In Defense of Rhetoric* (Oxford: Clarendon Press, 1988), p. 88, is clearly incorrect in saying so. Nor do I agree with Ober's view of the hostile attitude of the Athenians towards the orators (*Mass and Elite*, pp. 174 ff.), which is often contrary to his own statements and is manifestly so to that of Creon (*Thucyd.* 3.38.2–9). Nor does it follow that a distrust of orators (unless it is universal) means a distrust of rhetoric. See also *Gorgias* 517a, where Plato speaks of "the true rhetoric."

knew in the second century C.E. as "old shoes worn out except for the tongue." Here I consider those Sophists who engaged in philosophy and other disciplines as well as those who devoted themselves mostly to rhetoric. My argument is that all of them, as the educators of the fifth century, made a significant contribution to the study of rhetoric as we find it in the advanced critical work of Aristotle, Plato, and Isocrates.[29] Indeed, I find it of interest that both those acknowledged as philosophers and those known as rhetoricians were contributing (as I believe both should) to the development of rhetoric, particularly since shortly later (in the fourth century) there was to be a contentious split between rhetoric and philosophy that continued in Western thought until the eighteenth century.

The Sophists were recognized as the educators of Greece by their contemporaries (e.g., Plato's fear, Aristophanes' criticisms, Isocrates' comments) and by later scholarship. The word σοφιστής means, among other possibilities, professional educator or teacher. As a "teacher of rhetoric" it is so used by Plato, for example, in *Lysis* 204a, *Meno* 91a–d (and cf. 90a–95e), and *Protagoras* 341d.[30] Traveling about as teachers of traditional and also of new disciplines such as rhetoric, a goodly number came to Athens where they exercised an extensive influence: Anaxagoras with Pericles; and Protagoras drew up the laws for the Athenian colony at Thurii, where Hippodamus was the city designer, as he was of the Peiraeus in Athens.[31]

What were their teaching methods? We start, as always, with the fact that sophistic writings of any length are lost—with a few exceptions in the field of rhetoric: Gorgias, Antiphon, Thrasymachus. What we have is an abundance of fragments and revealing comments on sophistic rhetoric in Aristophanes, Isocrates, Plato, and Aristotle. For example, there are four

---

29. See A. Greene, *Moira* (Cambridge: Harvard University Press, 1944), pp. 251 ff., writing on Anonymous Iamblichus to the effect that the teachings, theories, and doctrines of specialists such as Protagoras, Socrates, Democritus, Prodicus, Critias, Antisthenes, Thucydides, Hippias, and Antiphon permeate their culture and become part of the possession of ordinary minds.

30. See O. Navarre, *Essai sur la rhetorique grecque avant Aristotle* (Paris: Hachette et cie, 1900), p. 24. He speaks of them as the first teachers of language and its allied disciplines in Athens. See also B. Vickers, *In Defense*, p. 149. R. Bolgar ("The Training of Elites," p. 29) says of education in Greece that the evidence, admittedly meager, suggests that systematic instruction for the young developed in the seventh century among the nobility and new citizen societies. On the popularity of the Sophists, cf. Plato, *Apol.* 20a–b and *Meno* 91a–92d. On them as teachers: Thucyd., 8.68.1 ff.; Aristotle, *Ethica Nicomachea* 1180b30–1181a17; Isocrates, *Antidosis* 79–83; Xenophon, *Anabasis* 2.6.16, *Memorabilia* 1.2.31.

31. On Hippodamus as a Sophist, see W. Schmid and O. Stahlin, *Geschichte der griechischen Literatur*, vol. 3 (Munich: C. H. Beck, 1940), p. 48.

methodological techniques in which they engaged and for which we have contemporary testimony. First there was the *epideixis* or public lecture in which they presented some problem or idea in well-structured language.[32] Isocrates notes in his *Antidosis* (46 ff.) that "some men prefer to write discourses on the world of Greece and the affairs of state, setting forth the content in an imaginative and well styled manner and listened to with great pleasure." Then there was *ex tempore* speaking, a readiness to discuss any subject.[33] This is rather amusingly illustrated by the opening passage of the *Gorgias* where Callicles says of Gorgias that surely he would be willing to enter into discussion with Socrates, but "there is nothing like asking him, Socrates, for this point in fact was a feature of the epideixis [he just gave]. At least a few moments ago he was urging those present to put a question about anything they might care to ask, saying that he would answer any and all questions." A third technique was the critical analysis of poetry, of which we have an example in Plato's *Protagoras* 339a–d, where Protagoras remarks: "And so now my inquiry will be on the same subject which . . . we have just been discussing, virtue. . . . [S]omewhere Simonides (the poet) says to Scopas . . . 'it is difficult for a man to be truly good.'" He then goes on to analyze a short part of the poem.[34] That poetry was not an uncommon pursuit of the Sophists is seen in Isocrates' comment in the *Panathenaicus* 18: "Three or four sophists of the ordinary sort were sitting around . . . conversing about poets in general and in particular about the poetry of Hesiod and Homer." Finally, there was their use of eristics, disputatious argument wherein one person seeks to make the other give absolute answers to statements which demand qualification as in, for example, Plato's *Euthydemus* 284c on whether πράττειν and ποιειν mean the same thing.[35] From the time

---

32. Plato, *Protag.* 320d–322e, *Hippias Major* 286a, *Phaedrus* 227a–234d; Xenophon, *Memorab.* 2.1.21–34.

33. Plato, *Protag.* 334e, 329b, *Gorgias* 447c–d, 449c, 461d, *Meno* 70b–c, *Hippias Minor* 363c–d; Aristotle, *Soph. Elenchis* 183b36–184a7.

34. Compare this with Aristophanes' parody of the method in the *Frogs* 1119 ff. See also Plato, *Protag.* 339–340b; Isocrates, *Antidosis* 46–47, *Panathenaicus* 18–19.

35. Isocrates, *Panath.* 26 f., with which compare Plato, *Rep.* 539b: the delight the young find in eristics; *Sophist* 232b: the sophist is an antilogist. Some general examples of it are the *Parmenides* and the *Euthydemus*, as well as the *Soph. Elenchis* of Aristotle (cf. Navarre, *la rhetorique grecque*, pp. 45–46). Kerferd (*Sophistic Movement*, ch. 6) describes two kinds of controversial discussion: eristics, how to win an argument one way or another; and antilogy, to seek verbal contradictions, or discover intrinsic contrariety in an argument (e.g., Plato, *Lysis* 216a). D. Laertius 3.37–57 cites a tradition that the whole *Republic* of Plato was to be found in the antilogies of Protagoras.

of Zeno (born ca. 490 B.C.E.), who very likely initiated the method, the Athenians engaged vigorously in disputation and discussion. Eristics is not something to be readily dismissed as trickery such as we find it in Plato's *Euthydemus.* First of all, in a good sense it is a kind of intellectual dueling that develops a sharpness of mind, clarifies problems, and helps to specify and define issues. Even in its bad sense it encourages the person subjected to the trickery to develop these qualities in self-defense.[36]

Related in a general way to eristics is the methodology of the *dissoi logoi,* namely, the idea that two opposing views exist with regard to any aspect of reality. It may have been used to deceive at times, but the positive side of it was that it considered a debated point in the round. As an educational technique it is simply the effort of looking fully at a subject to determine where the truth might possibly lie. In many respects this is the method used in the Platonic dialogue to try to determine an issue. In the process the objective ideally sought, as Socrates says in the *Phaedo* 91a–b, is to arrive at the truth, not to win.[37] In fact some believe[38] that Plato's choice of the dialogue form reflects this aspect of the *dissoi logoi* idea, i.e., its peirastic or probing character. This would indicate to me the pervasive character of their teaching and the regard in which it was held.[39] A strong witness to the effectiveness of their teaching in general is to be found in the excellent speeches of the orators of the fifth and fourth centuries: Pericles, Cleon, Lysias, Demosthenes, and Aeschines, to name a few.

There was one other pedagogical method of the Sophists. Cicero speaks about it (*Brutus* 46–47), attributing the statement to Aristotle: "[Aristotle says] that Protagoras wrote out and had ready for use discussions of noteworthy subjects, discussions which are now called *loci communes,* and that Gorgias

---

36. See G. Ryle, "Dialectic," pp. 40 ff. The ability to specify and define a thing as far as it is possible to do so is a critical foundation for intelligent thinking on the subject. In fact I am happy to find that Ryle (p. 61) agrees with something I stated a few times in the two volumes of my commentary, namely that Aristotle "produces definitions, mostly very good ones, of virtues, passions, temperaments."

37. See the *Tetralogies* of Antiphon, or the *agôn* between Helen and Hecuba in the *Trojan Woman* of Euripides, 890–1059.

38. S. Goldhill, *Reading Greek Tragedy* (Cambridge: Cambridge University Press, 1986), p. 231; and we might add that Socratic philosophy itself owes much to them. This view is similar to the one I am arguing here with regard to the development of rhetorical theory as we find it in the finished work of Aristotle, Plato, and Isocrates.

39. And they did not hesitate to criticize other Sophists who were inadequate or bad teachers, e.g., Isocrates, *Panathenaicus* 18, *Ag. the Sophists* 9.

did the same thing, . . . as did Antiphon of Rhamnus." Probably what is meant here is that the Sophists presented a collection of brief statements on common principles, problems, etc., on subjects such as we find in Aristotle's *Rhet.* 99a7: "What kind of movement is the soul?" or common to the discussions of the day: What is the just, the good? These formed a fund of general concepts and ideas. The effort on the part of the student to present a *topos* in an *epideixis* would be an invaluable educational experience. Akin to this exercise was the collection of proemia they made.[40]

What, then, was the object of these methodologies? Protagoras, speaking to Socrates and a number of Sophists about his profession, expressed rather well its objective:

> Sophistry is a τέχνη of long standing and those men of the ancient past who took it up, fearing the hatred in which it was held, disguised it, some as poetry, for example Homer and Hesiod . . . others as religious ritual . . . such as Orpheus and Musaeus. . . . [Y]our own Agathocles (who was a great sophist) cloaked it as music. . . . But I don't go along with them for I do not believe that they accomplished their purpose. . . . I admit that I am a sophist and an educator of men. . . . [T]he student who comes to me will learn nothing other than that for which he came. The learning is: good judgment in his own affairs . . . and in the affairs of the city that he may be most influential in managing and speaking on the city's public interests. (*Protag.* 316d–317a, 317b, 318e–319a)

That concluding remark is simply a restatement of a basic principle in the doctrine taught by the Sophists, namely, that ἀρετή is πολιτικὴ ἀρετή.[41]

---

40. The *Dissoi Logoi* take up a discussion on the teachability of wisdom and virtue. Other questions, such as what are the good/evil, the honorable/dishonorable, the just/unjust, and the true/false, are found in the διαλέξεις ἠθικαί. This document is not from the fifth century of Protagoras and his *Antilogies*, but from the latter part of the second century C.E. (175–200) and Sextus Empiricus. See Navarre, *la rhetorique grecque*, pp. 62 ff. There is no reason to think that these are not typical of what was done by Protagoras in his *Antilogica* and by Gorgias. This is so particularly since the themes clearly echo what we know to be sophistic topics, e.g., the nature of truth, knowledge, and appearance and reality. On the proemia see Radermacher, *Artium Scriptores*, B.17.1.

41. They did put their theory into practice: Protagoras wrote the constitution for Thurii, Gorgias and Hippias acted as ambassadors, Thrasymachus as a deliberative speaker would be occupied with State problems. Plato confirms this when he describes rhetoric as "the kind which shares in the royal science [*epistêmê*] and persuades men to justice" (*The Statesman*, 303a–304a).

This objective is not to be dismissed out of hand as shallow, vocational education. The Sophists, judging from the contemporary reports, were well-educated men who recognized the value of the sciences, the arts, philosophy, and theology. Hippias, for example, insisted that his students know arithmetic, geometry, astronomy, and music.[42] As a teacher he gave courses in these subjects and in mythology, history, painting, sculpture, the function of letters, syllables, and musical scales; he also wrote epic, tragedy, and prose of all kinds.[43] The impressive range of Sophistic interests can be surmised with some assurance from the fragments of their writings. We find there that rhetoric, as the τέχνη λόγων, is the art that integrates the other disciplines to form a solid liberal arts education, whose goal was the πολιτικὴ ἀρετὴ described above by Protagoras as "good judgement in one's own affairs and in the affairs of the city."

The following Sophists, with the exception of Alcidamas and Antisthenes, will be found in *Die Fragmente der Vorsokratiker*, and (in English) in *The Older Sophists*.[44]

Protagoras: like the Sophists in general he is an heir to the educational tradition of the poets, e.g., *Protag.* 338e ff. Such study of poetry instinctively leads one to the structure and the structuring character of language. This is particularly so in a highly inflected language. For similar sentiments regarding prose, see Isocrates, *Against the Sophists* 16–18. As one continues with the passage from the *Protagoras*, it becomes clear that through the analysis of the poem one is learning how to be clear and precise in one's language statements. Protagoras also studied the relations of language and music (e.g., *Hippias Major* 285d, *H. Minor* 368d), an area of study that interested other Sophists working on euphony, rhythm, the sounds of one's language. He studied a very common problem of the fifth century: the nature of φύσις and

---

42. Cf. Plato, *Hippias Minor* 366c–369a, on the vast number of his achievements as listed by Socrates. He was also a good ethicist, as Guthrie (*The Sophists*, p. 284) shows.

43. See Kerferd, *The Sophistic Movement*, pp. 46–48. Isocrates, *Antid.* 261 ff. remarks that while these subjects (geometry, arithmetic, etc.) are of no immediate practical aid, they help the person by developing mental sharpness and are a preparation for φιλοσοφία (as Isocrates understood it), just as literature and grammar are.

44. H. Diels and W. Kranz, *Die Fragmente der Vorsokratiker*, vol. 2 (Zurich: Weidmann, 1969); R. K. Sprague, ed. *The Older Sophists* (Columbia: The University of South Carolina Press, 1972).

νόμος. In the *Protagoras* 322a ff. he defends νόμος. A list of his works will be found in Diogenes Laertius 9.55; at 3.57 Laertius calls attention to a tradition holding that the whole of Plato's *Republic* is to be found in the *Antilogica* of Protagoras.

Gorgias: a gifted extempore speaker and the teacher of Isocrates, among others. Plato (*Meno* 70a–b) speaks of his success as an educator in Larissa, Thessaly. He found time to occupy himself with the philosophy of nature. His interest, however, was in the *logos* as our way in which to communicate with each other. The opening words of his *Helen* are: "The proper adornment of speech is truth" (κόσμος ... λόγῳ δὲ αλήθεια). This attitude may well explain his interest in the character of language: its verbal power and forcefulness, its right to employ poetic words for dignity, its proper use of tropes, metaphors, isocola, antithesis, homoioteleuton (these last three are the so-called Gorgianic figures), doubling of words (cf. Aristotle, *Rhet.*, 04a19 ff.). This concern with the character of language is well reflected in a comment of Leon Bloy: "It is indispensable that truth should be clothed in glory. Splendor of style is not a luxury, it is a necessity." The importance of Gorgias' view on language is confirmed by Aristotle's 12 chapters on style in *Rhet. III*. In the *Gorgias* (454c–e) we find that in rhetoric he admits that μάθησις is better than πίστις, that the rhetorician must have επιστήμη (460aff.), and finally that there is a rhetoric of knowledge and a rhetoric of belief (see Coulter in K. Erickson, *Plato: True and Sophistic Rhetoric*, Amsterdam 1979). Finally, in the *Helen* 8–9 Gorgias calls to our attention the important role of emotion in speech.

Thrasymachus: presented rather unattractively in Plato, *Rep. I*, followed Gorgias on the importance of emotion (e.g., his *Eleoi*, Plato, *Phaedrus* 267c–d, Aristotle, *Rhet.* 04a15) and of style in his observations on rhythm (Aristotle, *Rhet.* 09a2 ff.). Theophrastus claims that he discovered the middle style, as Dionysius of Halicarnassus writes in his *Demosthenes* 3. He has also been called the inventor of rhythmical prose. His *Subjects for Speeches* (Suidas, *DK* A. 1) may well have been a set of those brief disquisitions by the Sophists on varied topics of which Aristotle spoke, as reported by Cicero (*Brutus* 46–47). In the essay of Dionysius of Halicarnassus on *Demosthenes* 3, we have a partial speech of his *On the Constitution*. This offers a sharp contrast to Plato's report on his ideas in *Rep. I* (cf. Guthrie, *The Sophists.*, pp. 295–298). Another deliberative speech of his may be that for the people of Larissa (Diels-Kranz, B.2). There is also mention by Suidas of a *Textbook on Rhetoric*.

Prodicus: influenced by Gorgias, as was the historian Thucydides. He was a very popular professor. See, e.g., *Protag.* 315cd, a dialogue in which he hears Socrates, of all people, say: "I beg to be spared Prodicus' distinction of terms . . ." (358a–b). Socrates, in fact, called himself Prodicus' pupil in the careful use of words and their meanings (*Protag.* 341a; see also *Meno* 96d). Socrates also sent Prodicus pupils, surely a sign of the regard in which he held him (*Theaetet.* 151b). Like Gorgias he, too, was concerned with morphology, correctness of words (*orthoepeia*), a discriminating use of words, the gender of nouns (cp. the *Cratylus* of Plato). This concern with semantics is not as superficial as it may appear. Care in this area is very important in any kind of philosophical undertaking. This is an observation that is well attested to by Plato in his Socratic dialogues. In the ethical field we have a passage from Prodicus' *Choice of Heracles* (virtue versus vice) in Xenophon's *Memorab.* 2.1.21–34. He also produced a treatise on *The Nature of Man.* Prominent enough to be mentioned by Aristophanes (*Clouds* 361, *Birds* 692), he could also poke fun at himself, as he reveals with the story of himself throwing in a tidbit from his very expensive fifty drachma speech to wake up an audience about to go to sleep on him (Aristotle, *Rhet.* 15b15 ff.).

Antiphon: quite possible there was one, not two Antiphons—Antiphon of Rhamnus, and Antiphon the Sophist to whom *On Truth, On Concord, Politicus* are attributed. Antiphon of Rhamnus, rhetorician and sophist, is probably the author of these works and all the fragments. For a discussion of the question see J. S. Morrison in Sprague, *The Older Sophists*, pp. 108–110, and Guthrie, *The Sophists*, pp. 292–294. Owing to his birth early in the fifth century at the time of the Persian Wars ca. 480 B.C.E. (cf. his *Genos*), the reports that he was self-taught in the rhetorical *technê* are quite reasonable since the teachers of rhetoric would be few, if there were any, at that time. His writings are extensive and only a study of the evidence as it is presented by *DK* or Morrison, pp. 112–240, can give some idea of their variety, much wider in fact than those of Socrates, whom he knew rather well (Xenophon, *Memorab.* 1.6). Although he apparently was not exposed to any rhetorical training and did not engage very actively in actual court speaking, he is included in the list of the Ten Attic Orators. He was a logographer not only for those engaged in a trial at court, but also for those presenting a case to the Assembly. The testimonia in the fragments indicate this work in writing for others, as do also the speeches *On the Murder of Herodes, A Prosecution for Poisoning against a Stepmother*, and *On a Member of the Chorus*. On the other hand, the fragments indicate a sizable number of forensic speeches (i.e., legal, and for public debate). We have one speech, a deliberative one, which considers, it would appear, political matters and their ethical implication. We also have the twelve speeches in the three *Tetralogies*, which were apparently used as illustrative exercises, and the fragments of 17 court speeches and two Assembly speeches. The last two are written for others to deliver (all of these are to be found in Morrison). We also possess fragments of and extended references to his treatise *On Truth, On Concord, Politikos, On the Interpretation of Dreams* (e.g., in Galen, Aristotle, Oxyrhynchus Papyri, Stobaeus, Cicero, cf. Morrison). He is recalled as a very pleasant speaker and his style is commended in a number of places and described as "precise, persuasive and clever in its inventiveness" (Photius, *Bibliotheca*; Plutarch, *Lives of the Ten Orators*). Owing to his early date he is possibly responsible for the development of prose style and for the typical structure of a speech. His language is said to be grand but not overwhelming (Hermogenes, *On Kinds* [*of Literary Composition*]). Finally, we have fragmentary evidence of his speech in defense of himself on the charge of treason, brought as a result of his involvement in the activity of the Four Hundred and their overthrow of democracy in Athens in 411 B.C.E. The speech was apparently a brilliant job and is highly praised by Thucydides (as is Antiphon himself as a man, 8.68). In Aristotle's words Antiphon was esteemed for his outstanding political insight and good judgment (*Constit. of Athens*, 32.2). Like the other Sophists his interests cover a wide area, e.g., On the Mind and its Knowing, On Justice-Injustice, Geometry, Law and Nature, on Physical Reality (sun, moon, etc.), on Education, on Living one's Life.

Antisthenes: somewhat enigmatic since most of our evidence on him is late. This is strange because D. Laertius (*Vita* 6.15–18) lists 62 titles under his name, which range from works on style and expression, through books devoted to individuals (e.g., the *Sophists, Theognis, Cyrus*), to studies of philosophical problems (*On Justice, The Good, On Truth, On Nature*), to logic and epistemology (*On Contradiction, On Opinion and Knowledge, On Learning*), to works on varied subjects such as education, music, Homer, the *Odyssey*, etc. He lived about 450–360 and was a student of Gorgias (D. Laertius, 6.1), whom he later attacked apparently in his *Archelaus* (Athenaeus, *Deipnosophistae* 220d). He studied with and was close to Socrates (Xenophon, *Symp.* 8.4, *Memorab.* 3.11.17).

In the *Symp.* 4.34–44 of Xenophon he appears as an attractive person who is satisfied with what little he has. In fact Popper and Grote view him as "the only worthy successor of Socrates" (see Guthrie, *The Sophists*, p. 305). We are told that he encouraged his students to "become fellow pupils with him of Socrates" (D. Laertius, 6.2, Xenophon, *Symp.* 4.61). In itself this would suggest an influence of Socratic thinking on his own doctrine. His brief discussion with Socrates in D. Laertius 6.5 reflects Socrates' statements on friendship; and the observations on virtue and the wise man (6.11) attributed to him by Laertius are Socratic in character. At 6.10–13 Laertius speaks of varied aspects of his moral teaching and ends his comments with the observation (6.14): "This man alone of all the Socratics received the praise of Theopompus who states that he was a man of skill and able by the good taste of his discourse to win over anyone." Suidas calls him a "Socratic philosopher." Jerome (*Contra Jovinianum*) speaks of his many works on rhetoric and philosophy, and Athenaeus (*Deipnosophistae* 220c–e) gives a partial survey of some of his work. Some of his philosophical work was mentioned earlier. His doctrine that contradiction was not possible (only identical predication was possible, e.g., man is man) is mentioned by Aristotle (*Met.* 1024b32 ff.) who at 1043b23 ff. identifies the doctrine with the Antisthenians, whereas Plato associates it with those about Protagoras. Since he held that virtue can be taught (unlike Socrates), he must have held that it could be first known. Radermacher, *la rhetorique grecque*, B.XIX.1–13, presents the rhetorical fragments, among which we find the following comments: an investigation of words is the beginning of education (B.XIX.6 f), an "assertion" is that which makes clear what something was or is or will be (7). Guthrie, pp. 307–309 reviews his ideas on ethics, logic, politics, poetry and theology.

These summaries give some idea of the work of the Sophists. And so I will pass over Lycophron, Alcidamas, and Anonymus Iamblichus. Critias, included in their number by Guthrie, is not a Sophist, although Guthrie thinks that his "spirit" is that of a Sophist. Those I have dropped are omitted not because they have nothing to contribute but simply for the reason given, e.g., Alcidamas, a pupil of Gorgias, favored the rhetoric-philosophy idea of some Sophists; Lycophron's (Aristotle, *Politics* 1280b10 ff., calls him a Sophist) social contract theory is reviewed in Guthrie (pp. 139, 143–145); Anon. Iamblichus reflects what we know of the teachings of Antiphon, Antisthenes, Hippias, Critias, et al. I will conclude with the *Dissoi Logoi*.

Dissoi Logoi: written in the Doric dialect, it is dated about 400 B.C.E. but came to our notice substantially later. Our copy (whose beginning may be lost) was found in connection with the manuscripts of Sextus Empiricus (late 2nd century C.E. into 3rd century). The *Dissoi Logoi* are a form of the double argument, i.e., one argument for, one against a position, on the Protagorean principle that "there are two sides to every subject," cf. Euripides frag. 189: ἐκ παντὸς ἄν τις πράγματος δισσῶν λόγων ἀγῶνα θεῖτ᾽ ἄν, εἰ λέγειν εἴη σοφός (A. Nauck, *Tragicorum Graecorum Fragmenta Supplementum*, B. Snell, Hildesheim, 1964). This treatise, on the other hand, holds for the principle that the *logos* has a meaning secured by the reality it refers to and is not purely relativistic. It argues that the relation between truth and falsehood has an objective foundation. The theses of the antinomies contain the relativistic statement of which the following would be a typical example: "If shoes are worn out, this is good for the shoe repairer, bad for the wearer." The antithesis asserts that the two statements are different and by a reduction ad absurdum demonstrates that to say otherwise makes language and speech nonsensical. For example, in the citation given one can say that, since "good" and "bad" are the same, worn out shoes are good for the wearer and bad for the cobbler. Or in a more important area one can argue that justice is injustice (see antinomy 3). The first six of the *dissoi logoi* contain such statements. On the whole they do not appear to be as sharp and acute as those we meet in Plato's *Euthydemus*. But that not withstanding they do force one to ponder the statement, to try to distinguish where the error lies, and to give a reasonable resolution of the error. All of which makes for good mental exercise and a sharpening of one's logical astuteness. The six antinomies are followed by three more. The first is on sortition (a method used in mid-fifth-century Athens for the appointment of members to the Boule and the archonship). The next is on speech. Its opening sentence I believe should be noted: "I think it belongs to [the same man] and to the same art to discourse in the brief style and to understand [the] truth of things and to know how to give a right judgment . . . to understand the art of rhetoric and to teach concerning the nature of all things, their state and how they came to be." (The translation is Sprague's in *The Older Sophists*, p. 291). The last is on memory. A. E. Taylor (*Varia Socratica*, Oxford University Press, 1911, pp. 91–128) discusses the treatise and his view of it is that it shows "signs of Eleatic origin and of considerable Socratic influence," with an emphasis on the last. For example, see p. 106 ff. on the third antinomy and p. 114 on the just and unjust. He offers a slight reservation on p. 119 but at p. 128 restates his view on the presence of Socratic thinking because of the correspondences in the work with the *Protagoras* and *Meno* of Plato.

When we turn to the influence these Sophists had upon the work of Isocrates, Plato, and Aristotle we are faced in many instances, as I have noted, with the perennial problem of a lack of detailed knowledge of their works in rhetoric, philosophy, literature, theology, the sciences, music, sociology, etc. This problem, I should observe, is also true for the pre-Socratic philosophers. But as Kerferd points out,[45] there is a need for the same kind of detailed, scholarly study of individual Sophists as is given to individual pre-Socratic philosophers. In this way conclusions such as I will draw legitimately, I believe, from the evidence we now possess could be verified with more satisfaction. These conclusions are also drawn from the inescapable fact that not only were the Sophists the educators of the fifth century who "settled the main lines along which men's educational aspirations were to be satisfied . . . for centuries to come,"[46] but also that despite the negative comments[47] made about sophists by Isocrates, Plato, and Aristotle, the Sophists of whom I have spoken are clearly held in esteem by them. See, for instance, Aristotle at *Politics* 1305a10–15 on why the present leaders of the State are not tyrants: "In the old days the leaders of the people came from the generals. . . . [N]ow, however, since the art of rhetoric has grown in power men with speaking ability lead the people." Then we have Plato speaking in praise of Hippias in *Hippias Major* 282, or compare the *Gorgias* and the *Protagoras*, and Isocrates speaking with favor in *Antidosis* 197–198. From Xenophon's *Memorabilia* we know that Antiphon, Antisthenes, and Prodicus were friends of Socrates. On the other hand, I do not think that we can say that there were not Sophists who gave support to the negative criticism we hear, just as today we have hypocrites in the legal, medical, biological,

---

45. G. Kerferd, ed. *The Sophists and Their Legacy* (Wiesbaden: Steiner, 1981), p. 3.

46. Bolgar, "The Training of Elites," p. 39.

47. Isocrates wrote a work, *Against the Sophists*; Plato's antipathy calls for no documentation, but cf. *Laws* 937e–938c; Aristotle remarks in *Soph. Elenchis* 165a19–24: "But since to some people it is more serviceable to appear to be wise rather than actually to be wise and not to appear to be so (for the art of the sophist is apparent wisdom, not real wisdom) and the sophist is a money-operator on the basis of apparent, but not real wisdom. It is clear that for these people one must appear to do the task of the learned man rather than to do it and not to appear to do it."

advertising, educational, and other professions. But regarding the Sophists of whom we have been speaking, let us remember Gorgias' remark in his *Helen* 15: "For the things we see do not have the nature *which we wish them* to have, but the nature which each *actually* has"[48] (emphasis mine).

Perhaps one of the first things we notice is the ready reception of the argument from probability accepted by Isocrates and Aristotle and rejected by Plato. The only kind of reasoning Plato would accept is that based on absolute knowledge (ἐπιστήμη) and right opinion (δόξα ἀληθής; see *Meno* 97b–100c) supported by αἰτίας λογίσμῳ (98a). However, the very character of the subjects which are mostly met in discourse makes Plato's position untenable. For the subjects range over the whole area of the problematic, the uncertain. Efforts to resolve such subjects will be mostly grounded on probable reasoning. For Isocrates, *doxa* was that which was αλήθεια,[49] the truth. Aristotle admitted into rhetorical discourse both opinion and absolute knowledge. Arguments from both areas, certain and probable knowledge, are acceptable to him, and rightly so. There is as much play for rhetoric in philosophy as there is in a dubious forensic case. Probability arguments were a normal procedure because of the emphasis given to them by the Sophists. In the course of time we find them challenged by Plato as a source for rhetorical argumentation but reaffirmed by Aristotle.

It was Isocrates, however, who organized the Sophists' views on rhetorical education into a reasonable system integrating their ideas on *doxa*,[50] subject-matter, and the ultimate objective, *aretê*. His goal was ethical as well as political instruction assisted by the power of the *logos* as organizational

---

48. As translated by Kennedy in *The Older Sophists*, ed. R. Sprague. The statement sums up the character of much of the common criticism expressed against the Sophists from Plato to our own day.

49. His φιλοσοφία was not strictly philosophy as we would understand it. It was rather a form of general political and moral culture in which rhetoric was the integrating factor, for as he says in *Nicocles, The Cyprians* 7 (hereafter *Nicocles* 2): "We consider the ability to speak, as one should, the most significant sign of sound thinking; and discourse which is true, conformable to custom and law, and is just is the image of a good soul worthy of belief." "Sound thinking" (εὐ φρονεῖν) is Isocrates' acknowledgment of the role of mind in discourse.

50. *Helen* 5: "likely conjecture about useful things is far preferable to exact knowledge of the useless" (*Antid.* 271).

principle (*Nicocles II* 5–9, *Panegyricus* 48–49, *Antid.* 253–257). By *logos* he meant rhetoric, the τέχνη λόγων,[51] or as he called his education: τὴν παιδείαν τὴν περὶ τοὺς λόγους, i.e., a making of the cultivated, informed, responsible mind able to communicate with others on matters of the polis and morality (see, e.g., *Ag. the Sophists* 21: την των λόγων των πολιτικων ἐπιμέλειαν; also *Panathenaicus* 30 ff., *Alexander* 4–5). The content of this education follows the suggestions of the Sophists: mathematics, grammar, music, poetry (*Demonicus* 51–52, *Nicocles* 13–14), history (*Antid.* 266, 45–46), moral questions (*Ag. the Sophists* 8: ἡ ἐπιμέλεια τ ῆς ψυχ ῆς, a favorite phrase of Socrates). As a pupil of Protagoras and Gorgias, Isocrates was concerned with euphony and rhythm of language, the use of figures and tropes, and with eristics, geometry, and as-tronomy, as well as with the study of grammar and literature as helpful, but not directly so (*Antid.* 261 f., 267; see, however, *Demonicus* 51–52, *Nicocles* 13–14 on literature). This *logos* is closely related to *nous* (*Nicocles II* 7) and its objective is truth, as Isocrates understands ἀλήθεια (i.e., right opinion as clearly as it can be determined, cf. n. 50). As he says at *Antid.* 257: "We will discover that none of the intelligent actions we do are done without the help of speech." In short, our reasoned and reasonable actions are intimately related to our internal as well as our external speech. Hence his concern for truth in the *logos*, something he does not find in the sophists he criticizes in *Ag. the Sophists* 9. Finally, this *logos*, whether in the form of an essay, speech, dialogue, or *epideixis*, must be organic, a living whole with all of its parts systematically arranged (*Ag. the Sophists* 16), a point which Plato also emphasized in the *Phaedrus* 264–269. Isocrates' efforts to make speech —which in his mind was a most important element in human culture—into an effective instrument of communication greatly influenced the formation of Europe's prose style.[52]

---

51. His success as an educator is reflected in the list of distinguished students he sent forth: in history, Ephorus, Theopompus, Androtion; in eloquence, Lycurgus, Hypereides, Isaeus; in philosophy, Speusippus; in statesmanship, Timotheus. Later Isocrates was a strong influence on Cicero, who called him the "master of all rhetoricians" (*Brutus* 32; see also *De Orat.* 2.94).

52. The Sophists followed the teachings of the Presocratics on the nature of language, names for things, the rightness of the names, and the correctness of diction—e.g., Protagoras (in the dialogue named for him) on the poem of Simonides, or Prodicus on the definitions of words (337–41). Protagoras began, it would appear, the classification of words (Aristotle, *Soph. Elenchis* 173b17 ff.), of the parts of speech such as noun-verb. See P. B. Forbes, "Greek Pioneers in Philology and Grammar," *Classical Review* 47 (1933): 105–12.

With the same ease and efficiency with which Isocrates took over and developed the ideas of the Sophists on *doxa*, rhetoric, education, and style into a very successful educational program, so Plato and Aristotle incorporated Sophistic eristics, antilogy, and the double argument (*dissoi logoi*) into their statements on rhetoric. The result is admirably exemplified in Plato's dialogue form. If there was ever an instance of the *"anti Platon chez Platon,"* this is it. For the dialogue as used by Plato is the most forceful and suasive tool for making the word an efficient instrument of communication. The dialogue form itself is very likely the effect of the Sophists' use of question and answer. Earlier we saw Callicles say of Gorgias, "a few moments ago he was urging those present to put a question about anything . . . saying that he would answer any and all questions." This matter of question and answer can be seen in the Socratic dialogues, where the disputants are actors locked in a struggle as they try to define terms and establish meanings, working as they are from mutually opposed (or antilogistic) assumptions (e.g., *Laches, Lysis, Charmides, Euthyphro*). In such an exchange the consequences are far more substantial than the techniques used since they affect the auditors' thinking on moral issues, theology, society, ethics, and politics.

In a similar way Aristotle incorporates the elements of eristic and antilogy in his presentation of true and apparent argument by way of enthymeme (on the apparent, see *Rhet.* 2.24). We also find elements of the double argument (*dissoi logoi*) in his constructive analysis of the emotions. For the most part he sets contrary emotions side by side to contrast what can be said of the two closely related emotions. Later on he places together the contrasting attitudes of the young, old and middle aged (2.12 ff.). Earlier I wrote of the work of the Sophists as a "propaideutic for the informed and perceptive work in rhetoric of Plato, Isocrates, and Aristotle." I think the sophistication revealed by all three in integrating Sophistic concepts into their rhetorical presentations demonstrates the validity of that statement.[53] Aristotle and Plato intro-

----

53. For contrast, see Anaximenes' *Rhetoric to Alexander* as an example of the handbook method, or the work attributed to Cicero, the *Auctor ad Herennium.* Plato's understanding of truth as firmly fixed and unchangeable made probability unacceptable to him. As a consequence, what he presents negatively in the *Gorgias* and *Protagoras* and positively at the end of the *Phaedrus* as his theory of rhetoric makes it impossible for him to accept as part of his theory the world of possibilities confronting humans when absolute truth is inaccessible to them in the given situation. However, Plato did accept rhetoric as valid in the area of absolute truth when he admitted the possibility of true rhetoric (*Phaedrus* 272b) and the legitimacy of *psychagogia* (261a) or the appeal to the whole person: intellect, emotions, feelings, and attitudes.

duced the method of antilogy and double argument naturally into their larger schema for rhetoric. Plato does so in his dialogues with their discussion of truth-falsity, just-unjust, honorable-dishonorable, etc., while Aristotle incorporates some of the points just mentioned when he outlines the three kinds of oratory and their proximate τέλη.

All three men accepted the Sophistic position that rhetoric was closely related to the good of the State, that the citizens' *aretê* was πολιτικὴ ἀρετή. Isocrates did so fully, Plato indirectly, Aristotle directly and partially. Politics as the study of humans in society is the branch of ethics in which rhetoric is primarily interested. As we have seen, πολιτικὴ ἀρετή is also a major objective in Isocrates' pursuit of φιλοσοφία. The objective of Plato's dialogues is to determine what qualities become the good man whose first service is to the polis. And at *Rhetoric* 1356a25–30 Aristotle says: ". . . so it happens that rhetoric is a kind of offshoot of dialectic and the discipline of ethics which is correctly called politics. Wherefore rhetoric slips into the guise of the science of politics and those who lay claim to it do the same partly from ignorance, partly from presumption and other human causes."

Human Excellence, identified by the Sophists, as it was, with the excellence of the person as a member of the polis, was ultimately the objective of those who, like Plato, sought that excellence in the person himself. Like the other contributions of the Sophists—of which I have spoken and which, as far as I know from our evidence, is unique to them—this concept endowed the rhetorics of Isocrates, Plato, and Aristotle with a structural factor that enabled them to build a reasoned and competent system for the τέχνη λόγων, as they all called rhetoric. As a consequence, the rhetorical theory of each man was a synthesis that brought together in a reasonable way elements critical to the technique of rhetoric and each directed the art in a general way to an objective, human *aretê*. This objective was rightly proper to rhetoric since the *logos* itself is proper to man. Rhetoric was raised above and beyond a mere ἐμπειρία ("skill"). It was informed with the ability and the duty to seek out and discover the truth as far as it can be known in given instances in order to share it with others.

It may come as a shock to hear me dismiss as smart but incorrect the statement that "rhetorical excellence has no connection with moral excellence," that rhetoric is neither good nor bad, as Whitehead said of science. Related as rhetoric is so intimately with the *logos*, the very way in which a person gives expression to what he or she is—his or her aspirations, ideals, attitudes—it cannot escape from reflecting moral excellence. Indeed, there may well be more than we think in the use by the Greeks of the phrase τέχνη λόγων ("the *art* of the *logos*"). Art, apart from its meaning of a skill directed by reason, also produces something; and that artifact is an expression of the person of the artist. Rhetoric, as a liberal art for the Greeks, is ultimately engaged, as are all the arts, in the pursuit of reality, of truth, and truth carries no meaning save to the human. As Isocrates says, "discourse which is truthful, lawful, and just is the image of a good and trustworthy person," or again, "Elegance and artistry of language is the work of an intelligent mind" (*Antid.* 255; *Panegyr.* 48).

When he writes of the two dialogues much cited as instances of Plato's rejection of rhetoric, V. Tejera states fairly much what I have just said of rhetoric as *technê*: "Taking the *Gorgias* and *Phaedrus* together, while scrupulously respecting their contexts, Plato's Socrates can be seen to be saying that in the true art-and-science of rhetoric the technique of organizing a speech into a beautiful and effective whole must be informed by the purpose of promoting either justness or truthfulness in the hearer. . . . Without this rhetoric remains a mere skill; and the only questions that can arise about it are questions of technique."[54]

Aristotle, too, saw truth as one of the objectives of the rhetorical *technê*.[55] Where he differed from the view of Isocrates and Plato in his understanding of the discipline was that he saw rhetoric as the intelligent and effective use of language for communicating with others,[56] but without identifying the art with what it was not, with something other than itself, such as education for the polis, or dialectics. In itself rhetoric was a *technê* that demanded knowledge in these and other areas if one was to speak on them. This knowledge, generally speaking, was that of the normally intelligent, educated person, not that of the specialist.

Finally, we can say that to speak of rhetoric, as the Greeks did, as a τέχνη περὶ τοὺς λόγους (*Gorgias* 449d; Aristotle, *Rhet.* 54a12), or as the τέχνη λογοποιική, is to speak of it as a study of the ways in which to use both the spoken and written *logos* most efficiently for communication with others. The Sophists, as the educators of the fifth century, made the rhetorical theorists of the fourth century fully conscious of the importance of this. First of all, the Sophists raised questions about substantial human problems: the

---

54. "Irony and Allegory in the *Phaedrus*," in *Plato: True and Sophistic Rhetoric*, ed. K. Erickson (Amsterdam: Rodopi, 1979), p. 293.

55. W. Grimaldi, S.J., "Rhetoric and Truth: A Note on Aristotle, *Rhetoric* 1355a21–24," *Philosophy and Rhetoric* 11 (1978): 173–77. See *Gorgias* 508c.

56. Plato, in the *Phaedrus* 227b–c taken with 261a–b, 271c–d, makes this very same point.

gods, moral issues, the nature of man, political philosophy, the theory of knowing, the nature of society (*nomos* and *physis*), the apparent and the real. Secondly, they demonstrated that there were not always absolute answers to these problems (and so the necessity of probability argumentation). They developed ways of investigating a problem: the study of language and meanings of words, and the uses of the double argument, of antilogy, of the question-and-answer method of eristics.

The differences between the rhetorical theories of Isocrates, Plato, and Aristotle and those of the earlier, intervening *technai* (as we can gather from the criticism of them by all three men) indicates to me the active presence of the Sophists' thought (both the philosophers' and rhetoricians') to these fourth-century thinkers, and this thought influenced heavily the formation of their rhetorics.

Two

Extending and Correcting the Rhetorical Tradition:
Aristotle's Perception of the Sophists

John Poulakos

Students of antiquity wishing to inquire into the practices and notions of the Greek Sophists generally turn to Plato. In so doing, they leave out of the account Aristotle, an important source of insights on the itinerant teachers of the fifth and fourth centuries B.C.E. This learned preference is largely due to the belief that Aristotle mostly reiterated the views of his master or followed his lead. While it is true that many Aristotelian notions can be traced to Plato, it is also true that Aristotle had a mind of his own. That this is so is evident in the latter's perception of the Sophists, one that not only resembles but also deviates from Plato's.

In this essay I am mainly concerned with Aristotle's account of the Sophists. While this account can stand on its own, the question of its similarities to and differences from its Platonic forebear also merits attention. What Aristotle thought about the Sophists tells us two things: first, Plato's critique of the instructors of rhetoric and argument was carried on well after his death; and second, their contributions to the rhetorical tradition were more highly esteemed by Aristotle than they had been by Plato.

Using standards of historical significance and logical correctness, Aristotle arrives at the following assessment of the Sophists: because they had contributed to the cultural reservoir of rhetorical insights, they are historically important; but because their reasoning is often flawed, it needs to be corrected. This twofold assessment rests on Aristotle's view that all discoveries are the result of either elaborations on previously worked matters or original inventions (*Sophistical Refutations* 183b17–20). By his own admission, his *Rhetoric* constitutes mostly an elaboration of prior precepts: "On the subject of rhetoric there already existed much material enunciated in the past" (*Sophistical Refutations* 184a10–184b1). On the other hand, his *Topics* stands as an original invention: "Regarding reasoning *[syllogizesthai]* we had absolutely no earlier work to quote" (*Sophistical Refutations* 184b2). These remarks suggest that as a successor to the Sophists Aristotle responds to a twofold need. Insofar as the Sophists had left some of the earlier materials of rhetoric in a rather disorderly and incoherent state, Aristotle set out to systematize (*odopoiein*) them and render them coherent.[1] But inasmuch as they practiced argument and refutation without adhering to an explicit theory of dialectic, he sought to discover a method of arguing any point without contradiction (*Topics* 100a18–20)[2] and of defending any thesis consistently (*Sophistical Refutations* 183b5–6).

The Aristotelian perception of the Sophists, then, differs from its Platonic counterpart by its use of the standard of historical significance, a standard Plato never invokes. Another difference between the master and his most famous student is the way in which the student confronts his own critical task. Whereas Plato had written rhetorical compositions seeking to imitate, mock, refute, or outdo the Sophists,[3] Aristotle prefers to advance theoretical propositions, to allude to his newly devised rules of the *technai* of rhetoric and logic, and to judge the Sophists by these rules. But speeches as self-sufficient units of discourse addressing a particular issue are nowhere to be found in Aristotle. In his preserved texts, oratory (as it was known) is simply abandoned while the capacities for metarhetorical discussion and critical commentary are boosted. Consequently, while Aristotle praises the Sophists for their contributions to the rhetorical tradition, he himself does not carry it on the way, say, Isocrates does. Instead, he extends it by carving out a new direction, the direction of rhetorical theory.

Like Plato, Aristotle refers to the "older" as well as to his contemporary Sophists by name or collectively, as a class.[4] Often abstracting a general principle from many particulars, he also discusses, in the manner of Plato, "the Sophist" as a composite of several features, that is, as a type. Therefore, his remarks can be taken to refer to common rather than to individualistic traits and practices, except of course when he is discussing a named individual. Follow-

---

1. See *Rhetoric* 1.1.1.

2. See also *Sophistical Refutations* 183a37–38.

3. Consider, for example, the speeches in Plato's *Apology, Phaedrus, Symposium,* and *Menexenus.*

4. Concerning Aristotle's views on both the "older" and the second generation Sophists as well as his overall assessment of both groups, see Carl J. Classen, "Aristotle's Picture of the Sophists," in *The Sophists and Their Legacy,* ed. G. B. Kerferd (Wiesbaden: Franz Steiner Verlag GMBH, 1981), pp. 23–24.

ing Plato, Aristotle defines a *Sophist* as a practitioner of questionable rhetorical and argumentative techniques. But whereas Plato had defined the term with a dramatic sense of urgency, turning the act of defining into a venturesome expedition of hunting down a cunning beast, Aristotle defines the Sophist dispassionately, so as to fulfill his authorial obligation to his readers; to meet, that is, their expectations of informational clarity and intellectual decorum. Searching for the Sophist, the Plato of *The Sophist* encountered many obstacles, now finding and now losing him along the blurred lines separating philosophy from nonphilosophy, statesmanship from nonstatesmanship, rhetoric from nonrhetoric. But with Aristotle the lines of demarcation are made sharper, and as a result the Sophist is found more easily and defined with greater confidence.

While executing this task, Aristotle seems neither obsessed nor especially troubled by the Sophists the way Plato does. Although he, too, adopts a critical stance toward them, his critique does not exhibit the Platonic elements of hostility and outright rejection. Aristotle's Sophists are more an object of study and less the mortal enemies of the investigator. Treating them as a part of early Hellenic intellectual history, Aristotle pays them some attention and seeks to overcome what he regards as their shortcomings in rhetoric and to correct what he considers their errors in logic. Yet in his overall project, encompassing a wide range of historical, critical, and theoretical inquiries, the Sophists play only a minor role, the role of a peculiar intellectual phenomenon that somehow must be made intelligible and meaningful. Accordingly, Aristotle handles them as a given aspect of the Hellenic cultural heritage but does so without attaching to them the extraordinary significance they had been assigned in some Platonic dialogues. With Aristotle, in other words, the importance of the Sophists begins to diminish. For him, the "older" ones were not the sole perpetrators of the sociopolitical chaos of the fourth century that Plato had thought they were; rather, they represented an era of preliminary investigations in thought and language, investigations that now had to be reconsidered, straightened out, and brought to completion. As for the second-generation Sophists, they simply represented an extension of the earlier masters whose doctrines and practices they were perpetuating.[5]

---

5. Consider, for example, Bryson's claim, as expressed by Aristotle, that "no one ever uses foul language" (*Rhetoric* 3.2.13), a variation of Antisthenes' famous dictum that no one can contradict himself or another. Also consider Lycophron's notion that the law is "a guarantee of men's just claims on one another, but it is not designed to make the citizens virtuous and just" (*Politics* 1280b11–13). Thought to have been Gorgias' student, Lycophron can be said to be perpetuating his teacher's view that rhetoric is not concerned with instruction or matters of right and wrong (*Gorgias* 455a).

But in the context of the breadth and depth of Aristotelian intellectual inquiry, both the older and the younger Sophists lose some of their prominence and weight. Once the principal intellectuals of the culture, the Sophists are given in the hands of Aristotle the status of a single mention in a long list.

Beyond its respect for the tradition and its commitment to a new conceptualization of rhetoric, Aristotle's perception of the Sophists is also guided by distinctions he makes between rhetoric and other fields such as philosophy and politics.[6] Aristotle basically agrees with Plato's view that the Sophists imitate the philosopher. However, he puts the matter somewhat differently when he says that they practice apparent, but not real, wisdom.[7] Although it is difficult to say what exactly Aristotle means by "apparent" wisdom,[8] it is clear that "real" wisdom is what the philosopher possesses or practices.[9] On this matter, Aristotle and Plato think as one. Now if by "apparent" wisdom he generally means rhetoric, the art whose whole business is about appearances *(pros doxan)*, and by "real" wisdom he intends dialectic, Aristotle can be said to depart from Plato and to rework the relationship of the two faculties by making the one a counterpart of the other.[10] But if by "apparent" wisdom he means fallacious argument, and "real" wisdom correct argument, then the Sophists practice something that needs to be rectified by devising explicit rules of argumentation, not derided in the manner of Plato. In another vein, Aristotle refers to "truth" and "action" as the two aims that distinguish the philosopher from the orator and others like him: "philosophy

---

6. For Aristotle, philosophy and politics are two areas of activity that attract those rich enough to dispense with the troubles of ordering their own household or managing their slaves (*Politics* 1255b35–38).

7. See *Metaphysics* 1004b15–27. See also *Protrepticus* (45), where Aristotle differentiates between exactitude (as a form of real wisdom) and imitation: "The philosopher alone, of all men, imitates that which among all things is the most exact; for, what he looks at is originality and exactness itself, not merely imitation." See Anton-Hermann Chroust, *Aristotle: Protrepticus: A Reconstruction* (South Bend: University of Notre Dame Press, 1964), pp. 20–21.

8. It is not clear, in other words, whether "apparent" wisdom is apparent because the beholder perceives it to be so, or because the one professing it knows that it is not "real," or because it does not appear the way the philosopher (i.e., Aristotle) thinks it should. Moreover, to say that X is not Y does not say what X is.

9. For Aristotle's understanding of the philosopher's preoccupation with truth and falsehood, see *Metaphysics* 997a14–15; for his interest in first principles and causes, see *Metaphysics* 1003b18–19; and for his capacity to theorize on all subjects, see *Metaphysics* 1004a33–34.

10. See *Rhetoric* 3.1.5 and 1.1.1.

is rightly called a knowledge of Truth *[epistêmen tês alêtheias]*. The object of theoretic knowledge is truth, while that of practical knowledge is action; for even when they are investigating how a thing is so, practical men study not the external principles but the relative and immediate application" (*Metaphysics* 993b20–24). Similarly, while philosophy concerns itself with "the actual forms of things," rhetoric is interested in the way things participate in these forms: "For instance, the philosopher asks what is injustice, the orator states that so-and-so is an unjust man: the former inquires into the nature of despotism, the latter [into] what is a despot" (*Problems* 956b6–10).

Yet another point on which Aristotle converges with Plato concerns the distinction between enlightened politics and rhetoric. Whereas Plato had argued that the Sophists imitate the statesman and had subordinated rhetoric to knowledgeable political rule or statesmanship (*Statesman* 304), Aristotle claims that rhetoric, which the Sophists do practice, resembles, but is not the same as, political science. Aware that some Sophists confuse rhetoric with political science while others rank rhetoric as the superior of the two (*Nicomachean Ethics* 1181a14–15), he asserts in no uncertain terms that these two areas of study differ at least in rank: rhetoric is subordinate to political science (*Nicomachean Ethics* 1094b2–3).[11] When considering the question of who should teach the science of legislation, Aristotle notes that in most other sciences it is the experts and the practitioners who do the teaching. However, in the case of politics, which includes legislation, "the sophists, who profess to teach the science [of politics] never practice it" (*Nicomachean Ethics* 1180b35–1181a1). Asserting that knowledge of politics requires both experience and study, Aristotle observes that "those sophists who profess to teach politics are found to be very far from doing so successfully. In fact, they are absolutely ignorant of the very nature of the science and of the subjects with which it deals" (*Nicomachean Ethics* 1181a12–14). As we move from Plato to Aristotle, the explicit change from statesmanship to political science and the implicit change from practice to study should be obvious; but so should rhetoric's unchanged status. For both Plato and Aristotle, rhetoric is not simply different from politics; it is inferior to it.

Finally, Aristotle departs from Plato's view that the Sophists imitate the orator by suggesting that they, indeed, are orators.[12] In this capacity, they are

---

11. Even so, Aristotle acknowledges that rhetoric is not entirely foreign to political science. On the contrary, political science is a constitutive part of rhetoric: "Rhetoric is composed of analytical science and of that branch of political science which is concerned with Ethics" (*Rhetoric* 1.4.8).

12. However, recall Plato's view in the *Gorgias* (465c) that sophists and orators appear to be of the same class.

said to have engaged in various practices, some of which Aristotle regards as consistent with his own conception of the art of rhetoric, and
some of which he does not approve. For example, he endorses Prodicus'
way of waking up an audience dozing off (*Rhetoric* 3.14.9) and Gorgias'
witty response to the bird that let fall her droppings upon him (*Rhetoric*
3.3.4). Additionally, observe his advice to confound the opponents' earnest with jest and their jest with earnest (*Rhetoric* 3.18.7) and his
acknowledgement of Protagoras' contribution to the purity of style by
using gender-specific nouns (*Rhetoric* 3.5.5). By contrast, he disapproves
of Protagoras' promise to make the weaker argument stronger and finds
people's disgust with it justifiable (*Rhetoric* 2.24.11). Likewise, he considers Gorgias' style too affected by poetry to serve adequately the
purposes of prose (*Rhetoric* 3.1.9).

If, then, Plato rejected the Sophists, Aristotle sought to demonstrate
where they had erred or left matters more or less unfinished. This correcting and supplementing stance is not inconsistent with his treatment of
most of his predecessors, whom, as Cope notes, he "hardly ever
mentions . . . except for the purpose of finding fault."[13] The fault of the
Sophists in the field of rhetoric, Aristotle suggests, was their tendency to
disregard linguistic norms of proper usage and taste; in the field of argument it was their proclivity to ignore or violate the rules of correct reasoning.[14] Their disregard of proper language and their transgressions against
reason aside, the Sophists did what they could, according to Aristotle, to
advance the art of rhetoric, but they naturally left the task of its further
development to their successors. Himself one of their successors, Aristotle
seems to have reasoned that the Sophists' rhetorical precepts needed not
to be dismissed and ridiculed in the manner of Plato; rather, they needed
first to be taken into account as signposts of the rhetorical tradition, and
second to be elaborated and corrected.

---

13. E. M. Cope, *An Introduction to Aristotle's Rhetoric* (Cambridge: Macmillan
and Co., 1867), p. 43. Addressing Aristotle's attitude toward his predecessors,
Cherniss has identified many references in Aristotle's works that "demonstrate in
an uncontroversial manner his tendency to accommodate to his own doctrines
every possible early statement by a reinterpretation of its obvious meaning." See
Harold Cherniss, *Aristotle's Criticism of Presocratic Philosophy* (Baltimore: Johns
Hopkins University Press, 1935), p. 339.

14. Of course, Aristotle is relying on the linguistic uses and tastes of his age, and
on the rules of logic he articulates in his *Analytics*.

Attempting to show how his rhetorical inheritance had developed into his present theoretical views, Aristotle situates the Sophists at the beginnings of the history of rhetoric and acknowledges his debt to them, in effect according them the kind of respect commonly due the progenitors of a tradition. In so doing, he also places himself at the end of a long chain of development, a position carrying the obligation to extend and improve what one has inherited. This is how he puts the matter in his *Sophistical Refutations* (183b17–34):

In all discoveries, either the results of other people's work have been taken over and after having been first elaborated have been subsequently advanced step by step by those who took them over, or else they are original inventions which usually make progress which at first is small but of much greater utility than the later development which results from them. It is perhaps a true proverb which says that the beginning of anything is the most important; hence it is also the most difficult. For as it is very powerful in its effects, so it is very small in size and therefore very difficult to see. When, however, the first beginning has been discovered, it is easier to add to it and develop the rest. This has happened, too, with rhetorical composition *[peri tous rhêtorikous logous]*, and also practically with all the other arts. Those who discovered the beginnings of rhetoric carried them forward quite a little way, whereas the famous modern professors of the art, entering into the heritage, so to speak, of a long series of predecessors who had gradually advanced it, have brought it to its present perfection—Tisias following the first inventors, Thrasymachus following Tisias, Theodorus following Thrasymachus, while numerous others have made numerous contributions; hence it is no wonder that the art possesses a certain amplitude *[plethos]*.

Amplitude, however, does not mean completion or even adequacy; rather, it means, at least in this case, a wide availability of materials from which to choose and many options to consider while rearticulating one's heritage and giving it a new direction. Cognizant of the tradition he had stepped into, and seemingly indebted to the Sophists, Aristotle takes it upon himself to further the rhetorical art and thus to make his own contribution to it. Generally embodied in his *Rhetoric*, his contribution consists of a new arrangement of the available precepts and a bold step in a theoretical direction. But in addition to its novelty, Aristotle's elaboration is illustrated and given legitimacy by means of a multitude of citations from Homer, the tragedians, the Sophists, and the Orators, citations suggesting that his views about rhetoric are well grounded in the discursive practices of both his ancestors and his contemporaries.[15] However, what he has to say about sophistical rhetoric goes beyond his celebrated treatise and is to be found in many of his other works, including the *Topics, On Sophistical Refutations*, the *Ethics*, the *Politics*, and the *Poetics*.[16]

Considered together, the above comments suggest that in Aristotle's mind the Sophists' contributions to the art of discourse, however minimal or inadequate, must be valued because they at least stimulated further developments and shaped the understanding of subsequent thinkers and practitioners.

---

15. The overview and synthesis of the rhetorical tradition in Aristotle's hands were apparently more pronounced in his now-lost *Sunagôgê Technôn*. In an apparent reference to this treatise, Cicero observes (*De inventione* 2.2.6–7): "Aristotle brought together in a single compilation the ancient writers on the art of rhetoric, going right back to their founder and inventor, Tisias; with great care he sought out the main tenets of each author name by name, wrote them down clearly, and meticulously expounded the difficult passages. And with the charm and brevity of his diction he so excelled the inventors themselves that no-one looks to learn their precepts from the original books, but everyone who wants to understand what they were resorts to Aristotle as a far more convenient expositor. Thus Aristotle published his own views and also those of his predecessors, so that from this work we become acquainted both with his own views and with the others." Quoted in Jonathan Barnes, ed., *The Complete Works of Aristotle*, 2 vols. (Princeton: Princeton University Press, 1984), 1:2430.

Regarding the ways in which Aristotle changed the rhetorical tradition, see Friedrich Solmsen, "The Aristotelian Tradition in Ancient Rhetoric," in *Aristotle: The Classical Heritage of Rhetoric*, ed. Keith V. Erickson, (Metuchen, N.J.: Scarecrow Press, 1974), pp. 278–309.

On the impact of Aristotle's move from the practical to the theoretical level, E. M. Cope has observed: "The effect of this modification . . . is to withdraw the notion of the art in some degree from the exclusively practical application of it encouraged by the sophistical school, and to fix the attention rather upon its theory and method; in short, it tends to a more scientific treatment of the subject" (*Introduction*, p. 34). To Cope's observation we can add that Aristotle's attention to rhetorical theory and method also changed rhetoric's function from persuading to knowing or discovering the available means of persuasion (*ou to peisai ergon autês, alla to idein ta uparchonta pithana*) (*Rhetoric* 1.1.14).

16. For the connection between *Rhetoric* and *Poetics* see Solmsen, "Introduction," in *Aristotle: Rhetoric and Poetics*, trans. W. Rhys Roberts and Igram Bywater (New York: Modern Library, 1954), pp. xi–xiv. For the connection between the *Rhetoric*, the *Ethics*, and the *Politics*, see Christopher L. Johnstone, "An Aristotelian Trilogy: Ethics, Rhetoric, Politics, and the Search for Moral Truth," *Philosophy and Rhetoric* 13 (Winter 1980): 1–24.

Even if their views may seem somewhat odd or superficial to their successors, the Sophists are not to be dismissed lightly. Because early investigations are always problematic[17] and because subsequent generations are usually the beneficiaries of such investigations, the proper attitude toward the early contributors to an art is gratitude:

> It is only fair to be grateful not only to those whose views we can share but also to those who have expressed rather superficial opinions. They too have contributed something; by their preliminary work they have formed our mental experience. If there had been no Timotheus, we should not possess much of our music; and if there had been no Phrynis, there would have been no Timotheus. It is just the same in the case of those who have theorized about reality *[tôn peri tês alêtheias apophênomenôn]*: we have derived certain views from some of them, and they in turn are indebted to others (*Metaphysics* 993b12–19).

Part of Aristotle's attitude toward the Sophists can be discerned by two simple and warranted changes in this passage: first, replacing "those who have theorized about reality" with the phrase, "those who have done work in rhetoric"; and second, extending the logic of the Phrynis-Timotheus relation to read as follows: "If there had been no Sophists, we should not possess much of our rhetoric; and if there had been no rhetoric, there would have been no Aristotle." Inasmuch, then, as the Sophists were among the earliest practitioners and teachers of rhetoric, their initial observations are credited with having influenced the thinking of their successors, including that of Aristotle. But what sounds historically worthwhile to Aristotle as overviewer of the early days of rhetoric appears inferior to Aristotle as critic of public discourse. Interestingly, what makes the Sophists' views simultaneously worthy and inferior is one thing: their preliminariness. Preliminary discoveries, for Aristotle, are almost inherently tentative, incomplete, and inadequate. By contrast, subsequent findings, e.g. Aristotle's own, are more definitive, more complete, and more adequate. This is the Aristotelian system of development at work: successors generally outshine, outperform, and outdo their predecessors; or, the closer an idea or a practice is to its end, its *telos*, the better it is. Hence the general tendency of many traditional historians of rhetoric to regard Aristotle's *Rhetoric* as a refinement of previous versions of the art.

---

17. See also *Metaphysics* 993a15, where Aristotle notes that "the earliest philosophy speaks falteringly, as it were, on all subjects; being new and in its infancy."

Beyond Aristotle's expressed gratitude to sophistical rhetoric there lies the distant and impersonal discourse of a seemingly objective historian intent on describing the thinking and practices of the Sophists. This discourse is complemented by that of a scientist (really, a knower) whose novel discoveries are invoked so as to straighten out the warped rules of the Sophists' operations and to affirm the priority of the real over the apparent. In the *Rhetoric*, for example, Aristotle points out that the Sophists had perverted the art of persuasion by relying too much on its nonessential features *(prosthêkai or tôn exô tou pragmatos)*. As writers of technical handbooks *(technai)*, they gave inordinate emphasis to emotional appeals, personal appearances and stylistic techniques of delivery but ignored enthymematic reasoning, which is the body *(sôma)* of proof *(Rhetoric* 1.1.3). Further, they did not approach rhetoric methodically, that is, as an art with its own principles and rules. Because their main interest lay in practical matters and success in persuasion, they taught rhetoric not systematically but by relying on the various results of the art, not on the art itself *(Sophistical Refutations* 184a). In effect, they dealt mostly with rhetoric's countless particularities, not realizing that the totality of all these particularities does not amount to the essence of the art itself.

The same historico-critical tone is apparent in Aristotle's discussion of the Sophists' studies and practices in the field of reasoning. Generally, Aristotle charges the Sophists with espousing a fallacious logic and with juggling irrelevant arguments *(tois allotriois logois) (Eudemian Ethics* 1218b23).[18] Moreover, he notes that much of their argumentation is driven by their love of paradox. While discussing some of the difficulties arising out of the common opinions regarding virtuous behavior, Aristotle notes: "the sophists wish to show their cleverness by entrapping their adversary into a paradox, and when they are successful, the resultant chain of reasoning ends in a deadlock; the mind is fettered, being unwilling to stand still because it cannot approve the conclusion reached yet unable to go forward because it cannot untie the knot of the argument." To illustrate his point, Aristotle alludes to one of the Sophists' familiar arguments, which seeks to prove that "Folly combined with Unrestraint is a virtue. It runs as follows: if a man is foolish and also unrestrained, owing to his unrestraint he does the opposite of what he believes he ought to do; but he believes that good things are bad, and that he ought not do do them; therefore he will do good things and not bad ones" *(Nicomachean Ethics* 1146a22–30). Aristotle refutes this argument by means

---

18. See also *Sophistical Refutations* 169b21–25.

of a lengthy discussion of the character of restraint and unrestraint (*Nicomachean Ethics* 1146b8–1152a).

In addition to their paradoxical character, sophistical arguments are frequently contrary to generally-held views. One such argument is that "not everything which is has come into being or is eternal" (*Topics* 104b25–26). Aristotle counters one part of this claim by maintaining that "everything which is generated is generated from something and by something; and by something formally identical with itself." On the basis of this thesis, which is part of his larger discussion of the priority of actuality over potentiality, he reasons that "it seems impossible that a man can be a builder if he has never built, or a harpist if he has never played a harp; because he who learns to play the harp learns by playing it, and similarly in all other cases. This," he goes on to say, "was the origin of the sophists' quibble that a man who does not know a given science will be doing that which is the object of that science, because the learner does not know the science." Aristotle responds to this sophistical quibble by observing that "since something of that which is being generated is already generated . . . presumably the learner too must possess something of that science" (*Metaphysics* 1049b28–1050a1). Aristotle refutes several other sophistical arguments, but there is no need to list them all; nor is there any need to explore their nuances in detail. For our purpose, it suffices to say that in all his refutations the point is the same: when it comes to proper ways of reasoning, the Sophists falter often.

Thus far we have seen some of the ways in which Aristotle's perception of the Sophists resembles and differs from Plato's. We have also seen that Aristotle treats the Sophists as worthy of consideration both for their early discoveries in rhetoric and for their errors in reasoning. Convinced that their discoveries call for gratitude while their errors require correction, Aristotle attempts to redirect the rhetorical tradition and to rectify the sophistical mistakes in logic. In both cases, he searches for disciplinary rules whose observance promises to set both rhetoric and logic on the "proper" path to development. In what follows, I turn to Aristotle's treatment of the Sophists in the light of his understanding of philosophy. As we will see, this treatment echoes many Platonic themes suggesting that the Sophists are not philosophers.

Aristotle's philosophical outlook toward the Sophists is reflected in a few definitions and in several references to their epistemological claims, their rhetorical practices, their ways of reasoning, their enterprising spirit, their motives, and to various miscellaneous items. Although they are more or less internally consistent, all these elements of the larger picture lack brightness in color and fail to convey a vivid impression of the Sophists as men of words. On the other hand, they outline with remarkable specificity and clarity the parameters within which the Sophists and their practices are to be found. In and through his definitions of the sophist and sophistry, Aristotle manages to distinguish the sophist from other intellectuals and sophistry from the arts to which it bears a confusing resemblance. At a time when the public often confused rhetoric, sophistic, and dialectic, Aristotle took it upon himself to clarify each practice and to spell out the differences among them. However, putting an end to public confusion was only part of his motivation. A stronger motive seems to have been the wish to assert the primacy of philosophy. After all, Aristotle understands himself primarily as a philosopher, not as a rhetorician.

To begin with, Aristotle notes that sophists and dialecticians resemble the philosopher but are, in fact, different from him. The main difference is as wide as that between appearance and reality: the Sophists appear to be as wise as the philosophers and, along with the dialecticians, seem to be discussing the same subjects the philosophers are. In Aristotle's words, "dialecticians and sophists wear the same appearance as the philosopher, for sophistry is Wisdom *[sophia]* in appearance only, and dialecticians discuss all subjects, and Being is a subject common to them all." Further distinguishing sophists and dialecticians from the philosopher, he observes that "sophistry and dialectic are concerned with the same class of subjects as philosophy, but philosophy differs from the former in the nature of its capability and from the latter in its outlook on life. Dialectic treats as an exercise what philosophy tries to understand, and sophistry seems to be philosophy, but is not" (*Metaphysics* 1004b17–27).

In what seems to be an unmistakable reiteration of the Platonic separation of reality from appearance, the genuine from the counterfeit, Aristotle maintains that what the Sophists do has all the features of what the philosopher does—their wisdom appears like philosophy and sounds like philosophy. But in "reality" sophistical and philosophical wisdom are worlds apart even though inexperienced thinkers cannot tell the difference. One of the better-known practices of the Sophists is refutation. Like dialecticians, they entertain their interlocutors' claims in the give-and-take of critical discussion only to refute them, thereby demonstrating their expertise and superiority in argument. However, the principal problem with the sophistical kinds of refutation is that they are apparent, not real. In the opening lines of his *Sophistical Refutations* (164a23–164b27), Aristotle takes the distinction between appearance and reality as a given, and then applies it to refutative arguments:

> That some reasonings are really reasonings, but that others seem to be, but are not really, reasonings, is obvious. For, as this happens in other

spheres from a similarity between the true and the false, so it happens also in arguments. For some people possess good physical condition, while others have merely the appearance of it, by blowing themselves out and dressing themselves up like the tribal choruses; again some people are beautiful because of their beauty, while others have the appearance of beauty because they trick themselves out. . . . In the same way also reasoning and refutation are sometimes real and sometimes not, but appear to be real owing to men's inexperience.

Making yet another distinction between sophistry and philosophy, Aristotle points out that while the exclusive province of philosophy is to study the attributes of Being *qua* Being, sophistry, like dialectic, "deal[s] with the attributes of existing things, but not of things *qua* Being, nor . . . of Being itself in so far as it is Being" (*Metaphysics* 1061b8–9). In other words, while philosophy studies what is substantive and essential, sophistry concerns itself with what is superficial and incidental. Unlike the philosopher, whose aim is to study "the whole of reality in its essential nature" (*Metaphysics* 1005b6–7),[19] Aristotle holds that the sophist is preoccupied with the accidental *(to sumbebêkos),* which "is only, as it were, a name." Instead of dealing with reality as it is—instead, that is, of addressing the necessity of what is—the sophist addresses the non-necessity of what is not. Therefore, Aristotle concludes, "in a way Plato was not far from wrong in making sophistry deal with what is nonexistent; because the sophists discuss the accident[al] more, perhaps, than any other people."[20] In effect, he suggests that if something happens neither always nor usually, if it is outside the realm of necessity or custom, we may treat it as though it did not happen at all. Alternatively, we may treat it as misleading because it resides at the surface of things whereas the essence is to be found in their core.[21]

In addition to defining the Sophists by reference to their interest in appearances and their preoccupation with the accidental, Aristotle discusses

---

19. See also *Metaphysics* 993b20–24, 997a14–15, 1003b18–19, and 1004a33–34.

20. *Metaphysics* 1026b15–22. See also *Metaphysics* 1064b27–29. For Aristotle's definition of the accidental, see *Metaphysics* 1025a14ff.

21. For a discussion of the relationship between surface and core in Aristotle's *Rhetoric*, see John Poulakos, "Aristotle's Indebtedness to the Sophists" in *Argument in Transition: Proceedings of the Third Summer Conference on Argumentation,* ed. David Zarefsky, Malcolm O. Sillars, and Jack Rhodes, (Annandale, Va.: Speech Communication Association, 1983), pp. 27–42.

them in terms of their purpose, which, he claims, distinguishes them from the dialecticians but not from the rhetoricians. In the field of rhetoric, he notes, there is no distinction between one who speaks according to sound argument *(kata tên epistêmên)* and one who speaks according to moral purpose *(kata tên proairesin)*. However, "in dialectic it is the moral purpose that makes the sophist, the dialectician being one whose arguments rest not on moral purpose but on the faculty" *(Rhetoric* 1.1.14).[22] The distinction between sophists and dialecticians is also made in *Sophistical Refutations* (171b7–8), this time, however, in terms of the reality-appearance dichotomy: "The man who views general principles in the light of the particular case is a dialectician, while he who only apparently does this is a sophist." Again, the best a sophist can do is appear to be a dialectician.

Time and again, Aristotle claims that "the sophistic art consists in an apparent and not real wisdom, and the sophist is one who makes money from apparent and not real wisdom." By contrast, the "really" wise man is one who tries "to refrain from fallacious arguments about the subjects of his knowledge and to be able to expose him who uses them." The wise man (the philosopher) can make money too, if he so wishes, by capitalizing on his knowledge; but generally a philosopher does not care about money.[23] What he does care about is giving sound reasons for his claims and trying to extract sound reasons from others. But if this is so, Aristotle argues, "it is essential for those who wish to play the sophist to seek out the kind of argument which we have mentioned [the kind that gives reasons or refutes]; for it is well worth his while, since the possession of such a faculty [the faculty of reason-giving and refuting] will cause him to appear to be wise, and this is the real purpose which sophists have in view" *(Sophistical Refutations* 165a22–32).

---

22. In his explanation of this passage, J. H. Freese, the translator, states (p. 14): "The essence of sophistry consists in the moral purpose, the deliberate use of fallacious arguments. In Dialectic, the dialectician has the power or faculty of making use of them when he pleases; when he does so deliberately, he is called a sophist." See Aristotle, *"Art" of Rhetoric*, trans. J. H. Freese (Cambridge: Harvard University Press, 1975).

For Aristotle's additional comments on the distinction between capacity and deliberate purpose *(proairesis)*, see *Topics* 126a30–126b 3; *Nicomachean Ethics* 1127b15; and *Rhetoric* 1.13.10.

23. In this regard, Aristotle recounts a story about Thales, who made a large sum of money by relying on his knowledge of astronomy to predict a rich crop of olives, "proving that it is easy for philosophers to be rich if they choose, but this is not what they care about" *(Politics* 1259a6–19).

Clearly, Aristotle's wise man is not content simply to offer "real" proofs of what he claims; he also tries to expose the apparentness of the apparently wise, that is, of the sophist. This is precisely what Aristotle tries to accomplish in several of his works, especially in his *Sophistical Refutations*. The way he proceeds is first to work out a calculus of reasoning (i.e., in the *Analytics* and *Topics*) and then to show how the Sophists do not measure up to it.[24] However, Aristotle ultimately falls short of the goal of an air-tight distinction between the "real" and the "apparent" reasoner. For there is nothing to prevent the sophist from appearing to be doing "for real" all the things a wise thinker would be expected to do. Conversely, there is nothing to prevent the perception that a wise thinker is only practicing another form of "apparent" wisdom. Finally, as Aristotle himself observes, "there is nothing to prevent a man [from] accepting what are not facts rather than the truth" (*Topics* 161a31). But if this is so, Aristotle can only be said to have taken refuge in the domain of a reality he considered superior to that of the Sophists.

In this Aristotelian reality, reasoning and refutation are thought out well (without inconsistencies and contradictions) and carried out exactly.[25] By contrast, the kind of reasoning or refutation sophistry employs is not only apparent but also irrelevant: "By sophistical reasonings and refutations I mean not only the seeming but unreal reasoning or refutation but also one which, though real, only seems to be, but is not really, germane to the subject at hand."[26] Sophistry, in other words, often brings into a discussion materials not pertaining to the subject under consideration.[27] In doing so, it may succeed in contradicting the man under examination but it does not "make clear whether he is ignorant." Aristotle maintains that a question-and-answer procedure should engage the ignorant and should seek to expose their ignorance. The Sophists, however, do not limit themselves to the ignorant; they also try to

---

24. On this point, Classen ("Aristotle's Picture of the Sophists," p. 14) has argued that "Aristotle is not concerned merely to refute, let alone ridicule fallacious arguments of the sophists, but again and again to reveal the reasons for their fallacies and the basis for their errors."

25. For the meaning of *exactitude*, see Aristotle's *Protrepticus* (45).

26. See also *Eudemian Ethics* 1218b23.

27. This critical observation coincides with Aristotle's complaint in the *Rhetoric* (1.1.4) that litigants often talk about things that have nothing to do with the case, and with his wish that all courts should adopt the Court of the Areopagos' policy of restricting speech to what has a direct bearing on the case at hand.

entrap *(empodizousi)* with sophistical arguments "even the man of scientific knowledge" *(ton eidota)* (*Sophistical Refutations* 169b20–29).[28] Employing fallacies connected with the accidental *(to sumbebêkos)*, they often succeed in creating the impression that they have refuted even the specialists and the experts: "they argue with the men of science with reasonings based on accident, and the latter, being incapable of making distinctions, either give in when questioned, or think they have done so when they have not" (*Sophistical Refutations* 169b7–10).

Aristotle's attempts to specify who the Sophists are leads him to distinguish them from yet another class of "pseudo"-intellectuals: the Eristics. While both classes are interested in semblances and winning intellectual contests through similar arguments, the Eristics are after victory *(nikê)* while the Sophists are after an impressive reputation *(doxa)*. As Aristotle puts it, "those who behave like this [fighting unfairly in argument] merely to win a victory, are generally regarded as contentious and quarrelsome *[eristikoi anthrôpoi kai philerides]*, while those who do so to win a reputation which will help them to make money are regarded as sophistical." The difference between Eristics and Sophists, then, lies in their motives: "Quarrelsome people [eristics] and sophists use the same arguments, but not for the same reasons; and the same argument will be sophistical and contentious but not from the same point of view. If the semblance of victory is the motive, it is contentious; if the semblance of wisdom, it is sophistical; for sophistry is an appearance of wisdom without the reality" (*Sophistical Refutations* 171b25–34).

Having distinguished the Sophists from dialecticians, philosophers, and eristics, Aristotle gives several examples of their reasoning, which he generally finds erroneous. One of their argumentative practices is to exaggerate the principle of identity and thus to deny that "Koriscos" is the same as "good Koriscos" (*Eudemian Ethics* 1240 24–25). In effect, they argue that there is a difference between the individual thing and its essence, an argument which Aristotle disposes of by maintaining that at least "in the case of primary and self-subsistent terms, the individual thing and its essence are one and the same." Then he goes on: "It is obvious that the sophistical objections to this thesis [identity of the individual thing and its essence] are met in the same way as the question whether Socrates is the same as the essence of Socrates; for there is no difference either in the grounds of asking the question or in the means of meeting it successfully" (*Metaphysics* 1032a6–11).

------

28. Insofar as the men of knowledge were men of authority in Aristotle's culture, this sophistical practice was obviously undermining epistemological authority.

Another argumentative practice the Sophists engage in is to respond to questions demanding specificity by answering "'Partly yes and partly no,' 'Some are but some are not,' 'In one sense it is so, in another not.'" But when someone responds thus (that is, sophistically), Aristotle reports that "the hearers cry out against him as being in difficulty" (*Rhetoric* 3.18.4). This may be an indirect criticism of the notion of *dissoi logoi*, in whose spirit the Sophists were making double and opposing responses even when the request was for a single answer. It may also suggest Aristotle's solution to the problem of the doubleness of discourse: of any two opposing answers, one is always superior to the other. In either case, it is noteworthy that he himself engages in the same sophistical practice when addressing the meaning of "now" in his discussion of time and motion: "the 'now,' which is identical everywhere, itself *retains its identity in one sense, but does not in another* [my emphasis]; for inasmuch as the point in the flux of time which it marks is changing (and so to mark it is its essential function) the 'now' too differs perpetually, but inasmuch as at every moment it is performing its essential function of dividing the past and future it retains its identity" (*Physics* 219b13–15). To support his point that a thing can retain its identity and also be different (in terms of its relations), Aristotle refers to the sophistical argument that distinguishes "between Koriscos in the Lyceum and Koriscos in the market-place" (*Physics* 219b21–22).

Yet another sophistical practice Aristotle mentions—in fact, he calls it "the most sophistical of all frauds" *(to malista sophistikon sukophantêma)*—is one questioners use often and which "produces a striking appearance of refutation, when, though they have proved nothing, they do not put the final proposition in the form of a question but state conclusively, as though they had proved it, that 'such and such a thing, then, is not the case'" (*Sophistical Refutations* 174b9–12). This practice is termed sophistical because it does not follow the proper procedure: instead of asking a question, it makes a statement.

Having exposed the weaknesses of sophistical reasoning, Aristotle next questions the knowledge the Sophists claim to possess and impart. In his estimation, they can be said to know only accidentally *(kata to sumbebêkos)*; the true causation and necessity of things, the two elements of knowledge, generally escape them: "We consider that we have unqualified knowledge of anything (as contrasted with the accidental knowledge of the sophist) when we believe that we know (i) that the cause from which the fact results is the cause of that fact, and (ii) that the fact cannot be otherwise" (*Posterior Analytics* 71b9–12). However, this conceptualization of knowledge is foreign to the Sophists, who believe that to know is to have knowledge *(to epistasthai to epistêmên echein)* (*Posterior Analytics* 74b23). Accordingly, they assume they know something if the premises of their starting point are generally accepted and true. However, Aristotle objects, "the starting-point is not that which is generally accepted or the reverse, but that which is primarily true of the genus with which the demonstration deals; and not every true fact is peculiar to a given genus" (*Posterior Analytics* 74b24–25). Because the Sophists' knowledge is questionable, Aristotle observes, they demand their fees in advance; otherwise, "nobody would pay money for the knowledge which they possess" (*Nicomachean Ethics* 1164a32). The one exception to this financial arrangement was Protagoras, who "used to tell his pupil to estimate the value he set upon his knowledge, and accepted a fee of that amount" (*Nicomachean Ethics* 1164a25–27). This way, he avoided facing complaints from students about not meeting his promises and not fulfilling his part of the educational bargain.

Finally, Aristotle critiques the Sophists' use of language, charging them with using it improperly.[29] Their attempts to refute their opponents and create the illusion of demonstration are characterized by such linguistic fallacies as "equivocation *(omônumia)*, ambiguity *(amphibolia)*, combination *(sunthesis)*, division *(diairesis)*, accent *(prosôidia)*, and form of expression *(schêma lexeôs)*" (*Sophistical Refutations* 165b25–27). In and through these fallacious forms of language the Sophists succeed in creating the impression of refuting their opponents and in victimizing those inexperienced in the power of names *(tôn onomatôn tês dunameôs) (Sophistical Refutations* 165a17). In effect, the Sophists exploit not only the malleability but also the inadequacy of language, the fact that it does not have a name for every single thing: "names and a quantity of terms are finite, whereas things are infinite in number; and so the same expression and the single name must necessarily signify a number of things" (*Sophistical Refutations* 165a11–14). Assuming that understanding requires that one know exactly which one thing out of a number is signified, Aristotle suggests that the Sophists often frustrate their interlocutors' understanding by using names and expressions signifying more than one thing. In this regard, he notes that they often use homonyms (*Rhetoric* 3.2.7; *Sophistical Refutations* 165b30–166a6). Aristotle discusses the six fallacies that depend on language, offers examples of each, and proposes that the way to combat them is to advance "the opposite of that on which the argument [at hand] turns" (*Sophistical Refutations* 179a11–13).

----

29. For an extended discussion of Aristotle's views on language, see Richard McKeon, "Aristotle's Conception of Language and the Arts of Language," *Classical Philology* 41 (October 1946): 193–206, and 42 (January 1947): 21–50.

On a more specific note, he takes issue with the claim of Bryson the Sophist that (as Aristotle puts it) "there is no such thing as foul language, because in whatever words you put a given thing your meaning is the same." Aristotle counters: "This is untrue. One term may describe a thing more truly than another, may be more like it, and set it more intimately before our eyes. Besides, two different words will represent a thing in two different lights; so on this ground also one term must be held fairer or fouler than another. For both of two terms will indicate what *is* fair, or what *is* foul, but not simply their fairness or foulness, or if so, at any rate not in an equal degree" (*Rhetoric* 3.2.13).

In this essay, we have considered Aristotle's perception of the Sophists and some of the ways in which it resembles and differs from Plato's. What we have seen is that the Aristotelian perception is informed by two perspectives, the one historical-rhetorical, the other philosophical-logical. Aristotle the rhetorical historian and theorist treats the Sophists with the respect due the pioneers of a tradition. At the same time, he undertakes to correct some of their rhetorical precepts and to add to their contributions to rhetoric by marking out a new territory, the territory of rhetorical theory. On the other hand, Aristotle the philosopher and logician critiques the Sophists for being concerned with appearances rather than with reality and for dwelling on the accidental rather than on the necessary or the regular. Moreover, he faults their conception of knowledge and disapproves of their typical discourses for containing linguistic as well as logical fallacies. Further, he exposes the weaknesses of their refutative practices as well as their failure to give reasons. Finally, he calls into question their notion of discursive relevance, their love of paradox, and their disregard of the proper uses of language. Insofar as Aristotle sought to correct the reasoning of the Sophists, he can be said to have followed Plato's steps; but insofar as he attempted to extend the rhetorical tradition they had begun, he can be said to have marked out an independent path, one on which we travel still.

Three

Toward a Predisciplinary Analysis of Gorgias' *Helen*

Edward Schiappa

Gorgias' *Encomium of Helen* (hereinafter *Helen*) has earned a central place in the recent revival of interest in sophistic and neo-sophistic rhetorical studies. For its composition alone the speech has been the object of considerable controversy, with scholars as diverse as Dodds, Cole, Jebb, and Van Hook condemning Gorgias' stylistic "excesses,"[1] while Barrett, de Romilly, Crowley, and I have praised his artistry and creativity.[2] Descriptions and assessments of the theoretical content of the text are equally diverse. Scholars find evidence in the text of a psychological theory of *logos* (Segal), a magical account of discourse (de Romilly), an incipient "postmodern" theory of epistemology (Enos, Gronbeck, Untersteiner), a thinly-veiled defense of the art of Rhetoric (Poulakos), and a nonrepresentational theory of language and meaning (Mourelatos, Kerferd).[3] Despite the great interest the

---

1. E. R. Dodds, *Plato: Gorgias* (Oxford: Clarendon, 1959), p. 9; Thomas Cole, *The Origins of Rhetoric in Ancient Greece* (Baltimore: Johns Hopkins University Press, 1991), p. 73; Richard C. Jebb, *The Attic Orators from Antiphon to Isaeos*, 2 vols. (New York: Russell and Russell, 1962), p. cxxiv; Larue Van Hook, *Isocrates*, vol. 3 (Cambridge: Harvard University Press, 1945). p. 122.

2. Harold Barrett, *The Sophists* (Novato, Calif.: Chandler and Sharp, 1987); Jacqueline de Romilly, *Les Grands Sophistes dans l'Athenes de Pericles* (Paris: Fallois, 1988), translated into English by Janet Lloyd as *The Great Sophists in Periclean Athens* (Oxford: Clarendon, 1992); Sharon Crowley, "A Plea for the Revival of Sophistry," *Rhetoric Review* 7 (1989): 318–34; Edward Schiappa, "An Examination and Exculpation of the Composition Style of Gorgias of Leontini," *Pre/Text* 12 (1991): 237–57.

3. Charles P. Segal, "Gorgias and the Psychology of the Logos," *Harvard Studies in Classical Philology* 66 (1962): 99–155; de Romilly, *Les Grands Sophistes*; Richard Leo Enos, "The Epistemology of Gorgias' Rhetoric: A Reexamination," *Southern Speech Communication Journal* 42 (1976): 35–51; Bruce E. Gronbeck, "Gorgias on Rhetoric and Poetic: A Rehabilitation,"

text has generated, there is remarkably little agreement about even the most rudimentary interpretive issues, such as the genre to which it belongs, the role it played in fifth-century B.C.E. rhetorical praxis, and its theoretical significance. Resolution of all these issues is unnecessary and perhaps even undesirable. Nonetheless, I believe that recent developments in the historiography of the Sophists opens a space from which to consider the text anew.

This essay offers a predisciplinary historical analysis of Gorgias' famous speech. I call the analysis "predisciplinary" to indicate my belief that the texts of fifth-century Greek writers, especially those by the figures commonly referred to as the Older Sophists, ought to be approached with the awareness that certain "disciplines" were not yet formalized either in theory or in practice. In particular, the dichotomy often used to distinguish between "philosophical" and "rhetorical" discourse is simply not evident in the texts of the fifth century that describe sophistic education.[4] Fifth-century texts concerning *logos*—such as Gorgias' *Helen*—differ substantially from fourth-century texts concerning rhetoric *(rhêtorikê)*—such as Plato's *Gorgias*, Alkidamas' *On Those Writing Written Speeches*, the *Rhetoric to Alexander*, and Aristotle's *On Rhetoric*. Prior to the fourth century, one rarely finds a distinction between the art or skill of producing discourse that seeks "truth," and the art or skill of producing discourse that seeks persuasion. Accordingly, a predisciplinary approach attempts to avoid vocabulary and assumptions

---

Southern Speech Communication Journal 38 (1972): 27–38; Mario Untersteiner, *The Sophists*, trans. Kathleeen Freeman (Oxford: Basil Blackwell, 1954); John Poulakos, "Gorgias' *Encomium to Helen* and the Defense of Rhetoric," *Rhetorica* 1 (1983): 1–16; Alexander P. D. Mourelatos, "Gorgias on the Function of Language," *Siculorum Gymnasium* 38 (1985): 607–38; G. B. Kerferd, "Meaning and Reference: Gorgias and the Relation between Language and Reality," in *Hê Archaia Sophistikê: The Sophistic Movement*, papers read at the First International Symposium on the Sophistic Movement Organised by the Greek Philosophical Society, 27–29 September 1982 (Athens: Athenian Library of Philosophy, 1984), pp. 215–22.

4. Edward Schiappa, "*Rhêtorikê*: What's in a Name?: Toward a Revised History of Early Greek Rhetorical Theory," *Quarterly Journal of Speech* 78 (February, 1992): 1–15. See also Schiappa, *Protagoras and Logos: A Study in Greek Philosophy and Rhetoric* (Columbia: University of South Carolina Press, 1991), and David M. Timmerman, "Ancient Greek Origins of Argumentation Theory: Plato's Transformation of *Dialegesthai* to Dialectic," *Argumentation and Advocacy* 29 (1993): 116–23.

about discursive theories and practice imported from the fourth century when analyzing fifth-century texts.

My contention is that certain persistent questions about Gorgias' *Helen* yield different and perhaps unanticipated answers once the speech is repositioned as a predisciplinary text. I will revisit three questions: What is the speech's *purpose*? What are its contributions to fifth-century discursive *practices*? What are its contributions to fifth-century *theory*? I offer five arguments: (1) Identifying Gorgias' *Helen* as an "epideictic" speech is a somewhat misleading characterization; (2) the speech is not a veiled defense of the art of rhetoric; (3) Gorgias may have inaugurated the prose genre of *encomia;* (4) Gorgias advanced fifth-century B.C.E. "rationalism" by enacting certain innovations in prose composition; and (5) the *Helen*'s most significant "theoretical" contribution is to offer a secular account of the workings of *logos*—an account that functioned as an exemplar for later theorists.

What is the Speech's Purpose?

Because the speech makes no reference to contemporary events, there is no confident way to date the text with precision; estimates range from before 415 to 393 B.C.E..[5] The speech is written in the Attic dialect, not in Sicilian Doric or in the Ionic one might expect from a Leontinian, a choice that suggests the text was designed for oral performance in a variety of venues: "The Attic 'dialect' was the least provincial of all, avoiding the extreme harshness of the Doric and the softness of the Ionic, and tended to be more and more the language of cultivated Greeks."[6]

The stated goal of the speech is to exonerate the legendary Helen of the charge of deserting her husband Menelaus and running away with Paris—the act that precipitated the famous Trojan War. The topic was a familiar one, as discussions of Helen's culpability can be found, among other places, in Homer

---

5. See M. L. Orsini, "La cronologica dell' *Encomio di Elena* di Gorgia e la *Troiane* di Euripide," *Dioniso* 19 (1956): 82–93; and Friedrich Blass, *Die attische Beredsamkeit*, 2nd ed., vol. 1 (Leipzig: Teubner, 1887), pp. 72–75.

6. George Norlin, *Isocrates*, vol. 2 (Cambridge: Harvard University Press, 1928–1929), pp. 348–349 n; cf. Isocrates 15.296 and Thomas Cole, *Origins*, pp. 74–75. Of course, later Attic became the "common," or *koinê*, dialect for all Greeks.

(*Iliad* 3.164) and Euripides (*Trojan Women* 914–1032, *Helen*).[7] Some have supposed that Gorgias' account may have been an answer to Euripides or vice versa, but as D. M. MacDowell argues, "There is no resemblance in details, and no strong reason to link Gorgias' discussion of Helen with anyone else's."[8]

Gorgias begins with a clear statement of purpose: his task is to remove, through reasoning *(logismos),* the unjust blame that Helen has received (1–2). After providing a brief account of her birth, personal qualities, and marriage (3–5), Gorgias posits a list of four possible causes behind Helen's departure to Troy: chance and the gods, physical force, persuasion by *logos*, or passion (6). He then addresses each of the four causes in turn, arguing that each is such a powerful force that Helen should not be blamed for her behavior. The amount of space he spends on each cause is noteworthy: Gods and chance are dealt with in one paragraph (6), as is force (7), while *logos* is addressed in seven (8–14) and passion in five (9–19). He then concludes by summarizing the causes and suggesting that he has accomplished his purpose (20–21).

Beyond Gorgias' stated agenda, for what purpose was the discourse composed and performed? Most commentators categorize the *Helen* as epideictic rhetoric.[9] The verb *epideiknumi* is typically translated as "display" or "show," and *epideixis* denotes a particular exhibition or demonstration. Since ancient writers refer to *Helen* as an epideictic address, it is commonly assumed that the purpose of the speech was to show off Gorgias' oratorical abilities. Segal calls it a "mythological showpiece of rhetoric" and an

----

7. Frank J. Groten's study of various treatments of the Helen legend in Greek literature makes it clear that Gorgias was not the first to argue that Helen was blameless. Furthermore, the many previous sympathetic treatments of Helen call into the question the claim that Gorgias' *Helen* was an unprecedented effort to "radically reconstruct" history in order to "dislodge a mythic source for misogynism" (Susan C. Jarratt, *The Return of the Sophists: Classical Rhetoric Refigured* [Carbondale: Southern Illinois University Press, 1991], p. 74). For a reading that argues Gorgias' *Helen* "reiterates in oratorical discourse the general trend toward further subjugation of women" in ancient Greece, see Susan Biesecker, "Feminist Criticism of Classical Rhetorical Texts: A Case Study of Gorgias' *Helen*," in *Realms of Rhetoric: Phonic, Graphic, Electronic,* ed. Victor J. Vitanza and Michelle Ballif (Arlington, Texas: Rhetoric Society of America, 1990), pp. 67–82.

8. D. M. MacDowell, *Gorgias: Encomium of Helen* (Bristol: Bristol Classical Press, 1982), p. 12. See also Blass, *Die attische Beredsamkeit*, 1:56–57.

9. See Van Hook, *Isocrates*, 3:54. Also Segal, "Gorgias and the Psychology of the Logos," p. 100.

"epideictic encomium," John Robinson dubs it a "display piece," Poulakos says that Gorgias in the speech "indulges in the delights afforded by epideictic rhetoric," and Van Hook deems it a "brilliant *tour de force*."[10] Susan C. Jarratt classifies the *Helen* as "epideictic" and says that Gorgias "exploits the latitude offered by a rhetorical performance," while Scott Consigny argues that all of Gorgias' speeches are categorized properly as epideictic and that Gorgias "uses the epideictic primarily to advertise his own rhetorical skills."[11] The purpose of Gorgias' display of oratorical prowess, most commentators believe, was to attract more students of rhetoric.

A predisciplinary reading of *Helen* problematizes, though does not necessarily reject, such a conclusion. To begin with, it is not at all clear that Gorgias' extant texts ought to be limited by the apparently mutually exclusive choice of "philosophy" or "rhetoric." Certainly in the past the *Helen* has been appropriated in just such a limiting fashion. Though often cited in histories of rhetoric, the *Helen* is rarely, if ever, mentioned in histories of Greek philosophy. As has been argued elsewhere, categorizing texts from the fifth century B.C.E. exclusively as "rhetoric" or "philosophy" often risks anachronism.[12] The question is, what were Gorgias' speeches supposed to accomplish? Were they "display" speeches intended solely to entertain? Or were they, at least in some instances, efforts to theorize about issues later labeled "philosophical"? Interpretations that privilege one feature of the text over the other can neglect the obvious answer that Gorgias' speeches—like anyone else's—potentially can serve multiple functions. Locating the text as predisciplinary gives us reason to hesitate before assessing it with specific, disciplinary criteria.

For example, it is inappropriate to confine *Helen* to the Aristotelian genre of epideictic rhetoric. Even though one can refer to a performance of *Helen* by Gorgias as an *epideixis*, and despite the etymological link between *epideixis* and *epideiktikê*, identifying the speech as an "epideictic" oration is somewhat misleading. Assignment of fifth-century texts to a specific genre of

---

10. Segal, "Gorgias," p. 100; John M. Robinson, "On Gorgias," in *Exegesis and Argument,* ed. E. N. Lee, A. P. D. Mourelatos, and R. M. Rorty (Assen, The Netherlands: Van Gorcum, 1973), p. 53; John Poulakos, "Gorgias' and Isocrates' Use of the Encomium," *Southern Speech Communication Journal* 51 (1986): 300–307; and Van Hook, *Isocrates,* p. 54.

11. See Jarratt, *The Return of the Sophists,* p. 59; and Scott Consigny, "Gorgias' Use of the Epideictic," *Philosophy and Rhetoric* 25 (1992): 281–97.

12. See Schiappa, *"Rhêtorikê"* and *Protagoras.*

discourse may presume a greater degree of genre-related compositional expectations than were the case during Gorgias' career. Aristotle's well-known threefold taxonomy of rhetoric was not codified until his lectures, given decades after Gorgias' death.[13] Accordingly, one problem with characterizing *Helen* as epideictic is that a discrete genre of epideictic rhetoric is not clearly identified as such until well into the fourth century. In fact, Aristotle's conceptual formulation of epideictic rhetoric is almost certainly original. The earliest extant use of the word *epideiktikê* is in Plato's *Sophist* (224b5), where it is used to describe "the art of display" that helps to define the profession of the Sophists. The *Sophist* was one of Plato's later dialogues, however, and the prior absence of the word suggests that it is prompted by fourth-century Sophists and has been applied only with hindsight to sophistic speeches of the previous century. *Epideiktikê* might have been yet another example of Plato's original construction of an *-ikê* word to designate a specific art or skill.[14]

Thomas Cole contends that the word "epideictic" is part of a later standard terminology that has its roots in the "preanalytic stage" of the history of rhetoric. He suggests that what marks a speech as *epideixis* is that it is *written to be presented* rather than the quality of "showing off":

> Epideictic oratory will then be, in origin, what *epideixis* is in Xenophon's account of Prodicus: not the showing off one one's talents, but the displaying or revealing (orally) of what was already in existence beforehand—in the form of a prememorized piece. . . . And its ultimate use as a designation for ceremonial rather than judicial or political oratory will be a natural result of the fact that ceremonial occasions were the only ones at which recitation of a written (or prememorized) text would have been considered acceptable by a fifth-century audience. (p. 89)

Cole's claim may be supported by the following speculative morphological argument. I noted earlier that *epideiknumi* is typically translated as "display" or "show." I should add that the same is true of shorter verb *deiknunai*. Other meanings include "bring to light" and "to show forth." The noun *deikêlon* can designate a specific exhibition. The meaning of the prepo-

---

13. See George A. Kennedy, *Aristotle: On Rhetoric* (New York: Oxford University Press, 1991), pp. 299–305.

14. A. N. Ammann, *IKOS bei Platon* (Freiburg: Paulusdruckerei, 1953); Pierre Chantraine, *Etudes sur le vocabulaire grec* (Paris: Klincksieck, 1956), pp. 97–171; Schiappa, *Protagoras and Logos*, pp. 40–49.

sition *epi-* varies; it lacks the sort of core meaning that some prefixes have. Its sense depends on context and case; possible meanings include "upon," "at," "toward," "against," etc. The question becomes, Why was the preposition *epi-* compounded with *deiknumi* to create *epideiknumi?* It is difficult to say. Even in English, one can find prefixes that at one point might have conveyed an active sense of position or motion, but that later became a dormant appendage: one can *picture* an event, or *depicture* it. One can *cede* or *concede* a position. One can *limit* or *delimit.* One can *splay* or *display* a banner. We may conjecture plausibly that originally *epideiknumi* designated a special sort of "showing." It is certainly possible that, with respect to discourse, it had to be written in order for it to be some*thing* that could be "di-splayed." If Cole's argument is correct, then what later would be called epideictic speech originated with the recounting or recitation of an "exhibit" or "specimen" of written prose.

Whether Cole is correct or not about the original sense of *epideixis* before the formalization of rhetoric in the fourth century, emphasis on the predisciplinary character of the *Helen* leads to several conclusions. The most obvious implication is that there simply were not the same sort of formal, generic expectations for prose compositions of the fifth century as are found a century later.[15] Gorgias would not have felt any tension between writing a "theoretical" versus an "epideictic" speech, because there had not yet arisen a particular need to distinguish prose texts on the basis of instruction versus entertainment. And *epideixis* or "demonstration" could strive for both. While there is no doubt that he intended his distinctive style to be entertaining, there is no reason to doubt that Gorgias also wanted to instruct—just like other early Greek writers, including "philosophers" such as Parmenides, Empedocles, and Heraclitus.[16] Gorgias adapted and transformed poetic styles and genres of composition and in the process created texts that now appear to us as rhetorical "hybrids." Gorgias' innovation was not so much stretching a *given* set of prose genres as it was *taking* certain poetic forms and *creating* texts that "fuse" certain rhetorical goals and forms of composition that would soon be separated

---

15. Cf. John Poulakos, "Gorgias' and Isocrates' Use of the Encomium," where it is argued that Gorgias "creates a hybrid rhetorical form" by deliberately "stretching" the traditional form of the encomium to include the justificatory features of *apologia.*

16. Cf. Havelock's discussion of the multiple agendas of the writings of presocratic philosophers. Eric A. Havelock, "The Linguistic Task of the Presocratics," in *Language and Thought in Early Greek Philosophy,* ed. Kevin Robb (LaSalle, Ill.: Hegeler Institute, 1983), pp. 7–82.

by later prose writers. Isocrates' comment about the competing needs of *apologia* and *encomium* (*Helen* 14–15 in Van Hook 67) would have struck Gorgias as strange.

Carter argues that epideictic rhetoric played an important ritualistic function in ancient Greek culture. The funeral oration *(epitaphios)* in particular is credited with creating an "extraordinary," transcendent knowledge for its participants, generating a strong sense of community, and guiding behavior toward accepted norms.[17] Similarly, Perelman and Olbrechts-Tyteca suggest that the function of epideictic rhetoric is not to change beliefs or attitudes but to "increase the adherence to values held in common by the audience and speaker."[18] There is no evidence that any of these objectives are pursued by Gorgias in the *Helen*, at least not in the sense in which they are explained by Carter or Perelman and Olbrechts-Tyteca. And there is no evidence that the *Helen* was ever given in anything approaching a setting that would be conducive to performing ritualistic functions. Rather than concluding that Gorgias is somehow a "failed" epideictic speaker,[19] a predisciplinary reading challenges the assumption that—prior to epideictic's formalization—an address such as *Helen* would have been expected to increase adherence to community values or perform ritualistic functions.[20]

A further consequence of resituating the speech as predisciplinary is that historical interpretations of *Helen* that presume rhetoric was a discrete discipline or a clearly demarcated body of literature are anachronistic. The best example of such an interpretation is Poulakos', which argues that the Helen portrayed in Gorgias' speech is actually "the personification of rhetoric."[21] Recalling that Gorgias is said to have alluded to an analogy between Penelope and *philosophia*, and noting that both *rhêtorikê* and *philosophia* are feminine nouns, Poulakos suggests

---

17. Michael F. Carter, "The Ritual Functions of Epideictic Rhetoric: The Case of Socrates' Funeral Oration," *Rhetorica* 9 (1991): 209–32.

18. Ch. Perelman and L. Olbrechts-Tyteca, *The New Rhetoric: A Treatise on Argumentation*, trans. John Wilkinson and Purcell Weaver (Notre Dame: Notre Dame University Press, 1969), p. 52.

19. Blass (1:68), for example, criticizes certain stylistic choices by Gorgias as being foreign to epideictic eloquence.

20. It also may be the case that Carter is simply wrong to characterize all Greek epideictic rhetoric as ritualistic, though I suspect he is right about the functions of the *epitaphios*.

21. Poulakos, "Gorgias' *Helen*," p. 4. To be fair, though Poulakos offers "historical" grounds for his reading, he retreats in his conclusion to the position that *Helen* "may be read" as a defense of rhetoric, regardless of whether the Helen-rhetoric analogy "even crossed [Gorgias'] mind."

(p. 10) that Gorgias, "although talking about Helen, is really referring to rhetoric." Reading Helen as rhetoric is plausible, he claims, since "both are attractive, both are unfaithful, and both have a bad reputation" (pp. 4–5).

Poulakos' reading is dubious history on three counts. First, the available evidence suggests that the Greek word for rhetoric—*rhêtorikê*—had not yet been coined when Gorgias wrote *Helen*.[22] Even if *rhêtorikê* had been in use at the time, it would have been so novel as to make pretext unnecessary and the allusion unsuccessful. Second, Poulakos' "historical explanation" for the need for pretext on behalf of Gorgias is weak. He claims (p. 7) that "Gorgias must have been aware of the Athenian practices of intolerance; frequent banishments and condemnations, the burning of books in public, and excommunications by exile must have dictated that he approach his task indirectly." Such a characterization exaggerates Athenian "intolerance" and supposes that certain poorly attested legends, such as the burning of Protagoras' books, are true.[23] Third, if there had been an urgent need for pretext, Gorgias' speech certainly would have failed. Poulakos cites the names of Aristophanes' *Frogs*, *Wasps*, and *Birds* as examples of the artistic masking of purpose, but there was no mistaking the playwright's message as anything other than a bombast directed toward specific politicians and policies.[24] The powerful leader Cleon, for example, was ridiculed by Aristophanes even though—perhaps even *because*—Cleon was sitting right there in the audience! Likewise, the power of speech is an explicit and developed theme of *Helen*. If there had been intolerant censors lurking about in Athens, it is highly unlikely that they

---

22. According to Werner Pilz, "*rhêtorikê* findet sich nicht vor Plato." See *Der Rhetor im attischen Staat* (Weida: Thomas, 1934), p. 15. Other sources concluding that Plato's *Gorgias* is the earliest extant use of the word *rhetoric* include J. W. H. Atkins, "Rhetoric, Greek," *The Oxford Classical Dictionary* (Oxford: Clarendon, 1949); H. Hommel, "Rhetorik," *Der Kleine Pauly*, vol. 4 (München: Druckenmuller, 1972); Wilhelm Kroll, "Rhetorik," *Pauly's Real-Encyclopdie der classischen Altertumswissenschaft* Supp. 7 (1940): 1039–1138; H. G. Liddell and R. Scott, *A Greek-English Lexicon*, 9th ed. (Oxford: Clarendon, 1940); and Josef Martin, *Antike Rhetorik: Technik und Methode* (München: Beck, 1974). For the claim that Plato may have coined the word *rhêtorikê*, see Cole, *Origins*, p. 2; Schiappa, *Protagoras*; and Egil A. Wyller, "Plato's Concept of Rhetoric in the *Phaedrus* and its Tradition in Antiquity," *Symbolae Osloenses* 66 (1991): 51–69.

23. See Kenneth J. Dover, "The Freedom of the Intellectual in Greek Society," *Talanta* 7 (1976): 24–54; Schiappa, *Protagoras*, pp. 144–45; I. F. Stone, *The Trial of Socrates* (New York: Anchor Books, 1988), pp. 231–47.

24. See Kenneth J. Dover, *Aristophanic Comedy* (Berkeley: University of California Press, 1972).

would have considered Gorgias "harmless and nonthreatening" simply because he omitted the word "rhetoric." After all, Critias the Tyrant's alleged ban on discourse instruction is described by Xenophon as a prohibition of *logôn technê*, not *rhêtorikê* (*Memorabilia* 1.2.31).

Poulakos, of course, is not the only one who has read *Helen* as being primarily about rhetoric. W. J. Verdenius suggests that in composing the *Helen* "the analogy between oratory and poetry clearly preponderates in [Gorgias'] mind."[25] And Jacqueline de Romilly suggest that Helen's defense is a pretext for a defense of Gorgias' art: "Under the vindication of Helen pierces a cry of pride of the master of rhetoric."[26] Such descriptions are undermined by the text; they overemphasize and overparticularize one set of purposes and contributions while they underestimate other possible agendas.

Practical Contributions of Gorgias' *Helen*

Once the disciplinary expectations and nomenclature of classical rhetoric are set aside, Gorgias' role as an innovator in prose composition is more easily discernible. There are no clear examples of a prose composition being called an "encomium" prior to Gorgias' *Helen*.[27] It is not until after Gorgias' death in the fourth century that one finds texts such as the *Rhetoric to Alexander* describing "rules for the genre."[28] As Dover notes, "*encômion* and *encômiazein* are freely used in the fourth century of formal praise in prose or verse, but in fifth-century usage *encômion* is especially a poem celebrating someone's victory."[29] Such use is found in Pindar, Hesiod, and Aristophanes, but not in

---

25. W. J. Verdenius, "Gorgias' Doctrine of Deception," in *The Sophists and Their Legacy*, ed. G. B. Kerferd (Wiesbaden: Franz Steiner, 1981), pp. 116–17.

26. de Romilly, *Les Grands Sophistes*, p. 103: "Sous la justification d'Helene perce un cri de fierte du maitre de rhetorique." Janet Lloyd translates this as "Under the guise of justifying Helen, the master of rhetoric proclaims his pride in his skills" (*The Great Sophists*, p. 67). See also de Romilly, p. 108; and Heinrich Gomperz, *Sophistik und Rhetorik* (Leipzig: Teubner, 1912), pp. 36–37.

27. Noted by Thomas Shearer Duncan, "Gorgias' Theory of Art," *Classical Journal* 33 (1938): 405. See also Blass, *Die attische Beredsamkeit*, 1:72.

28. Kenneth J. Dover, *Plato: Symposium* (Cambridge: Cambridge University Press, 1980), p. 12.

29. Kenneth J. Dover, *Aristophanes: Clouds* (Oxford: Clarendon, 1968), p. 237. For examples see Aristophanes, *Clouds* 1205, fragment 491; Hesiod, *Works and Days* 344; Pindar, *Olympian Odes* 2.47, 10.77, 13.29; *Pythian Odes* 10.53; and *Nemean Odes* 1.7.

any prose writer. Though it is possible that "encomium" was added to the formal title at some later date, Gorgias' explicitly calls his discourse "an encomium of Helen" in the final sentence of the speech—a self-reference that suggests Gorgias was aware of the relationship between his speech and the poetic tradition. The most probable inference is that Gorgias helped to inaugurate a tradition of prose encomia that was infamous less than a century later, when we learn in Plato's *Symposium* (177a–c) that speeches of praise had been composed on subjects as diverse as Heracles and salt. It does not really matter that we would now classify Gorgias' speech as *apologia* or as a rhetorical "hybrid" rather than as an encomium. It is not unusual for writers to contribute to the formulation of canons and genres in ways they did not, and could not, anticipate.

Gorgias' *Helen* is also noteworthy for being an early and masterful example of the apagogic method of argument by which an advocate enumerates a series of possibilities and addresses each in turn. Kennedy's summary warrants quotation in its entirety:

After a brief introduction in which Gorgias seeks to justify the choice of subject—it is right to praise the praiseworthy and defend the maligned—he states (6) that Helen must have yielded to Paris either through fate or the wishes of the Gods, or else she was ravaged by force or persuaded by words or maddened by love. No other possibilities are presumed to exist. Each of those enumerated is examined in turn and it is demonstrated by what Aristotle would call enthymeme or example within the limits of probability that in each case Helen cannot be blamed for her action. The most interesting discussion is that of persuasion by words (8 ff.), where Gorgias develops an analysis of psychological effects. The speech ends with a brief conclusion echoing the statements of the introduction. In four and a half pages Gorgias has given a vivid, even unforgettable, example of the same logical method which he employed in his famous discussion of being. He refers to the little work as a *logismos* or "reasoning" in section two, and this seems entirely appropriate. . . . It is playful in mood, but it also has a serious purpose in demonstrating a method of logical proof.[30]

It is easy to fixate on Gorgias' exotic style and his "magical" use of language and, as a result, to neglect his "rationalistic" side. Such neglect is

---

30. George A. Kennedy, *The Art of Persuasion in Greece* (Princeton: Princeton University Press, 1963), pp. 167–68, note omitted.

a mistake. There is an unmistakable parallel in ancient Greek discourse between the transition from poetic to "purer" prose styles and the gradual rise of formal modes of reasoning. Because many texts of this era tend to combine elements of "rationalistic" prose and "mythic" poetry, there is a tendency to see such a "mixed" style as a fault of the writer rather than as evidence of rapid changes in modes of composition. For example, Parmenides tried to employ the meter of Homeric poetry in the service of philosophical analysis. Though some commentators praise Parmenides' ability to express himself in verse, others argue that the vocabulary and syntax of poetry were very much in tension with his goals and that Parmenides had to struggle to adapt his ideas to an unsuitable medium.[31] Gorgias was similarly situated in and influenced by an oral-poetic culture. His unique prose was transforming the uses to which written discourse was being put, thereby contributing to what is often called the shift from *mythos* to *logos*.[32]

Gorgias says in his introduction, "I wish to offer reasoning by particular arguments to free the accused of blame, to reveal that her critics are lying, and to show the truth and to halt the ignorance."[33] It is significant that Gorgias identifies "reasoning" *(logismos)* as his method. *Logismos* is not a very common word in fifth-century texts. A typical early use is Democritus' advice to "Drive out by reasoning the unmastered pain of a numbed soul."[34] Aristophanes uses the word only once—to make fun of rational argument in the plays of Euripides (*Frogs* 973). The word occurs sixteen times in the works attributed

---

31. Barnes complains that "it is hard to excuse Parmenides' choice of verse as a medium for his philosophy. The exigencies of metre and poetical style regularly produce an almost impenetrable obscurity." Jonathan Barnes, *The Presocratic Philosophers*, rev. ed. (London: Routledge and Kegan Paul, 1982), p. 155. The most thorough discussion of Parmenides' composition style is in Alexander P. D. Mourelatos, *The Route of Parmenides* (New Haven: Yale University Press, 1970), pp. 1–46, 264–68. See also David Gallop, *Parmenides of Elea* (Toronto: Toronto University Press, 1984), pp. 4–5; A. H. Coxon, *The Fragments of Parmenides* (Assen: Van Gorcum, 1986), pp. 7–8; W. K. C. Guthrie, *A History of Greek Philosophy*, vol. 2 (Cambridge: Cambridge University Press, 1962), pp. 3–4; and Eric Havelock, *The Literate Revolution in Greece and Its Cultural Consequences* (Princeton: Princeton University Press, 1982), pp. 220–60, and "The Linguistic Task."

32. Wilhelm Nestle, *Von Mythos zum Logos*, 2nd ed. (Stuttgart: A. Kroner 1941).

33. All passages quoted from Gorgias' *Helen* are based on George A. Kennedy's most recent translation (*Aristotle: On Rhetoric*, pp. 284–288), with my slight alterations.

34. DK 68B290. Translation by Jonathan Barnes in *Early Greek Philosophy* (London: Penguin, 1987), p. 283.

to Hippocrates, where it usually has the sense of careful analysis (see, e.g., *On the Art* 11). Though Herodotus never once uses the word, Thucydides employs it thirteen times—always to connote calculation, logical decision-making, or reflection.[35] Accordingly, Gorgias' self-conscious identification of his method as "reasoning" positions his text as contributing to the pursuit of what we would now term "rational argumentation." Though his style is highly poetic, it is also highly rationalistic for its time.

By calling the speech "rationalistic" I do not mean to imply that Gorgias was a "rationalist" in the modern philosophical sense. There are all sorts of "rationalities" that are performed in different ways at different times in different cultures.[36] Though Gorgias' manner of composition may strike some readers as "irrational" or "nonrational" compared to Aristotle's prose, for example, the more relevant comparison is with the sorts of compositions produced immediately prior to Gorgias and in his own generation. In doing so we will come closer to understanding the "Other" sort of rationality found uniquely in the writings of Gorgias. Specifically, Gorgias' speech contains a number of literate characteristics that clearly mark it as an example of fifth-century "rationalism"; for its time, the *Helen*'s "argumentation is didactic, obvious, and academic."[37] Gorgias' arrangement of arguments is "remarkably orderly and well-signposted," and his introductory forecast, clear transitions, and summarizing conclusion could serve as a model for persuasive speeches today.[38] Swearingen contrasts the beginning of the *Helen* with the mythologized narrative that begins Parmenides' famous poem, and concludes that the two reveal "vastly different" styles of composition:

> Gorgias' text exemplifies several "literate" features: definition of attributes, contrasts, and opposites; explicit statement of authorial/rhetorical purpose; and explicit identification of Gorgias as the composer and originator of the defense. There is no trace of even a vestigially formulaic attribution to the Muse or a god, except perhaps in the

---

35. See sections 2.11.7.3; 1.40.3.3; 2.40.5.2; 3.20.3.6; 3.83.2.3; 4.10.1.6; 4.92.2.3; 4.108.4.5; 4.122.3.2; 5.68.2.6; 6.34.4.9; 6.34.6.2; 8.57.2.1.

36. See Alasdair MacIntyre, *Whose Justice? Which Rationality?* (South Bend: Notre Dame University Press, 1988); and Richard Rorty, "A Pragmatist View of Rationality and Cultural Difference," *Philosophy East and West* 42 (1992): 581–96.

37. Barrett, *The Sophists*, p. 17.

38. MacDowell, *Gorgias: Encomium of Helen*, p. 17.

repetition of the story of Zeus as Helen's real father. But most of all, observe how Gorgias' argument is clearly marked *as an argument*, with metalinguistic terms and phrases that define structural and logical relationships among its statements.[39]

Furthermore, style and content in Gorgias are interrelated and complementary in a manner unlike Parmenides. Barrett notes that his use of the apagogic method "was clearly a stimulator of listener involvement and response. It insisted on a battle among ideas, on an agonistic clash promoting excitement. Thus in *Helen*, Gorgias structured an 'adversary' relationship among ideas in testing arguments. . . . Through form, Gorgias built in agitation and competition of reasons; form contributed to substance."[40]

Finally, it should be noted that Gorgias identifies himself *as a writer*— a self-identification that is very rare and unusual for a fifth-century author. He ends his speech with these words: "I wished to write a speech as Helen's encomium and my own recreation." One is far more likely to encounter verbs of saying and hearing when sixth- and fifth-century texts describe the role of the author/speaker. It is exclusively in the texts and fragments of a small number of "philosophers" such as Diogenes of Apollonia that one finds statements like "as will have been shown clearly in this written composition" *(suggraphêi)*.[41] Gorgias' self-conscious identification of himself as the author of the text is remarkable for its time. Moreover, his combination of an epic theme, a highly poetic style, systematic reasoning, and self-conscious writing provides reason to doubt "great divide" theories that portray oral/mythopoeic and literate/rationalistic styles and mindsets as wholly distinct. Such schemata simply do not work when one examines the texts of various Sophists.[42]

The practical contributions of Gorgias' *Helen* can be summarized best by describing them as advancing the art of written prose in general, and of argumentative composition in particular. Though the subject matter is ostensibly mythical, the *modus operandi* of the discourse supplants the qualities of traditional, oral-poetic composition with such humanistic-rationalistic practices as the apagogic method of argument. Finally, it is possible that Gorgias helped to inaugurate the practice of composing encomia in prose.

---

39. C. Jan Swearingen, "Literate Rhetors and Their Illiterate Audiences: The Orality of Early Literacy," *Pre/Text* 7 (1986): 149.

40. Barrett, *The Sophists*, p. 17.

41. DK 64B4.

42. See Jarratt, *Sophists*, pp. 31–61.

Toward an Analysis of the Theoretical Contributions of Gorgias' *Helen*

My intent in this section is not to provide a detailed commentary on the text, which already has been done admirably by MacDowell and others. Nor will I attempt the sort of extended argument that outlines and defends a Gorgian theory of this or that based on Gorgias' extant texts. Instead, I shall focus on the portion of the text that is of most interest to historians of rhetorical theory: the discussion of *logos* in paragraphs 8–14. *Logos* is a notoriously polysemous term in ancient Greek. Throughout this section I leave *logos* untranslated to as to avoid overly modernistic or reductionistic renderings. In most fifth-century sophistic texts the term is meant quite broadly, as with the current term *discourse*. Because the term is often set in opposition to *mythos*, "reasoned speech" is not too far off the mark. Some scholars (for example, Duncan, p. 407) suggest that for Gorgias *logos* means simply "expression in prose."

I want to address several hermeneutic practices that have obscured some of the ways Gorgias' *Helen* affected the content and practice of later theorizing. Specifically, I want to identify those features of the text that can be described as *paradigmatic*; that is, that serve as exemplars for later theorists. Kuhn describes *exemplars* as "shared examples": practical, concrete "problem solutions," the methods or procedures of which are imitated by others.[43] The virtue of such an approach is that it emphasizes that theorizing is a form of *praxis*. Gorgias' *Helen* is not only a set of interesting concepts; it is also a way of conceptualizing. His text not only provides us with another chapter in the history of thought, but in the fifth century B.C.E. it enacted a novel means of thinking. In short, in addition to asking the question "What did Gorgias *say*?" we need to ask, "What did his speech *do*?" Advancing new ways of theorizing about the world is at least as important as the content of the specific theories we might associate with specific figures. It well may be the case that Gorgias' most important theoretical contribution is his act of *theorizing* rather than any particular theoretical statement per se.

Though Gorgias' speech is filled with statements that we now find theoretically provocative, propositions of the form "Gorgias had a theory of X" are potentially misleading. There is a tendency to read even a few sentences about a concept by an early Greek writer as indicating that the writer

---

43. Thomas S. Kuhn, *The Essential Tension* (Chicago: University of Chicago Press, 1977), p. 298.

"held a theory" about it. So, for example, Duncan titles his article "Gorgias' Theories of Art" and suggests he held "theories of style" as well as a theory of catharsis.[44] Enos and Engnell contend in separate articles that Gorgias developed "theories of rhetoric."[45] Verdenius says that Gorgias held a "theory of knowledge," and Gronbeck believes Gorgias defended a specific "theory of language" consistent with contemporary existential phenomenology.[46]

Such statements are potentially misleading in two ways. First, they *overestimate* the maturity of theory development by implying more coherence and completeness than can be demonstrated with the available evidence. The term *theory* has many meanings, of course, but it seems reasonable to stipulate that a "theory" is made up of a constellation of beliefs that attempt to explain particular phenomena or to solve some specific intellectual problem. It probably exaggerates the degree of development of a person's thought to impute to him or her a full-blown "Theory of X" on the basis of one or two sentences that predicate certain qualities of a given "X." Accordingly, it is more appropriate at times simply to identify a statement as a "belief" or "hypothesis" rather than as a "theory."

Second, and more important, the attribution of a number of theories to ancient writers on the basis of isolated statements mischaracterizes the process of intellectual investigation in ancient Greece during the sixth and fifth centuries. By the late *fourth* century, the scientific and philosophical vocabulary, syntax, and available models of studies had developed to the point where one can identify competing "schools of thought" about various "theories" in more or less distinct "disciplines." Aristotle's accounts of earlier philosophy give us the impression that such was the case fully two centuries earlier. However, as the important work of Cherniss and Havelock has demonstrated, Aristotle's "history" is both inconsistent and misleading.[47] Aristotle presupposes that the conceptual categories and patterns of explanation available to him and his students were also available to his predecessors. In the

---

44. Duncan, "Gorgias' Theory of Art," pp. 406–8, 412.

45. Enos, "The Epistemology of Gorgias' Rhetoric," 35, 45; Richard A. Engnell, "Implications for Communication of the Rhetorical Epistemology of Gorgias of Leontini," *Western Journal of Speech Communication* 37 (1973): 175.

46. Verdenius, "Gorgias' Doctrine of Deception," 116; Bruce E. Gronbeck, "Gorgias on Rhetoric and Poetic," *Southern Speech Communication Journal* 38 (1972): 27–38.

47. Harold Cherniss, *Aristotle's Criticism of Presocratic Philosophy* (New York: Octagon Books, 1935); Havelock, *The Literate Revolution* and "The Linguistic Task."

search for historical anticipations of his theories, Aristotle often radically retranslates earlier thinkers' notions into his own vocabulary. As Havelock argues, something important is lost in the translation: "Such vocabulary subtly distorts the story of early Greek thought by presenting it as an intellectual game dealing with problems already given and present to the mind, rather than as a groping after a new language in which the existence of such problems will slowly emerge."[48] One of the major tasks of earlier thinkers was to develop the analytical tools required before "philosophical" or "scientific" investigation could take place. As Friedrich Solmsen suggests in his study of the fifth-century Greek "Enlightenment," the most important advances may not "necessarily take the form of doctrines" or "programs of reform," but rather were experiments in ways of thinking about things.[49] In particular, what we call in hindsight the birth of Western philosophical thinking is the effort to describe the world with generalizations that privilege secular explanations of causes.[50]

In short, we *underestimate* the significance of the earlier writers' efforts to come to grips with the *process of theorizing itself* by overestimating the sophistication of such early "theories." When predisciplinary theoretical efforts are treated as if the authors were educated in methods and language developed much later, their role in *transforming* intellectual practices is missed.

In the case of Gorgias, the single most important theoretical contribution of the *Helen* is that it engaged in rational—i.e., systematic, secular, physical—explanation and description. He is clearly trying to give a serious account of the workings of *logos* and the mind. With respect to *logos*, Gorgias enumerates its qualities, describes its effects, and explains (crudely) how it works. The *Helen* is the earliest surviving extended discussion of *logos* and certainly the most sophisticated of its time. Prior to Gorgias the most we have are a few fragmentary aphorisms by thinkers such as Heraclitus and Protagoras that simply posit declarations about *logos*. Gorgias begins the relevant section of the *Helen* by making a similar type of declaration: "*Logos* is a powerful lord that with the smallest and most invisible body accomplishes most godlike works. It can banish fear and remove guilt and instill pleasure and enhance pity. I shall show how this is so" (8). But then Gorgias goes on to do what no one before him (that we know of) did: explain how *logos* works. The

---

48. Havelock, "The Linguistic Task," p. 57.

49. See Friedrich Solmsen, *Intellectual Experiments of the Greek Enlightenment* (Princeton: Princeton University Press, 1975), p. 4.

50. Guthrie, *History* 1:26–38.

effort may seem crude in contrast to the relatively sophisticated vocabulary and theories of Aristotle or the later dialogues of Plato, but the analysis provided by the latter would not have been possible without the efforts
of intellectuals such as Gorgias. The writing of systematic treatises was
exceedingly rare prior to the mid–fourth century. The scope and complexity of Gorgias' analysis is impressive when compared with his contemporaries and predecessors, even if it seems faltering compared to some of
his successors.

To explain the power of *logos*, Gorgias compares its effect with that of
poetry: "All poetry I regard and name as *logos* having meter. On those who
hear it come fearful shuddering and tearful pity and grievous longing as the
psyche, through *logos*, experiences some experience of its own at others'
good fortune and ill fortune" (9). Aside from providing what we might now
call a psychological account of the effects of oral discourse (as Segal has
described it), the passage is remarkable for containing a potentially unprecedented propositional form: a definition. Elsewhere I have claimed that "the
practice of definition has its recorded start in the dialogues of Plato,"[51] but the
statement "all poetry I regard and name as *logos* having meter" clearly ought
to count as a stipulative definition. Gorgias' *Helen* may be our earliest example of the practice of explicating precisely what a particular word means
in one's own discourse. That Gorgias defined a word is itself a significant
advance in the practice of theorizing.

The succeeding sentences have been the basis for various commentators' descriptions of Gorgias as a defender of an "irrational" or "nonrational"
account of language: "Divine sweetness transmitted through speech is inductive of pleasure, reductive of pain. Thus by entering into the opinion of the
psyche the force of incantation is wont to beguile and persuade and alter it
by witchcraft, and the two arts of witchcraft and magic are errors of the
psyche and deceivers of opinion" (10). Enos, among others, describes Gorgias
as articulating a "nonrational epistemology" and says that Gorgias "did not
stress rational methods for attaining krisis but, rather, used nonrational, stylistic procedures for gaining the assent of listeners."[52] However, as was noted
earlier, such characterizations underestimate the "rational" aspects of Gorgias'
texts. Furthermore, as Solmsen argues, accounts such as Gorgias' are better

----

51. See Edward Schiappa, "Arguing About Definitions," *Argumentation* 7 (1993):
406.

52. Richard Leo Enos, *Greek Rhetoric Before Aristotle* (Prospect Heights, Ill.:
Waveland, 1993), pp. 85, 88.

understood as attempts to rationalize language and thought "on a purely secular basis, with no need for divine causation."[53] Unlike storytellers who depend on the Muses for mystical inspiration, Gorgias' account implies that speakers have a "self-conscious relation" to their speech.[54] As de Romilly points out (p. 20), Gorgias "was deliberately shifting magic into something rational." In *Helen*, Gorgias proceeds to provide a secular explanation of why such "magic" works:

> If everyone, on every subject, had memory of the past and knowledge of the present and foresight of the future, *logos* would not do what it does, but as things are it is easy neither to remember the past nor consider the present nor predict the future; so that on most subjects most people take opinion as counselor to the psyche. But opinion, being slippery and insecure, casts those relying on it into slippery and insecure fortune. (11)

Gorgias then spends the equivalent of two paragraphs arguing that Helen is blameless because *logos* is so powerful that its use amounts to the use of force. First, he identifies *logos* as the powerful vehicle of *peithô*, persuasion:

> What is there to prevent the conclusion that Helen too, when still young, was carried off by *logos* just as if constrained by force? Her mind was swept away by persuasion, and persuasion has the same power as necessity *(anagkê)*, although it may bring shame. For *logos*, by persuading the psyche that it persuaded, constrained her both to obey what was said and to approve what was done. The persuader, as user of force, did wrong; the persuaded, forced by *logos*, is unreasonably blamed. (12)

Second, he proves just how powerful *logos* can be by providing a series of examples of how easily humans are persuaded by competing *logoi*:

> To understand that persuasion, joining with *logos*, is wont to stamp the psyche as it wishes one must study, first, the arguments of the astronomers who, substituting opinion with opinion, removing one and instilling another, make what is incredible and unclear appear true to

---

53. Solmsen, *Intellectual Experiments*, p. 5.

54. Jarratt, *Sophists*, p. 57.

the eyes of opinion; second, the forceful contests of argumentation, where one side of the argument, written with skill but not spoken with truth, pleases a large audience and persuades; third, the debates of rival philosophers, in which swiftness of thought is also exhibited, making belief in an opinion easily changed. (13)

The key contribution here is the act of raising a provocative theoretical question: When does persuasion amount to force? The question is both unusual and interesting because Greek literature prior to Gorgias usually treated persuasion and force, *peithô* and *bia*, as antithetical. As Kirby puts it: "I will try to persuade you, but, failing that, I will force you. Such a disjunction is rooted in our most fundamental concepts of civilization. The wild beasts settle their disputes by *bia*; it is a mark of our humanity, we feel, that we can use persuasion to effect change, that we are not limited to the use of coercion."[55] Kirby goes on to suggest that "the *peithô/bia* axis is at the basis of some of our most ancient literary and rhetorical formulations."[56] From the standpoint of intellectual history, it is arguably the case that Gorgias' questioning of a taken-for-granted dichotomy is a more important step in developing new modes of inquiry than any particular claim he makes about *logos*, *peithô*, or *bia*.

In the process of describing the persuasive/forceful workings of *logos*, Gorgias develops an analogy that proved to be influential: "The power of *logos* has the same effect on the condition of the psyche as the power of drugs on the nature of the body; for just as different drugs dispel different secretions from the body, and some bring an end to disease and others to life, so also in the case of *logos*—some bring pain, others pleasure, some bring fear, others instill courage in the hearers, and some drug and bewitch the psyche with a kind of evil persuasion" (14). De Romilly contends (p. 16) that "Gorgias' magic is technical. He wants to emulate the power of the magician by a scientific analysis of language and its influence. He is the theoretician of the magic spell of words." Gorgias theorizes in this case by drawing the analogy to the increasingly secular, "rational," and "scientific" art of medicine (see de Romilly, p. 20). The analogy functioned para-

---

55. John T. Kirby, "The 'Great Triangle' in Early Greek Rhetoric and Poetics," *Rhetorica* 8 (1990): 215.

56. Kirby, "Triangle," 216. See also R. G. A. Buxton, *Persuasion in Greek Tragedy: A Study of Peithô* (Cambridge: Cambridge University Press, 1982), pp. 58–63.

digmatically in the sense that both Plato's *Gorgias* and Aristotle's *On Rhetoric* later sought to explain the art of persuasion by comparing it to the developing art of medicine. Gorgias' effort at analogy may seem simplistic by contrast to the relatively sophisticated vocabulary and theories of Aristotle and the later dialogues of Plato, but the analysis provided by such later theorists would not have been possible without the efforts of intellectuals such as Gorgias.

Based on the passages in the *Helen* that discuss *logos* and passages in other Gorgianic texts, theorists have likened Gorgias' claims to contemporary aesthetic, psychological, and speech-act theories of language. Such readings have produced conflicting accounts of Gorgias' description of *logos,* among which I will not try to arbitrate. There are at least five distinct categories of readings: Psychological (Segal), Magical (de Romilly), Epistemological (Untersteiner, Enos, Gronbeck), Dramatistic (Verdenius, Rosenmeyer), and Sematological (Mourelatos, Kerferd). Each reading tends to tease out of selected phrases a distinct theory of *logos*, language, rhetoric, etc. As helpful as these treatments are, I think the "content" of Gorgias' account is remarkably straightforward and stands on its own. Though it is useful to interpret and reposition Gorgias' account into contemporary terminology, *Helen* also deserves to be understood, insofar as possible, in its own context and to be appreciated for what it contributed to its own generation of intellectuals. Once so positioned, we may find its most profound influence is not a particular "idea" per se, but a metaphor picked up by a later author, or a problem he poses. In terms of the history of rhetorical theory, we must remember that the writing of systematic or theoretical treatises was exceedingly rare prior to the mid–fourth century. The scope and complexity of Gorgias' analysis is impressive when compared to his contemporaries and predecessors, even if it seems crudely metaphorical compared to some of his successors.

Conclusion

This essay is part of a continuing effort to redescribe fifth-century–B.C.E. texts in light of the belief that Plato's and Aristotle's disciplinary and technical vocabulary—including the distinction between "Rhetoric" and "Philosophy"—is an inappropriate terministic screen with which to examine such texts historically. In recent studies, scholars guided by such a belief have advanced a number of claims that are adding up to a major redescription of the origins of Greek rhetorical theory. The traditional story that Rhetoric originated with Corax and Tisias has been challenged, as has the historical basis for the theory of a distinct and monolithic "Sophistic Rhetoric."[57] "Predisciplinary" readings of Protagoras' fragments and of Gorgias' text *On Not Being* have been offered that attempt to identify the texts' contributions to fifth-century theorizing and to the later development of both Philosophy *and* Rhetoric.[58] Plato's role in the "origin" and "disciplining" of both Rhetoric and Dialectic has also received recent attention.[59]

Gorgias' teachings surely belong to the history of the development of rhetorical theory and practice, but his precise place in that history is more complex than most treatments suggest. Gorgias wrote and spoke a generation before rhetoric was recognized as a distinct "discipline" upon the coining and popularizing of the word *rhêtorikê*. His discussion of *logos* is more precisely characterized as a set of beliefs about discourse in general than as a "theory of rhetoric" in the classical sense. Nonetheless, it is obvious that Gorgias significantly influenced the early theoretical articulation of the discipline of rhetoric by theorizing about the workings of persuasive discourse. Enos suggests that "rhetoric's origin as a formal discipline is best understood as an evolution of compositional techniques."[60] If so, then the *Helen* demonstrates that Gorgias played an important role in that origin. Though, strictly speaking, the speech should not be labeled "epideictic" in the Aristotelian sense of the word, Gorgias advanced fifth-century B.C.E. "rationalism" by enacting certain innovations in prose composition. These include the apagogic method of argument, identifying his means of persuasion as "reasoning" *(logismos),* identifying himself as the writer of the speech, probably inaugurating the prose genre of *encomia*, and offering a secular account of the workings of *logos*. There are many ways of making Gorgias' *Helen* meaningful by reading it as a historical text and as a source of inspiration for contemporary neo-sophistic theorists. As a complement to such readings, I hope that examining the *Helen* as predisciplinary underscores the text's historical significance by situating it in fifth-century Greek compositional and theoretical practices and by avoiding the imposition of fourth-century categories and expectations.

------

57. See Thomas Cole, "Who was Corax?" *Illinois Classical Studies* 16 (1991): 65–84; also Schiappa, "The Beginnings of Greek Rhetorical Theory," in *Rhetorical Movement*, ed. David Zarefsky (Evanston: Northwestern University Press, 1993), pp. 5–33, and "Sophistic Rhetoric: Oasis or Mirage?" *Rhetoric Review* 10 (1991): 5–18.

58. Schiappa, *Protagoras*; also E. Schiappa and Stacey Hoffman, "Intertextual Argument in Gorgias' *On What is Not*: A Formalization of Sextus, *Adv Math* 7.77–80," *Philosophy and Rhetoric* 27 (1994): 156–61.

59. Cole, *Origins*; Timmerman, "Ancient Greek Origins."

60. Enos, *Greek Rhetoric*, p. 42.

Four

Agency, Performance, and Interpretation In Thucydides' Account of the Mytilene Debate

Michael C. Leff

In a recent essay, Dilip Gaonkar offers an interesting and useful perspective on the issue I want to address. Classical rhetoric, Gaonkar argues, differs from contemporary rhetoric because it stresses production and action rather than interpretation and understanding. The old rhetoric looks toward doing and making, while the new rhetoric assumes a hermeneutic function—it operates as a metadiscourse that deciphers things said and done. Moreover, the old view of rhetoric as practical/productive art entails not just a set of techniques, but an "ideology of human agency," which Gaonkar defines in terms of the following interconnected set of presuppositions:

> a view of the speaker as the seat of origin rather than a point of articulation, a view of strategy as identifiable under an intentional description, a view of discourse as constitutive of character and community, a view of audience positioned simultaneously as "spectator" and "participant," and finally, a view of "ends" that binds speaker, strategy, and discourse in a web of purposive actions.[1]

The issue is whether this ideology of agency, connected with the performative stress in classical rhetoric, remains useful for the current purposes of hermeneutic inquiry. Gaonkar expresses skepticism on this matter, since he notes that classical theory (i.e., *rhetorica docens*) directs itself to pedagogy; it consists of precepts that apply to performance, and it does not

---

1. Dilip Gaonkar, "The Idea of Rhetoric in the Rhetoric of Science," *Southern Speech Communication Journal* 58 (1993): 258–95.

openly engage questions of interpretation or cultural analysis.[2] This skepticism is, perhaps, warranted insofar as we center attention on the preceptive, "theoretical" tradition. Nevertheless, the classical rhetorical consciousness appears in other venues, most notably in the writing of history. Classical historiography productively complicates matters since it sometimes expresses itself as a rhetorical performance designed to do interpretative work. In such instances the "ideology of human agency" is represented in action and placed within the context of opposing forces such as chance and necessity. The historian's own rhetoric serves to test, limit, and interpret the role of human agency as it is displayed within the larger frame of political and cultural developments.

Thucydides offers a clear example of just such a rhetorically complex approach to history.[3] In what follows, I hope to demonstrate that his work invites reflection about the nature and limits of agency and illustrates the interpretative power of a performative rhetoric. Obviously, space does not allow a full consideration of this matter, and so I will concentrate on a single incident in his *History of the Peloponnesian War*, the revolt of Mytilene, which Thucydides narrates in the opening sections of book 3.[4]

During the third year of the war (i.e., 428 B.C.E.), Mytilene, an independent ally of Athens, attempted to free itself from the Athenian league. When the Athenians responded by attacking and besieging the city, the Mytilenian government, then under the control of an aristocratic faction, armed the commons in hopes of beating back the enemy. The commons, however, almost immediately turned against the government, and the city was forced to capitulate, surrendering to the Athenian commander, Paches, on the condition that he would take no action until a Mytilenian embassy pled its case before the Athenian Assembly.

---

2. This matter, however, is more complicated than it appears on the surface. Some of the problems involved in sorting out "agency" in "productive" as opposed to "interpretative" approaches to rhetoric are sketched in my essay, "The Idea of Rhetoric as Interpretative Practice: A Humanist's Response to Gaonkar," *Southern Speech Communication Journal* 58 (1993): 296–300.

3. More properly it does so if we accept a view of Thucydides' *History*, similar to that of W. Robert Connor, that the text "elicits responses and shapes its audience." See *Thucydides* (Princeton: Princeton University Press, 1984), p. 13. Connor, in his introductory chapter, offers a useful summary of the controversy surrounding interpretation of Thucydides.

4. 3.1–50. All quotations in this paper are taken from the Crawley translation (New York: Random House, 1951).

As it turned out, the Assembly proved unreceptive to the ambassadors. Caught up in "the fury of the moment," it passed a Draconian measure, decreeing the execution of the entire adult male population of Mytilene and the enslavement of its women and children. A ship was dispatched to inform Paches of the decision.

The next morning, Thucydides reports, many Athenians began to repent their decision when they considered "the horrid cruelty of a decree, which condemned a whole city to a fate merited only by the guilty." The assembly reconvened and a new debate commenced. There was, Thucydides says, "much expression on both sides," but he singles out two speeches to represent the controversy—one by Cleon, "the most violent man at Athens," and the other by Diodotus, about whom we know nothing aside from the speech that Thucydides places in his mouth.

Thucydides' representation of the debate has attracted great attention for a variety of reasons, but for my purposes its most important feature is the reflexive turn it takes. The process of rhetorical deliberation becomes a subject of contention and, as Gomme notes, "the quarrel between Diodotus and Kleon is as much about how to conduct a debate in the ecclesia as it is about the fate of Mytilene."[5] Thus, this debate about debate offers a ground for understanding Thucydides' views about the proper conduct of public discourse, and, as I hope to show, these views involve a subtle and complex attitude about rhetorical agency.

Cleon's speech reflects the violent temperament that Thucydides attributes to the man. He opens on a petulant note, denouncing the whole proceeding and chastising his audience. The very fact of reconsideration, he complains, illustrates the greatest weakness of an imperial democracy. Deceived by the comity of internal politics, the Athenians tend to act toward their "allies" as they would toward one another. In truth, however, the empire is "a despotism," and the obedience of its subjects depends upon force, not loyalty. Failing to understand this reality, the *dêmos* exhibits a misguided sensitivity and, under the spell of sentiment, policy wavers inconstantly. Furthermore, such irresolution opens the Assembly to the clever arguments of oratorical performers, who undermine the stable common sense of ordinary folk. The fact is, Cleon declares, "that bad laws which are never changed are better for the city than good ones that have no authority," and "unlearned loyalty is more serviceable than quick-witted

---

5. A. W. Gomme, *A Historical Commentary on Thucydides*, vol. 2 (Oxford: Oxford University Press, 1956), p. 315.

insubordination." By reconsidering the decree, then, the Athenians have called forth an oratorical contest, where the speakers behave as though they are athletic rivals and the people are induced to judge on the basis of performative skills rather than their own vital interests.

This introductory section of Cleon's speech invites comparison with the speeches of Pericles, which appear in the first two books of the *History* and which probably embody Thucydides' standard for judging good political rhetoric. In one respect, the comparison is favorable, for Cleon, like Pericles, does not attempt deception by currying favor. He is willing to confront and criticize the *dêmos*. On the other hand, Pericles had celebrated the rationality and intellectual dexterity of the Athenians, comparing them favorably in this respect to the Spartans. Cleon's argument is not only anti-intellectual, but his maxim about "unlearned loyalty" seems almost to repeat Pericles' description of the Lacedaemonian character.[6] This difference between the two orators indicates a fundamentally different attitude about the nature of Athenian democracy, and Cleon's view suggests a form of deception more subtle and insidious than a simple effort to pander to the audience. But before we can assess this matter, we need to consider the second half of Cleon's speech, where he turns to the question at hand.

As he justifies his original and severe policy, Cleon invokes the two conventional *topoi* of deliberative oratory—the honorable and the expedient. In respect to the first, he maintains that the punishment fits the crime. The Mytilenians rebelled through free choice and not through compulsion. Their act was calculated, prompted by good fortune that led to false confidence, encouraged by the belief that "might makes right," and it eventuated in a decision where ambitions overwhelmed realistic judgment. The offense, therefore, was "not involuntary," and "mercy is only for unwilling offenders." In respect to expediency, Cleon insists that harsh punishment is necessary as a deterrent against future rebellions. Should the Mytilenians escape with a lesser penalty, other cities would be encouraged to defy Athenian authority, since "the reward of success is freedom and the penalty of failure nothing so very terrible." Hence, Cleon concludes that his policy is "just toward the Mytilenians and at the same time expedient."

We are now in a position to note, as almost all commentators have, the thoroughly deceptive character of Cleon's discourse. His speech enacts the

---

6. My comparison and contrast between Pericles and Cleon follows J. H. Finley, *Thucydides* (Cambridge: Harvard University Press, 1942), pp. 173–78, and Cynthia Ferrar, *The Origins of Democratic Thinking: The Invention of Politics in Ancient Athens* (Cambridge: Cambridge University Press, 1988), pp. 158–77.

same kind of rhetoric that it deplores, since he uses "all the tricks of the orator's trade to denounce oratory."[7] But is this deception conscious, the product of the agent's cunning? On this point, we cannot be certain. It is quite possible that Cleon's inconsistency results not from a planned effort to subvert the debate, but from an unconscious habit of mind—a narrow, partisan impulse that renders him incapable of balanced judgment and action.

Indeed, blatant inconsistencies in the argument of the speech suggest a fractured and self-deceptive consciousness. Cleon urges the *dêmos* to be skeptical of innovation and to hold a steady course, but he also encourages their impulsive anger toward the Mytilenians. Thus, he simultaneously advocates self-control and intemperate emotional reaction. Likewise, his account of the fall of the Mytilenians seems to recoil against the policy he supports for Athens. The Mytilenians, he explains, were deceived by momentary good fortune and, believing that might makes right, they acted impulsively without prudent consideration of the situation as a whole. Yet Cleon, in advising the Athenians, gives momentary anger priority over rational deliberation, and he argues that might and not right ought to direct imperial policy. When read in the context of the entire *History*, Cleon's maxim that prosperity leads to arrogance offers a diagnosis of the fall of Athens, and Cleon violates the maxim even as he utters it.[8]

In short, Cleon's speech is an exercise in special pleading, and it works to subvert the possibility of an effective democratic rhetoric as Thucydides conceives that possibility. Cleon's rhetoric corrodes civic deliberation not only because it promotes narrowly partisan ends but, more importantly, because it casts suspicion on any appeal to common interests. When he impugns the motives and character of rival speakers, he makes domestic politics take on the "aura of fear and intrigue" that he uses to describe imperial relations.[9] If this toxic rhetoric is not the result of a calculated effort to deceive the public, then the problem is all the more serious, since Cleon, Thucydides tells us, was the man "most powerful with the people" at that time. His success, then, indicates that he has absorbed the corruption of his environment. He has no need to pander to the audience because he embodies its disease; he is a patient, not an agent.

Diodotus, fully recognizing the fundamental threat posed by Cleon's rhetoric, begins with a defense of the deliberative process:

---

7. A. Andrewes, "The Mytilene Debate: Thucydides 3:36–39," *Phoenix* 16 (1962): 75.

8. See Ferrar, *Origins*, pp. 169–70.

9. Ferrar, *Origins*, p. 170.

> As for the argument that speech ought not to be the exponent of action,
> the man who uses it must be either senseless or interested; senseless if
> he believes it possible to treat of the uncertain future through any other
> medium; interested if wishing to carry a disgraceful measure and
> doubting his ability to speak well in a bad cause, he thinks to frighten
> his opponents by well-aimed calumny. What is still more intolerable is
> to accuse a speaker of making a display in order to be paid for it.

Thus, whether they reflect bad judgment or deliberate malice, accusations of
corrupt motives have a debilitating effect. Where corruption is suspected or
assumed, those who would speak out of honorable motives must either remain silent or abandon candor:

> Plain good advice has thus come to be suspect no less than bad; and the
> advocate of the most monstrous lies is not more obliged to use deceit
> to gain the people, than the best counsellor is to lie in order to be
> believed. The city [Athens] and the city alone, owing to these
> refinements, can never be served openly; he who does serve it openly
> always being suspected of serving himself in some secret way.

Diodotus' argument is compressed and aphoristic, but its gist seems
reasonably clear, and we might translate it into more contemporary terms as
follows:[10] Since political rhetoric deals with indeterminate social issues, it
cannot be contained within a determinate system of rules and procedures.
Consequently, political rhetoric constitutes the very medium in which it operates. When fear about the result of the process or accusations of corrupt
motive become prevalent, the deliberative exchange becomes corrupted, since
this kind of cynicism taints perception of the medium which conveys the
exchange. Consequently, if a democratic rhetoric is to work, the public must
believe that the agents who participate in it are capable of speaking candidly
about the common good. When secret motives are assumed, however, the
process collapses, since the false currency of deception drives candor out of
the public arena. If an appeal to civic motives cannot be accepted on its face,
even the civic-minded must practice deception. In this unhappy circumstance,
deception is piled upon deception until the rhetorical medium corrupts its

---

10. My comments here are influenced by Eugene Garver's account of prudence in
Machiavelli and the History of Prudence (Madison: University of Wisconsin Press,
1987).

own purposes and destroys the possibility of effective deliberation about contingent issues.

In the second half of his speech, Diodotus turns to the Mytilene issue and begins by making a surprising move. Adopting a calculus even more starkly realistic than Cleon's, he narrows the debate to the topic of expediency, maintaining that considerations of the honorable ought not to enter into the decision. The guilt of the Mytilenians, he argues, is irrelevant; the whole question hinges on a proper understanding of Athenian interests, and here Cleon errs, for he argues that the extreme punishment is expedient. Diodotus then proceeds to develop a nicely wrought argument that capital punishment, whether directed toward individuals or toward states, does not act as an effective deterrent against criminal acts. No punishment, he argues, can prevent rebellion, and so it follows that the harsh policy toward Mytilene can only have counterproductive results. Insurrections would still occur, and when they did, those involved "would hold out to the last, if it is all one whether . . . [they] surrender soon or late." The more expedient course, then, is to execute only the leaders of the Mytilenian rebellion and to leave the commons undisturbed. Pushing his argument still farther in the direction of *realpolitik*, Diodotus asserts that leniency toward the commons is advisable without regard for justice: "Even if they were guilty, you ought not to notice it, in order to avoid eliminating the only class still friendly to us." Thus, Diodotus holds that Cleon's claim to meet the requirements of the honorable and the expedient is inconsistent with the realities of the situation. Leniency is the better course, not because of pity or compassion, which Diodotus rejects as emphatically as his adversary, but because the practical merits of the case recommend it.

As he is represented by Thucydides, Diodotus emerges as a more sympathetic figure than Cleon. Yet, Diodotus also falls short of the Periclean standard, and John Finley has noted the most salient difference: "The idealistic tones of the Funeral Oration are missing now, and the advocate of simple decency had no other course than to talk in terms of calculation."[11] Assessed strictly as a response to the immediate situation, Diodotus' suppression of appeals to pity and compassion seems justifiable. As Thucydides' narrative makes clear, these emotions already were working in Diodotus' favor, and so it was a sound tactic to direct his effort toward the calculative side of the issue, where his position was less secure. Nevertheless, Diodotus does not simply de-emphasize these emotional factors: he categorically eliminates any

---

11. Finley, *Thucydides*, p. 177.

consideration of honor or justice. This exaggerated response suggests that Diodotus' speech is, just as much as Cleon's, an elaborate work of deception, though its intent is probably more honorable. If we assume that Diodotus' motive is simple decency, then the speech itself belies that motive. He denies the sense of compassion that prompts his effort and that he knows to have a strong influence on those who are likely to support his position. His well-calculated effort to reduce the apparent issue to purely rational calculation is a sign of a distorted and fragmented rhetorical environment. The balance between reason and emotion, deeply embedded in Pericles' oratory, disappears from public view. Although Diodotus suppresses the topic of the honorable in order to promote an honorable cause, his rhetoric voices a narrowed, one-dimensional consciousness, its strict appeal to rationality disguising the motives that guide it and the sentiments that fuel its persuasive force. Diodotus may be a decent man, but he cannot appeal to decency.

In sum, Diodotus proves unable to escape the problem he diagnoses in the first part of his speech. Once honorable rhetorical motives are debunked, the orator has no choice but to deceive whenever questions of justice and public sentiment arise. In order to save the immediate situation, Diodotus must join the conspiracy to subvert the process; he also must debunk the honorable, but as his own introductory argument implies, rhetorical deliberation becomes debased once it disregards the force of honorable civic motives and appeals. The circumstances constrain Diodotus, limit his power as an agent, and force him to act against what appears to be his own better judgment.

As I understand it, the problem Thucydides wants to highlight is not that a narrowing of the range of discourse to factional motives and calculative reasoning proves harmful because it eliminates considerations of abstract justice. In other words, I do not believe that he is an idealist who displays a "false consciousness." Rather, he seems to believe that the harm occurs because a truncated rhetoric subverts the adaptive, practical function of the deliberative process. The medium must sustain both rational considerations of advantage and sentimental attachments to honor because both elements inform the human world where the decision-making process occurs. Human communities do not act strictly on a rational basis, and they should not, since reason cannot encompass the contingencies of political life—chance, necessity, and collective psychology all enter into politics, and they exert a force that reason cannot control. Reason can modify sentiment by conditioning it in favor of prudential judgment. Within certain limits, prudential judgment can find means to cope with necessity and chance. But prudential judgment is itself a delicate blend of reason and sentiment, and in a democratic community, where it must proceed through the pluralistic medium of public deliberation, prudential judgment is a fragile thing, constantly in jeopardy of tearing itself apart and constantly threatened by the external force of chance and necessity.

In his account of the Mytilene debate, Thucydides shows how the pressure of events has begun to erode the deliberative process. The necessities of the war and chance factors, most notably the plague, have begun to alter the Athenian capacity to make collective judgments, and the leaders of the state are unable or unwilling to re-establish a balanced perspective. In the place of Pericles, Cleon emerges as the most prominent leader of the people, and his intemperate appeals to emotion lead to Diodotus' equally unbalanced appeals to sheer calculative rationality. As these appeals are set in opposition, the rhetorical process works against connections needed to sustain prudent deliberation. And once caught in this divisive tension, a democratic polity is driven toward catastrophe, since no outside force can correct the self-constituting agency of the rhetorical medium. Thucydides demonstrates this point as his *History* proceeds. In the Melian dialogue of book 5, we find the Athenians employing a calculative rationality that is as imprudent as it brutal, and in book 6, Nicias, though apparently an honorable and patriotic citizen, must adopt his opponents' tactics and weave a web of deceit that yields disaster both for himself and for Athens.[12]

How, then, does this interpretation of Thucydides bear on the problem of the "ideology of human agency" and rhetorical hermeneutics? As I understand his position, Thucydides clearly subscribes to this ideology. His *History* focuses upon agents acting in specific situations, and he represents their rhetoric as a crucial element in the unfolding historical drama. Moreover, the drama itself emphasizes the rhetorical environment at Athens, and the degeneration of the state is connected with the way that the performers become corrupt and ineffective. But he does not conceive agency as a detached moral or intellectual quality of individual performers. Agents are constrained by the complex circumstances that frame their rhetorical acts and by the evolving internal history of the deliberative process. Chance and necessity exert pressure on this process and, beyond a certain point, agents lose the capacity to direct or modify the course of events; they merely reflect the forces that impinge upon their actions.

Read in this way, the *History* interprets the interaction between human agency and impersonal historical circumstances. For Thucydides, the story is

---

12. For a more detailed account of the relationship between the Mytilene debate and later developments in the *History*, see Ferrar, *Origins*, pp. 174–77; and Connor, *Thucydides*, pp. 89–91.

one of an erosion of agency that follows from the momentum of events coupled with a network of misguided actions. Periclean Athens represents both the starting point of this process and the norm for Thucydides' judgment. It is normative precisely because the democratic polity then offered the maximum opportunity for human agency to work constructively within the deliberative process. Under this condition, the human community exercised its greatest freedom, for it was best able to control what human agents can control—their own processes of rhetorical exchange. But there are real and unavoidable limitations on the power of free deliberation, since it is circumscribed by social history and extra-verbal reality. When the limits of this power are not respected, arrogance replaces prudence, and the self-constituting rhetorical medium becomes increasingly vulnerable to the forces that operate beyond deliberative control. Ultimately, the fragile balance needed to maintain the role of democratic agency breaks apart, and deliberative agents yield to necessity and chance.

In one sense, this history is tragic. The force of events seems to lead inexorably to the demise of Athens and to the destruction of the community's power to direct its own fate. Yet, Thucydides' work also has a didactic purpose: its own rhetoric teaches those who study it about the limits of rhetorical agency and about how it collapses when agents fail to account for the constraints on their actions. The readers of the *History*, then, become better equipped to assume the role of agent, for they are better able to interpret that role not just at the moment of action but also from within an understanding of history.

Five

Greek Oratorical Settings and the Problem of the Pnyx: Rethinking the Athenian Political Process

Christopher Lyle Johnstone

The criticism of public address during the past decade or more has become increasingly preoccupied with text. Particularly with the advent of deconstructionism and close textual analysis, efforts to understand and evaluate public utterance concentrate on the sources, structure, and linguistic forms of expression. Certainly the influence of context has not been ignored, but consideration of contextual factors has concentrated on the political, social, philosophical, and other historical forces that shaped the formation and presentation of public discourse.[1] Little if any attention has been paid to the physical context within which oratory is presented and experienced.[2]

---

1. See William Norwood Brigance, ed., *A History and Criticism of American Public Address,* vols. 1 and 2 (New York: McGraw Hill, 1943), vol. 3 edited by Marie K. Hochmuth. More recently, see the collected studies of American political rhetoric in Michael C. Leff and Fred J. Kauffeld, eds., *Texts in Context* (Davis, Calif.: Hermagoras Press, 1989). Even Jebb in his encyclopedic treatment of the Attic Orators pays no heed whatever to the physical contexts within which speech was delivered. See J. C. Jebb, *The Attic Orators,* 2 vols. (New York: Russell and Russell, 1962).

2. One of the very few exceptions to this observation is Marie Hochmuth (Nichols), "The Criticism of Rhetoric," in *Speech Criticism: Methods and Materials,* ed. William A. Linsley (Dubuque, Iowa: William C. Brown, 1968), pp. 63–64: "we must consider the function of *place.* Place, of course, is not merely a physical condition. It is also a metaphysical condition, an ideological environment. . . . [However,] I do not intend to minimize the purely physical aspect of place, for this is sometimes important, of course. Comfort and discomfort, audibility or inaudibility may take on considerable proportions. . . . In evaluating speeches, the aspect of place must be recognized as a conditioning factor."

The setting for public address, nonetheless, is an important consideration in understanding and appraising oratory. If the invention of techniques of persuasion, arrangement, and expression is best understood in terms of the historical and cultural circumstances in which speech occurs, clearly the verbal style and active presentation of the matter of speech owe at least something to physical setting. Indeed, if the rhetorical examination of speech is principally concerned with how discourse functions in practice (as I take it to be), then certain characteristics of the setting—including time of day, the configuration of audience seating, and the acoustical properties of the speech location—are important insofar as they affect verbal style and vocal delivery. Other aspects of the physical context, including the architectural style of the auditorium, have been acknowledged as contributing to the rhetorical experience of listeners.[3]

It seems obvious that both speakers' technical choices and auditors' experience of oratory are affected by setting. The symbolic importance of speaking about civil rights from the steps of the Lincoln Memorial was not lost on Martin Luther King Jr., and it is reasonable to assume that the audience would have been attuned to this symbolism even if King had not called explicit attention to it in his speech. Similarly, the rhetorical impact of Lincoln's speech at Gettysburg was no doubt augmented by the stillness and sanctity of the surrounding battleground—and, as with King, the setting was explicitly invoked by the speaker. In such cases as these, the speech text is overtly connected to the physical setting and to its symbolic values. And the listener's experiencing of the discourse is no doubt also affected by these values.

The oratorical event—that is, the utterance, reception, and interpretation of public speech—is affected by its setting in still another way: delivery must take account of the physical and acoustical features of the speaking environment. Thus do such vocal aspects as volume, rhythm, rate, and the timing of pauses owe something to the distance between speaker and audi-

---

3. "Auditorium" is used broadly here as including any structure in which speeches were presented and listened to, including open-air assembly places.

Studies of Hitler's uses of oratory and the mass meeting note the importance of setting, including architecture, in effecting desired audience responses. See, for instance, Ross Scanlon, "Hitler and the Technique of Mass Brainwashing," in *The Rhetorical Idiom: Essays in Rhetoric, Oratory, Language, and Drama*, ed. Donald C. Bryant (New York: Russell and Russell, 1966), pp. 201–20.

That the subject matter of criticism is the "rhetorical experience" I infer from I. A. Richards' comment that "criticism . . . is the endeavor to discriminate between experiences and to evaluate them." See *Principles of Literary Criticism* (New York: Harcourt, Brace and World, 1925), p. 2.

ence, the depth and breadth of the area in which the audience assembles, and the acoustical properties of the structural or natural setting in which speech is uttered.[4]

Beginning with such observations as these, this essay describes salient features of several types of public speaking venues in Greece during the Classical Period and then considers the particular oratorical problems associated with the place where the Athenian assembly met, namely, the Pnyx. The acoustical limitations of this meeting-place, at least during the fifth century B.C.E., raise important questions about the role of public address in Athenian political deliberation during this period.

I

Despite the fact that it plays such a prominent role in the production, reception, and interpretation of public utterance—a speech, after all, is as much an adaptation to its surroundings as to audience and occasion—physical setting has been virtually ignored in our scholarship, though a number of archaeological studies consider the physical features of public auditoria in ancient Greece.[5] Nonetheless, if we are to appreciate fully the ways in which public discourse functioned and was experienced during the period when

---

4. A number of contemporary studies consider delivery as an element in the oratorical event, though none examines it in connection with the physical setting in which speech occurs. See Charles L. Balcer, "The Vocal Aspect of Delivery Traced Through Representative Works in Rhetoric and Public Speaking, *Communication Studies* 11 (1959): 27–34; John Waite Bowers, "The Influence of Delivery on Attitudes Toward Concepts and Speakers," *Communication Monographs* 32 (1965): 154–58; William W. Fortenbaugh, "Aristotle's Platonic Attitude Toward Delivery," *Philosophy and Rhetoric* 4 (1986): 242–54; D. F. Gunderson and Robert Hopper, "Relationships between Speech Delivery and Speech Effectiveness," *Communication Monographs* (June 1963): 105–7; James H. MacBath and Nicholas M. Cripe, "Delivery: Rhetoric's Rusty Canon," *Journal of the American Forensic Association* 2 (1965): 1–6; Ray Nadeau, "Delivery in Ancient Times: Homer to Quintilian," *Quarterly Journal of Speech* 50 (1964): 53–60; and Robert P. Sonkowsky, "An Aspect of Delivery in Ancient Rhetorical Theory," in *Aristotle: The Classical Heritage of Rhetoric,* ed. Keith V. Erickson (Netuchen, N. J.: Scarecrow Press, 1974), pp. 251–66.

5. General descriptions of ancient Greek speaking sites can be found in Paul MacKendrick, *The Greek Stones Speak* (New York: Norton, 1981); R. E. Wycherley, *How The Greeks Built Cities* (New York: Norton, 1976); and Wycherley, *The Stones of Athens* (Princeton: Princeton University Press, 1978).

rhetoric first flourished as a form of public political activity, we must be familiar with the types of settings in which oratory was presented and heard during the fifth century. While it is beyond the scope of the present discussion to consider these settings in detail, a brief survey will illuminate both their variety and the sorts of problems and potential resources they might have presented to the orator.[6]

If we take Aristotle's three-fold division of oratory as a framework, we might consider oratorical settings as they served epideictic, forensic, and deliberative purposes. The case of epideictic address is the least documented and consequently the least instructive. It seems likely that most epideictic speeches were delivered in the open air at places appropriate to the occasions on which they were given. Funeral orations *(epitaphioi)*, for example, were apparently delivered at graveside, taking Pericles' famous speech as typical.[7] Little can be said about such sites except to observe that, as with Lincoln at Gettysburg, the setting furnished the speaker with reference points and contributed to the psychological atmosphere in which auditors experienced these speeches. Physical and acoustical characteristics are in most cases impossible to determine owing to alterations in the sites, but relevant factors that might survive include such topographical features as structures (tombs, walls, buildings, monuments) and natural hillsides and concavities that could serve as crude amphitheaters. Efforts to reconstruct these features, at least in imagination, can yield insight into the physical circumstances to which speakers had to adapt their presentations.

Local festivals such as the *Panathenaia* at Athens and Dionysian celebrations in most cities and towns, as well as the great panhellenic festivals at Olympia, Ithsmia, Delphi, and Nemea, provided another type of epideictic occasion. As Kennedy notes, "we hear of a speech which Antisthenes intended to give at an Isthmian festival criticizing the Athenians, Thebans, and

----

6. For a detailed account of such settings, see William A. McDonald, *The Political Meeting Places of the Greeks* (Baltimore: Johns Hopkins University Press, 1943).

7. George Kennedy notes that Pericles delivered funeral orations in 440 and 431, the latter being the speech attributed to him by Thucydides. See *The Art of Persuasion in Greece* (Princeton: Princeton University Press, 1963), p. 155. Thucydides (2.35) places the speech at the *dêmosion sêma*, the public burial ground along the road from the Dipylon Gate to the Academy. Philostratus also can be taken to put Gorgias' *Funeral Oration* at this location (*Lives of the Sophists* 1.9.5): the speech "was delivered at Athens, [and] was spoken over those who fell in the wars, whom the Athenians bury at public expense with eulogies." For a detailed discussion of this site, see Wycherley, *Stones of Athens,* esp. pp. 223, 257–60.

Lacedaimonians. . . . [And] Gorgias delivered at least one striking speech at both a Pythian and an Olympian festival."[8] Of such oratorical events we might surmise that they were delivered in public spaces where sizable crowds could gather. These would include both the outdoor setting of the *agora*—the marketplace and/or civic center of the Greek *polis* that served as a public square—and the semi-enclosed circumstances of the *stoa*—the roofed colonnade or portico that attained great importance in city planning during the fifth century.[9] Both settings figured prominently in oratorical activities during the Classical Period, as we shall see shortly.

The chief advantage of the agora as a speech venue was, of course, that it could accommodate large gatherings of people—upwards of five thousand in only a limited section of the Athenian Agora, for example.[10] Presumably the orator usually addressed the crowd from a kind of speaker's platform that raised him somewhat above the audience. Plutarch (*Solon* 8.2) tells a story of how Solon "leaped forth suddenly in the Agora" and, when a crowd had gathered, mounted the "herald's stone" to address them. Later (during the second century B.C.E.) the Romans constructed a formal *bêma* (speaker's platform) on the northern side of the Athenian Agora. In any event, the market-squares of most Greek cities afforded an appropriate locale for the sort of oratorical displays for which Gorgias and other Sophists were known.

------

8. Kennedy, *Art of Persuasion*, p. 166. Fragments of or references to Gorgias' speeches are included in Rosamond Kent Sprague, ed., *The Older Sophists* (Columbia: University of South Carolina Press, 1972).

9. Philostratus (*Lives of the Sophists* 1.9.4) describes Gorgias delivering the *Pythian Speech* "from the altar at the temple of the Pythian god [Apollo]." As was true of all Classical Greek temples, of course, the altar was outside the eastern entrance to the temple, on a stone terrace the area of which was great enough to accommodate several hundred people. See H. Berve and G. Gruben, *Greek Temples, Theatres, and Shrines* (London: Thames and Hudson, 1973).

We might also infer from the example of Plato's *Symposium* that epideictic oratory was occasionally presented in private homes to small groups, and sophists were said to have made formal speeches even when meeting in houses. See Kennedy, *Art of Persuasion*, pp. 167 ff, and Plato's *Gorgias* 447c. Since such speech settings can hardly be called "public," however, it is beside the present point to consider the private home as a venue for public address.

10. See Homer A. Thompson and R. E. Wycherley, "The Agora of Athens: The History, Shape, and Uses of an Ancient City Center," *The Athenian Agora*, vol. 14 (Princeton: The American School of Classical Studies at Athens, 1972), p. 48. The *agorai* of other Greek cities provided similar accommodations for public speaking. See McDonald, *Political Meeting Places*, esp. ch. 4, "The City Assemblies in Post-Homeric Times."

They were not ideal, however: the absence of any artificial means of amplifying the human voice meant that the distance between speaker and listeners had to be kept within certain limits, and this limited the size of the audience. Moreover, ambient noise from elsewhere in the marketplace might have intruded, again circumscribing the number of listeners who could hear the speaker adequately. And finally, as with any outdoor venue, weather (heat, rain, hail) could interfere with or even terminate a speech event.

Some of these problems were overcome when the speech setting was moved from the open agora into the stoa. The stoa, as Wycherley notes, was a multipurpose building of first-rate importance: "It could form an entrance porch, or a facade; it could be placed on one or more sides of a court and could form an internal or external peristyle."[11] In such configurations, the stoa served as the location for a variety of civic and commercial enterprises: it contained shops, dining rooms, and commercial offices; housed commemorative paintings and artifacts; provided office space for civic officials; functioned as a meeting-place for teachers and their students; was employed as a law court; and gave sophists a place to display their art.[12] Indeed, "the Athenian orators constantly include the stoas among the glories of the city; Demosthenes couples them with the masterpieces of the Acropolis, the Propylaea and the Parthenon, and with the ship-shed of Peiraeus."[13]

The architecture of the stoa creates some interesting conditions for the orator. Long and narrow, walled along the back (and sometimes on the ends), with an open colonnade along the front, high-ceilinged, and constructed typically of stone, the stoa provided a place out of the elements in which a large assembly of people could be gathered.[14] Moreover, its dimensions sometimes

---

11. Wycherley, *How the Greeks Built Cities*, p. 110. He continues, "the prominence of the stoa in Greek architecture is easily explained. It suited the climate of Greece, offering welcome shade from the heat and ready shelter from wind and squalls; it was easily adaptable to a variety of purposes in public life and possessed great artistic possibilities" (p. 111). See also J. J. Coulton, *The Architectural Development of the Greek Stoa* (Oxford: Oxford University Press, 1976).

12. All these functions were served by stoas built in the Athenian *agora* during the fifth century. See John M. Camp, *The Athenian Agora* (London: Thames and Hudson, 1986).

13. Wycherley, *How the Greeks Built Cities*, p. 110.

14. Of the Painted Stoa in Athens, built to house paintings depicting scenes of Athenian military exploits, Camp observes: "Of all the stoas of Athens it holds the preferred location, along the north side of the Agora square, looking right up the Panathenaic Way to the Acropolis. It has the southern exposure recommended for stoas in order to take advantage of the warmth of the low winter sun while presenting its back wall to the cold north wind" (*Athenian Agora*, p. 66).

created something of the effect of a concert hall: in the larger stoas sound echoes and reverberates.[15] This effect is amply demonstrated in the rebuilt Stoa of Attalos on the east side of the Athenian Agora. Reconstructed in 1956 on its second-century–B.C.E. foundations with the same materials as and according to the plan of the original building, this structure (which now houses the excavation offices and museum) is a striking example of stoa architecture. The acoustical effects of its design are pronounced, and they would have presented the orator with both a challenge and a resource. While the reverberation of sound within the structure might have distorted the speaker's voice, it also amplified and enriched vocal qualities and rhythms. Indeed, an experienced speaker might have selected his cadences so as to take advantage of the building's acoustical properties.[16]

The importance of the stoa as an oratorical setting becomes clearer still when we turn from epideictic to forensic address. This is especially true in Athens, where legal requirements concerning jury size (a minimum of 201 persons served, typically 501, and in politically significant trials as many as 1,500 or more) demanded spaces that could accommodate large audiences.[17] Whereas the ancient homicide courts met in various traditional places according to the nature of the case,[18] from the early fifth century

---

15. Stoas were of various sizes, but in general they were long, narrow buildings, walled along the length in back and usually along the width at both ends, and open along the length in front, the open side being distinguished by its row of columns supporting either a roof or a second storey. Size during the 5th century ranged from the relatively small Royal Stoa (about 18 m long and 7.5 m wide), to the middle-sized Painted Stoa (not fully excavated yet, but estimated at 40 m long and known to be about 12 m wide) and the Stoa of Zeus Eleutherios (45 m x 10.5 m), and finally to the larger (80 m x 15 m) South Stoa I. See Camp, *Athenian Agora*, and Thompson and Wycherley, "Agora of Athens."

16. I am intrigued by the possibility that a speaker such as Gorgias, whose verbal style was noted for its rhythmic quality, might have spoken in one of the Athenian stoas, of which there were four in the *Agora* during the time he was at Athens. Surely, just as a great operatic performer will adjust his or her voice to take best advantage of the concert hall in which a performance is given, so as polished an orator as Gorgias could adjust his voice, pace, and verbal style to suit the acoustical peculiarities of the auditorium in which he spoke.

17. For a general, brief account of the courts see A. R. W. Harrison, *The Law of Athens, Procedure* (Oxford: Oxford University Press, 1971), pp. 36 ff.

18. Pausanias 1.28. See also D. MacDowell, *Athenian Homicide Law* (Manchester: Manchester University Press, 1963) and Thompson and Wycherley, "The Agora of Athens", esp. pp. 52 ff.

onward most civil law was practiced in stoas and peristyle-type buildings in the area of the Agora.[19]

The oldest and largest of the Athenian lawcourts during the Classical Period—the Heliaia—was probably located in the southwest corner of the Agora, near other civic buildings.[20] Possibly the lawcourt in which Socrates was tried, this building (which may have initially been a simple walled enclosure designed to shut out the bustle of the nearby market square)[21] gives some evidence of having at one time had the form of a peristyle or cloister—a stoa wrapped around an open courtyard.[22] The size of this building—it had interior measurements of about 26.5 m x 31 m—suited it for the largest Athenian juries.

In addition to the stoas themselves and to peristyle buildings, the forensic speech setting in Athens included during the late fifth century and into fourth a large rectangular, unroofed enclosure (22 m x 41 m).[23] Little remains of this structure, and it was superceded by a square peristyle building during the fourth century.

What we know of fifth- and fourth-century Athenian lawcourts as oratorical settings, then, is that they usually (but not always) incorporated the

---

19. Two inscriptions of the middle of the fourth century mention lawsuits tried in the Painted (*Poikilê*) Stoa before a jury of five hundred. *Inscriptione Graecae* 2.2 1641, 1670. The other stoas also served as lawcourts. See Camp, *Athenian Agora*, pp. 107–13, and Wycherley, *Stones of Athens*, esp. ch. 2.

20. The identification of this building remains conjectural. It is based on the several literary references to the presence of the *Heliaia* in the *agora*, on the configuration of the building itself, on the presence of an adjacent water-clock, and on the absence of alternative candidates. See Thompson and Wycherley, "Agora of Athens," pp. 62–65; Camp, *Athenian Agora*, pp. 46–47; Wycherley, *Stones of Athens*, p. 35; and John M. Camp, ed., *The Athenian Agora: A Guide to the Excavation and Museum*, 4th ed. (Princeton: The American School of Classical Studies at Athens, 1990), pp. 180–81.

21. See Thompson and Wycherley, "Agora of Athens," pp. 62–63.

22. Wycherley envisions it this way, at least during the Hellenistic period. See *How the Greeks Built Cities*, p. 85. Camp (*The Athenian Agora: A Guide*) also notes this: "Around the middle of the 2nd century B.C. a complete peristyle was inserted, and the building would seem to have been roofed with a lantern to provide light and air while assuring privacy" (p. 181). A clearer example of such a structure can be found in the larger square peristyle of the fourth century, located in the northeastern corner of the *Agora*.

23. See Thompson and Wycherley, "Agora of Athens," pp. 56–57. The identification of this building as a lawcourt rests principally on the discovery on its floor of a number of bronze jurors' ballots.

design of the stoa, they were partially or wholly open to the sky, and they were large. These features created physical relationships between speakers and audiences that could affect both the content and the delivery of forensic address. The acoustical characteristics of these structures, in particular, served (it would seem) to augment the force of the human voice, even as they created certain challenges to the orator. In any event, more can be said about these matters only after systematic study of these sites.[24]

The final class of ancient Greek oratory—deliberative—brings us to the last two types of oratorical settings to be considered here: the council house or *bouleutêrion,* and the public assembly place. The *bouleutêrion* was a common feature of the agora in Greek cities.[25] Even in non-democratic *poleis* and in such religious sanctuaries as Olympia and Delphi, policy- and lawmaking bodies met in buildings designed specifically as chambers in which moderately large groups (up to five hundred or more in some places) could be addressed by individual speakers. These buildings were typically square or rectangular, and they usually provided tiered seating and interior columnar arrangements so that speakers had line-of-sight access to auditors. High-ceilinged, their open-raftered terracotta roofs rested on walls generally constructed of stucco-covered, unbaked brick—though from the third century B.C.E. onwards a number of these buildings had walls of dressed stone.[26]

Two features of these buildings are pertinent to the present discussion. First, the dimensions and seating arrangement of the *bouleutêrion* provided for a spatial relationship between the speaker and his often large audience that was surprisingly intimate. In the Old *Bouleutêrion* at Athens, for ex-

---

24. At present, the most detailed descriptions of these buildings are to be found in MacDonald, *Political Meeting Places,* and in Camp, *Athenian Agora* and *The Athenian Agora: A Guide.*

25. See McDonald, *Political Meeting Places,* for a useful compendium of such structures and their locations.

26. See Wycherley, *Stones of Athens,* pp. 27–35. Also J. Camp and W. B. Dinsmoor Jr., *Ancient Athenian Building Methods* (Princeton, N. J.: American School of Classical Studies at Athens, 1984), pp. 6–8. Of course, little remains of the *bouleutêria* of the sixth–fourth centuries, since all but their limestone foundations have disappeared. However, stone council chambers of the Hellenistic period at several sites in Asia Minor are in a remarkably good state of preservation. Of particular interest in this connection are the *bouleutêria* at Miletus and Ephesus and the *ekklêsiastêrion* at Priene. For fuller accounts of these structures, see McDonald, *Political Meeting Places,* and A. W. Lawrence, *Greek Architecture* (Baltimore: Penguin Books, 1957).

ample, which was constructed at the beginning of the fifth century to accommodate the five hundred members of the newly-constituted *Boulê* (as a result of Kleisthenes' reforms), the distance between the speaker's position and the last row of seats is only about ten meters.[27] Thus could a speaker employ an ordinary speaking voice in addressing a fairly large audience, and thus could he make the sorts of asides and sotto voce comments that would be ineffective in a less intimate setting. Second, the use of wooden benches for seating and of stuccoed walls meant that sound reverberation would have been minimal (since neither material is highly reflective of sound). Even in council houses where stone was used in walls and seats, the presence of an audience (whose clothing and bodies would absorb sound) would have minimized the acoustical distortions normally associated with such materials.[28] The classical *bouleutêrion*, then, apparently provided an almost perfect speech setting, as the persistence of this design over several centuries attests.

The other principal deliberative setting to be considered here—and the one that will bring us soon to the specific focus of the present study—is the open-air assembly-place or amphitheater. In virtually all Greek *poleis*, though the citizens' assembly (the *ekklêsia*) met initially in the agora, it convened later in an amphitheater of more-or-less formal design and construction.[29] It

---

27. The Old and New *Bouleutêria* at Athens are described well in McDonald, *Political Meeting Places*, pp. 171 ff. See also Camp, *Athenian Agora*; John Travlos, *Pictorial Dictionary of Ancient Athens* (New York: Praeger, 1971); and Ida Thallon Hill, *The Ancient City of Athens* (London: Methuen, 1953).

28. For elaboration of the acoustical properties of various building materials and configurations, see George C. Izenour, *Theater Design* (New York: McGraw-Hill, 1977).

29. McDonald, *Political Meeting Places*, notes (p. 40) that "in post-Homeric times, before theaters were constructed (usually apart from the agora), the political assembly of most cities continued to hold its regular meetings in the agora." When the growth of commercial activity interfered with the business of the *ekklêsia*, it was moved to a quieter place. Typically, this was elsewhere in the open air, and eventually to an amphitheater of some sort.

There are at least two and perhaps three exceptions to this generalization that should be noted. One is the Thersilion at Megalopolis. This extraordinary building, constructed during the second quarter of the fourth century B.C.E. as the assembly hall for the "Ten Thousand" of the Arcadian League, was a roofed building with an interior area of some 3000 sq m. It could, indeed, have accommodated ten thousand standing or six thousand sitting spectators. The most distinctive feature of this structure, apart from its unusal size for a roofed building, is the ingenious arrangement of interior support columns, which were placed in such a way as to minimize visual and auditory obstruction between speaker and audience. For

is with the latter that we are presently concerned. Because the agora was deficient in several ways as a venue for meetings of the assembly, by the fifth century the theater was the scene of the regular political assemblies in almost all Greek cities.[30] In most cases, theaters served both as an assembly place and as the setting for dramatic performances. They were typically large,[31] and as their design was improved over two centuries their acoustical properties served their purposes more and more adequately.[32]

---

further details, see McDonald, *Political Meeting Places*, pp. 200 ff; D. S. Robertson, *A Handbook of Greek and Roman Architecture*, 2nd ed. (Cambridge: Cambridge University Press, 1945), pp. 174–75; and E. F. Benson, "The Thersilion at Megalopolis," *Journal of Hellenic Studies* 13 (1892–93): 319–26.

A second exception is the *bouleutêrion*-like *ekklêsiasterion* at Priene in present-day Turkey, near ancient Miletus. This stone building, with seating for seven hundred, was constructed on the lines of the council-house in other cities. The assembly of Priene, a small *polis*, had no need for a larger assembly place.

The other possible exception is the use during the ascendancy of the Thirty Tyrants at Athens in 405–4 B.C.E. of the Odeion of Pericles as a meeting place for the assembly. However, as McDonald observes (p. 46), "this building would have been suitable enough for... a limited assembly, and it would have been possible to exclude undesirable persons. But it could scarcely have accommodated the whole Athenian assembly, and... references to an 'assembly in the Theater at Munychia' [i.e., near the harbor-town of Peiraieus] during the time of the Thirty indicate that this was then the regular meeting place."

30. See Wycherley, *How the Greeks Built Cities*, and McDonald, *Political Meeting Places*. The latter observes (pp. 40–41) that "the agora in its ordinary form in cities of the Classical period and later would have been ill-suited to regular political assemblies, which often lasted several hours and required some sort of fixed seating arrangements. Moreover, the difficulty of seeing the speaker when all were standing on the same level would have been intolerable, unless there was a raised platform (*bêma*). But the building of a permanent bema in the agora is unknown until the Hellenistic period, and such an arrangement seems never to have been popular with the Greeks."

31. The late-fourth-century theatre at Argos, for example, could accommodate some twenty thousand, that at Megalopolis twenty-one thousand, and that at Epidauros— the acoustics of which are unusually good—fourteen thousand. The Theater of Dionysos at Athens could accommodate during the fifth–fourth centuries about fifteen thousand to seventeen thousand persons. See Robertson, *A Handbook of Greek and Roman Architecture,* and Wycherley, *How the Greeks Built Cities.*

32. The Greek theater originated during the seventh–sixth centuries as an orchestra—usually a circular area in which dances and choral odes were performed—in the *agora* of the city. As dramatic performances became more elaborate, and as audience

These properties are among the most salient features of such structures when we consider their use as meeting places for the *ekklêsia*. The most important, and obvious, of these properties is that the conical shape of the *cavea* or seating-area of the theater functions megaphone-like to amplify sound. It does so, moreover, with a minimum of echo or other acoustic distortion, so that in the best-designed theaters (e.g., at Epidauros) auditors in the uppermost rows of seats (under good weather conditions, at any rate) can hear quite clearly speakers and actors in the orchestra far below. In theaters where the slope of the *cavea* is less pronounced, of course, this effect is diminished. A second important acoustical feature of the amphitheater was that, when it was properly oriented, it sheltered auditors from the wind, which could also interfere with sound-transmission.[33] In circumstances where either of these features was less than optimal, orators addressing large audiences faced what may have been insurmountable obstacles to being heard by all present.

A final observation to be made about the amphitheater as a setting for political speech is that, at least in some instances, the topographical features of the site provided both speaker and auditor with significant reference points

---

size and commercial use of the marketplace grew, this orchestra was moved (ideally) to a flat area at the bottom of a hillside on which audience members could sit. The slope of the hill, especially when it was in the form of a curved cavity, provided for both visual access to the orchestra and enhanced transmission of sound. This occurred at Athens, for instance, early in the fifth century, and at other cities somewhat later. Successive improvements at such sites led finally to the development of the conical *cavea*, with its rows of stone seats, that is now associated with Greek theaters of the Classical and Hellenistic Periods. See Izenour, *Theater Design*, and MacKendrick, *The Greek Stones Speak*, esp. ch. 4.

33. Izenour, in *Theater Design* (p. 257), remarks that, "as for weather [as a factor in ambient conditions in theaters], the wind is the only element of importance because rain . . . certainly cancelled the performance. . . . [No] matter which way [the wind] blows, the fact of its creating an ambient disturbance that adversely affects each spectator as it blows past his ear lobes only adds to the masking effect of background noise over speech and is always more of a hindrance than help (no matter which direction it blows) in carrying the voice along to help it reach the upper seats. Scientifically there is little doubt . . . that even when absolute quiet prevailed, the acoustical difficulties encountered in these large outdoor theaters were severe and ever-present, and to overcome them performers . . . certainly measured the cadence of speech and to achieve adequate projection must have had to exert all the vocal power they could."

for invoking civic duties, accomplishments, and aspirations. The amphitheater (as at Argos, Megalopolis, and Athens, for instance) often allowed the audience to look out over the agora and at important civic monuments and cult temples. Just as with King at the Lincoln Memorial and with Lincoln at Gettysburg, such a circumstance permitted the orator to include in his speech specific references to the setting as a means of evoking appropriate associations in the audience.

Deliberative settings in classical Greece, then—at least when restricted to the meeting-places of citizens' assemblies—presented the political orator with both resources and obstacles. When we consider the latter in particular, certain questions arise concerning the conduct of public deliberation in democratic *poleis*. These questions are particularly provocative in the case of the meeting-place of the Athenian assembly: the Pnyx.

II

The deliberative assembly, which Aristotle termed "the supreme element in states" (*Politics* 1299a1), was in Greek democratic *poleis* the sovereign body whose function was to debate and vote on proposed laws and policies.[34] This was nowhere more true than in Athens during most of the fifth and fourth centuries. The process of public deliberation, in particular, has come to us through Thucydides, Xenophon, and others as one in which oratory is the essential mode of activity by which collective decision is reached. From these writers we learn of speeches made at the Pnyx on such momentous matters as the conduct of the Peloponnesian War (e.g., Thucydides' accounts at 1.139–145 of the debate on the Spartan ultimatum in 432/31 and at 6.8–26 of the debates on the proposed Sicilian expedition in 415), the management of the Athenian empire (e.g., the Mytilene debate of 427, in Thucydides 3.36–49), the maintenance of military discipline (see Xenophon, *Hellenika* 1.7.7–35 on the Arginoussai debate of 406), and the abandonment of democracy for oligarchy in 411 (Thucydides 8.53–54).

Contemporary historians, too, often promote the view that public deliberation in the *ekklêsia* consisted in a series of speeches presented by *rhêtores* who advocated or opposed specific proposals, which speeches were listened

---

34. "The deliberative element," Aristotle says at *Politics* 1298a4–6, "has authority in matters of war and peace, in making and unmaking alliances; it passes laws, inflicts death, exile, confiscation, elects magistrates and audits their accounts."

to attentively by the assembled citizens and then the proposals voted on.[35] This version of Athenian political debate is rendered problematic, however—at least during the fifth century—when we consider the implications for speech of the Pnyx as an oratorical setting. The position to be developed in the remainder of this paper is that the acoustical defects of the Pnyx in its first phase (i.e., during the fifth century) made it likely that speakers could not be heard adequately by a significant portion of their audience, and thus that our understanding of the role of oratory in Athenian public deliberation must be revised.

Debate in the *ekklêsia* was, in principle, a series of speeches, each composed and delivered by a citizen–*rhêtor*, each listened to attentively by an audience of several thousand who then voted on the issue under consideration. While, between speeches, there may have been some discussion among members of the audience about what they had heard and about the matter at hand,[36] each auditor was to consider independently the individual cases that had been made for and against a proposal. The problem with this account of the deliberative process is that it is predicated on speakers being heard adequately by all or most present. This would certainly be possible in a venue where the acoustical conditions were conducive to the projection of the human voice—and the amphitheaters used in most Greek *poleis* from the early fourth century on certainly meet this requirement to greater or lesser degrees.

---

35. See, for instance, M. I. Finley, *Democracy Ancient and Modern*, rev. ed. (New Brunswick: Rutgers University Press, 1985), p. 54: "the normal procedure was for a proposal to be introduced, debated, and either passed (with or without amendment) or rejected." "Debate," he continues (pp. 56–57), "designed to win votes among an outdoor audience numbering many thousands means oratory, in the strict sense of the word. . . . [Citizens] went up on the Pnyx, and . . . they listened to the debates and made up their minds." Similarly, Hansen contends that, "in an assembly attended by 6,000 citizens it was impossible to have an open discussion. The debate was bound to take the form of a string of speeches of varying length." See M. H. Hansen, *The Athenian Assembly in the Age of Demosthenes* (Oxford and N. Y.: Basil Blackwell Ltd., 1987), p. 56. See also C. E. Robinson, *Everyday Life in Ancient Greece* (Oxford: Clarendon, 1964); and A. H. M. Jones, "Athens and Sparta," in *The Greeks*, ed. Hugh Lloyd-Jones (Cleveland: World Publishing, 1962), pp. 56–69.

36. In his discussion of "acclamation and heckling" during debate on the Pnyx, Hansen notes that "participants sitting next to each other could in whisperings interchange views on the speech delivered from the platform or on the debate at large" and that "the participants took the liberty to interrrupt the speakers by cheers, by cries of protest, or by laughter" (*The Athenian Assembly*, p. 70).

In Athens, however, the move from the Pnyx to the Theater of Dionysos did not occur until the last half of the fourth century.[37] Moreover, even though the the Pnyx during each of its three phases was configured as a shallow amphitheater, during the fifth century—when many of democratic Athens' most important public debates took place—the Pnyx was decidedly unfriendly to oratory for a mass audience.

There are two ways to argue for this claim, one employing direct evidence and the other indirect. The best evidence, of course, would come from having an actual speech delivered to a real audience at the Pnyx as it was during the fifth century, or at least in an approximate reconstruction of those circumstances.[38] A second kind of direct evidence would involve taking acoustical measurements at the site as it now exists in order to determine its characteristics as a setting for public speech. However, in the absence of an audience such measurements would be misleading, owing to the impact on sound absorption and transmission of clothing and bodies.[39]

The second method of considering the acoustical features of the Pnyx is less direct and involves examining the behavior of vocal sound within the dimensions and configuration of the auditorium as it was in the fifth century. This is the method to be employed here. After fixing the physical characteristics of the Pnyx, we can examine the salient features of the production, transmission, and reception of the human voice in order to determine (within

---

37. For a survey of the epigraphical evidence of this move, see McDonald, *Political Meeting Places*, pp. 47 ff.

38. During a 1991 visit to the Pnyx with about fifteen students I approximated this approximation; that is, since the Pnyx has been excavated down to bedrock, and since the rock surface is largely if not wholly the same as it was during the first (fifth-century) phase of the structure, by standing at the downhill side of the excavated slope, where the original *bêma* was, and having the "audience" position itself along the arc of the first amphitheater's rear boundary, I was able to test both my speaking voice and the transmission of vocal sound at the site. Even taking into account the greater ambient noise in modern versus classical Athens, what we found was that, short of shouting, a speaker could not be heard clearly from the rear of the audience area. At the very least, this raised a question about the suitability of Pnyx I as an oratorical setting.

39. As Izenour points out (*Theater Design*, pp. 259–60), "a false conditioning element influencing modern judgment of ancient theaters acoustically (particularly the Greek theater) is that contemporary acoustical measurements are invariably made when they are empty; the results are very different when they are full. . . . [Full], the hard surfaces of seats and risers are covered over by an absorbtive audience, yielding an entirely different environment."

certain limits) the probable quality of this setting as an auditorium for a mass audience.

The Pnyx underwent two major reconstructions during its approximately two centuries of service as the principal meeting place of the Athenian assembly. Starting in the late sixth or early fifth century, the sloping stone hillside just southwest of the Agora was in use until the last part of the fourth century.[40] During the first period the natural hillside, gently sloping downward to the northeast, was used as the theater cavea. The surface was evened off by quarrying out the limestone, while on the northern side a straight retaining wall was built to hold the earth filling brought in to create a level place for a *bêma* (see fig. 1). Facing the city, some five thousand citizens stood or sat on the slope.[41]

In the second period the arrangement of the auditorium was reversed. A semicircular retaining wall was built to the north to support an earthen embankment that sloped gradually down to the southwest—in the opposite direction from the original slope of the hill. The speaker's *bêma* was shifted to the southern side of the site. The audience now sat (apparently on the embankment—there is no direct evidence that stone or wooden benches were

---

40. Excavation by the Greek Archaeological Society in 1910 definitely confirmed the identification of the site as the Pnyx where the Athenian *ekklêsia* convened. The detailed study of the history and the architecture of the Pnyx as well as of the topography of the adjoining area was made by Homer A. Thompson, who carried out large-scale excavations at various times between 1930 and 1937 in collaboration first with K. Kourouniotes and later with R. L. Scranton. Though the literature on the site is fairly extensive, the most useful discussions can be found in Kourouniotes and Thompson, "The Pnyx in Athens," *Hesperia* 1 (1932): 96–217; Thompson and Wycherley, *Agora of Athens*, pp. 48 ff.; McDonald, *Political Meeting Places*, pp. 44 ff.; and G. Joyner, "The Pnyx and the Ekklesia in Athens," in *Hellenika: Essays on Greek Politics and History*, ed. G. H. R. Horsley (New South Wales, Australia: Macquarie University Press, 1982), pp. 121–30. In the last of these, an appendix includes a list of ancient sources on the Pnyx and the assembly, with extracts from speeches reportedly given there. McDonald provides useful citations of epigraphical evidence.

41. On the attendance at and capacity of the Pnyx, see Thompson and Wycherley, *Agora of Athens*, pp. 48 ff.; McDonald, *Political Meeting Places*, p. 69; and M. H. Hansen, "How Many Athenians Attended the Ecclesia?" *Greek, Roman, and Byzantine Studies* 17 (1976): 115 ff. For contemporary accounts of the meetings on the Pnyx, see Aristophanes, *Acharnians* 19–33; *Knights* 754, 783; and *Wasps* 31–33, 42; and Thucydides 8.72. Figures 1 and 3 are adapted from Kourouniotes and Thompson, "The Pnyx in Athens," and are used with permission from the Harvard University Press and from the American School of Classical Studies at Athens.

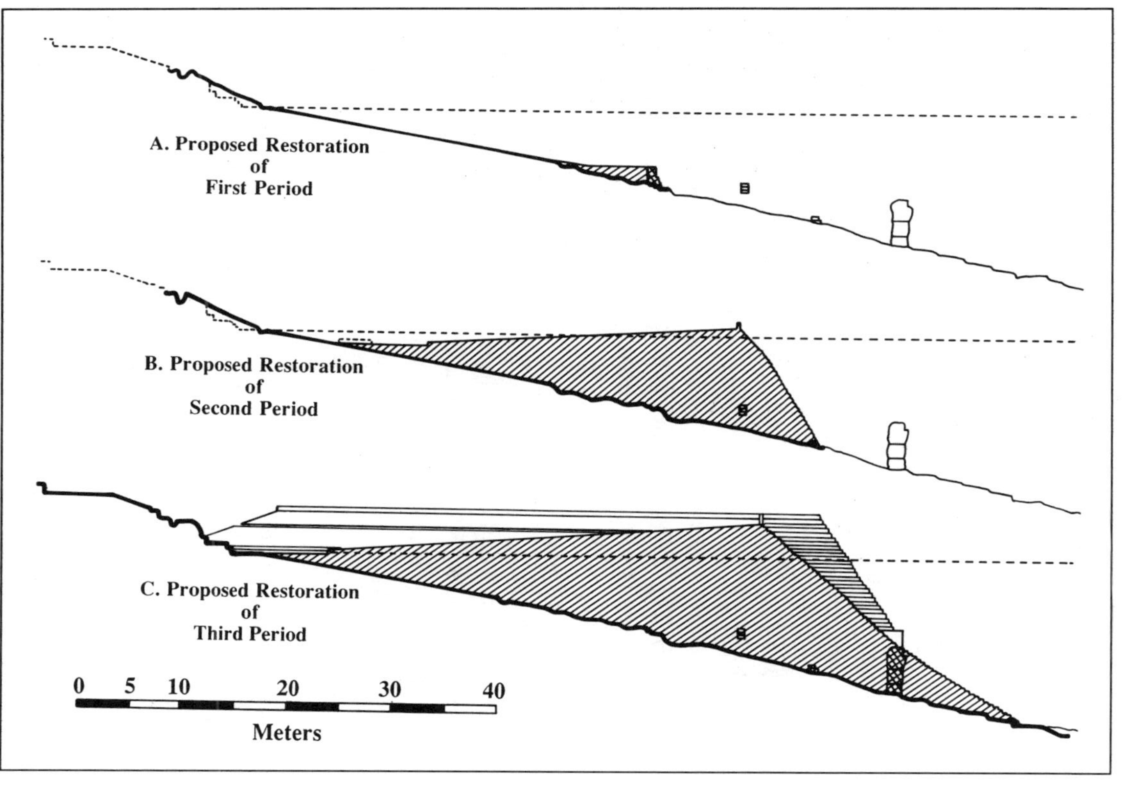

Figure 1. The three phases of the Pnyx (adapted from Kourouniotes and Thompson, *Hesperia*)

ever used on the Pnyx except adjacent to the speaker's platform, and these were for officials)[42] with their backs to the city, sheltered from the north wind by the retaining wall, no longer distracted by the sight of the Agora and their houses and fields (as Aristophanes satirizes the situation in the *Acharnians* of 425 B.C.E.). This new arrangement can be dated to 404–3, when the Thirty Tyrants shifted the location of the *bêma* (see Plutarch, *Themistocles* 19). The alteration of the theater provided for no significant increase in audience size.

The third and final stage occurred following the expansion of the *cavea* during the time of Lykourgos (i.e., 330–326 B.C.E.) and was contemporary with other modifications of the site.[43] The curved retaining wall was moved northward and raised to a height sufficient to contain an earthen embankment that sloped to the southwest (as in Period 2). At the same time, the southern edge of the auditorium was moved further back from the retaining wall, and a scarp was cut into the limestone hillside more or less along the diameter of the retaining wall at each end to a stone *bêma* in the center (see fig. 2). This enlarged audience area would have measured some 5550 sq m, and it would have accommodated ten thousand seated persons— "probably," as Kourouniotes and Thompson write, "a liberal estimate of the number of those interested in politics at the time of the reconstruction."[44]

Our present concern is with the first of these three configurations, that is, with the Pnyx as it was during the fifth century when such noted leaders as Themistocles, Pericles, Kleon, Nikias, and Alkibiades exercised political power through force of eloquence. In this crudest phase the auditorium on the Pnyx was some 40 m deep opposite the speaker's *bêma* and about 80 m wide

---

42. McDonald (*Political Meeting Places*, pp. 69–75) considers the question of seats in some detail, and concludes that during the third period of its history the Pnyx might have had some fixed seats for at least some portion of the audience (see p. 75).

43. The dating of the second reconstruction is discussed in McDonald, *Political Meeting Places*, p. 80. At about the same time the enlargement of the *cavea* occurred, preparations were made for the addition of two stoas to the southwest of the auditorium, higher up on the hillside. These stoas were apparently never completed.

44. "The Pnyx in Athens," p. 158. McDonald (*Political Meeting Places*, pp. 76–79) also describes the reconstructed amphitheater in some detail. Figure 2 is adapted from Thompson and Wycherley, *Agora in Athens*, and is used courtesy of the American School of Classical Studies at Athens.

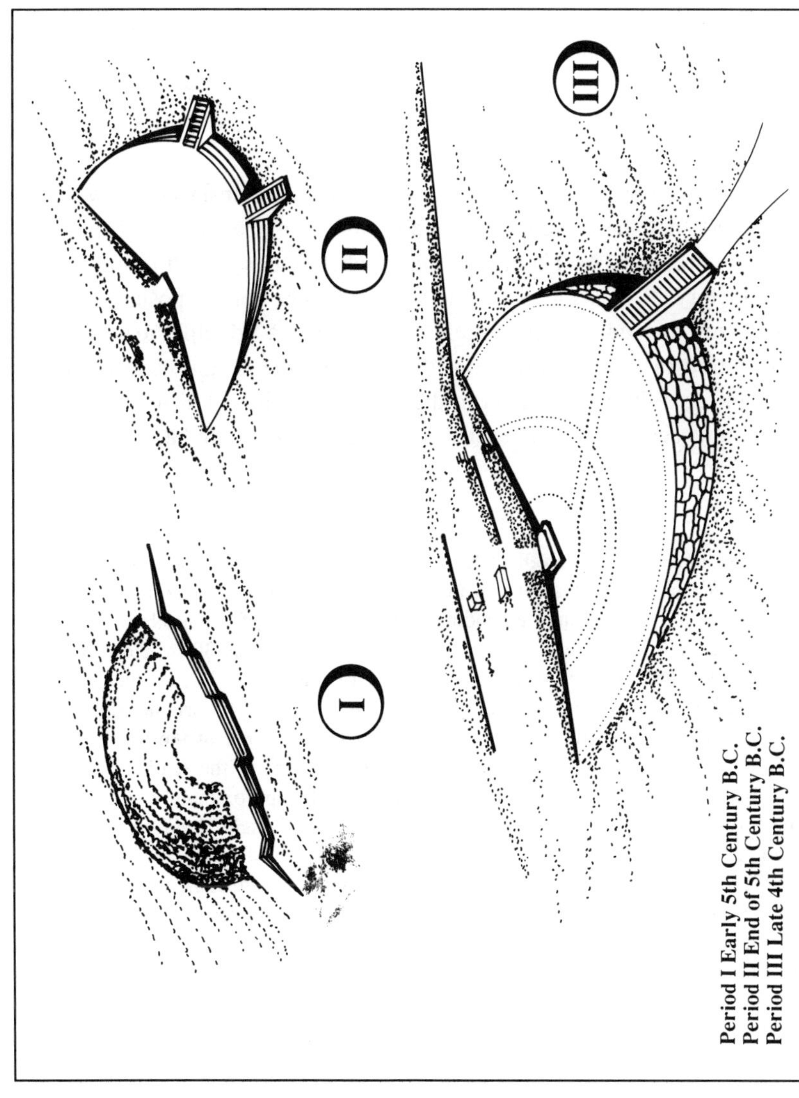

Figure 2. Pnyx (after J. Travlos)

across the back (see fig. 3). The resulting seating area was approximately 2,400 sq m, which would have accommodated at least five thousand citizens sitting, as Aristophanes suggests (*Knights*, 754, 783), on the bare rock.[45] The slope, while it was steeper than in either of the two later phases, was still relatively flat compared to the theaters of the fifth and fourth centuries, including the Theater of Dionysos to which the *ekklêsia* eventually moved. The original auditorium, in any event, would have done little if anything to augment the speaker's vocal projection, especially when the assembly was well attended.

What are the obstacles facing the orator in such circumstances? Several factors suggest that these were considerable much of the time, and insurmountable on occasion. As Thompson and Wycherley observe, "the site was never satisfactory."[46] This was due in no small measure to its exposure to the northeast winds. Indeed, it seems likely that this was a principal reason for the reorientation of the auditorium in 404–3, since the seating area of the second period was little larger than in the first. But a second difficulty with the site lay in its acoustical deficiencies. Even had the wind not been a factor,

---

45. The dimensions given here reflect Kourouniotes' and Thompson's sketch and description of the first period, shown in figure 3. Their report in *Hesperia* notes that the depth of the dressed area extending from the middle of the northern retaining wall (i.e., out from the presumed position of the *bêma*) is 30 m. However, they also observe that the later cuttings at the base of the Period 3 scarp have destroyed what there may have been of earlier stone dressing. The original dressed seating area extended to within a meter or two of the great *bêma* of the third period. The width of the auditorium is greatest where the arc of the seating area intersects the line of the two wings of the retaining wall—approximately 80 m. See "The Pnyx in Athens," especially p. 104. See also McDonald, *Political Meeting Places*, pp. 68–70.

The audience size noted here is taken from the maximum attendance at a fifth-century assembly according to Thucydides 8.72. McDonald, however, suggests (p. 69 n. 126) that this number might be too small for at least some meetings of the *ekklêsia*. Though Kourouniotes and Thompson (p. 104) assert that "there is no reason to suppose a greater capacity" than the five thousand mentioned by Thucydides, Hansen ("How Many Athenians Attended the *Ecclesia?*") argues that "the figure 5,000 must . . . be viewed with scepticism," and that "6,000 was a normal attendance, at least in the fourth century" (pp. 123–24). He acknowledges, however, that attendance during the Peloponnesian War may have been lower than normal.

46. *Agora of Athens*, p. 49. They attribute the problem largely to the wind. Joyner, too, comments on "the exposure of the site, especially to winds from the Northeast" ("The Pnyx and the Ekklesia in Athens," p. 122).

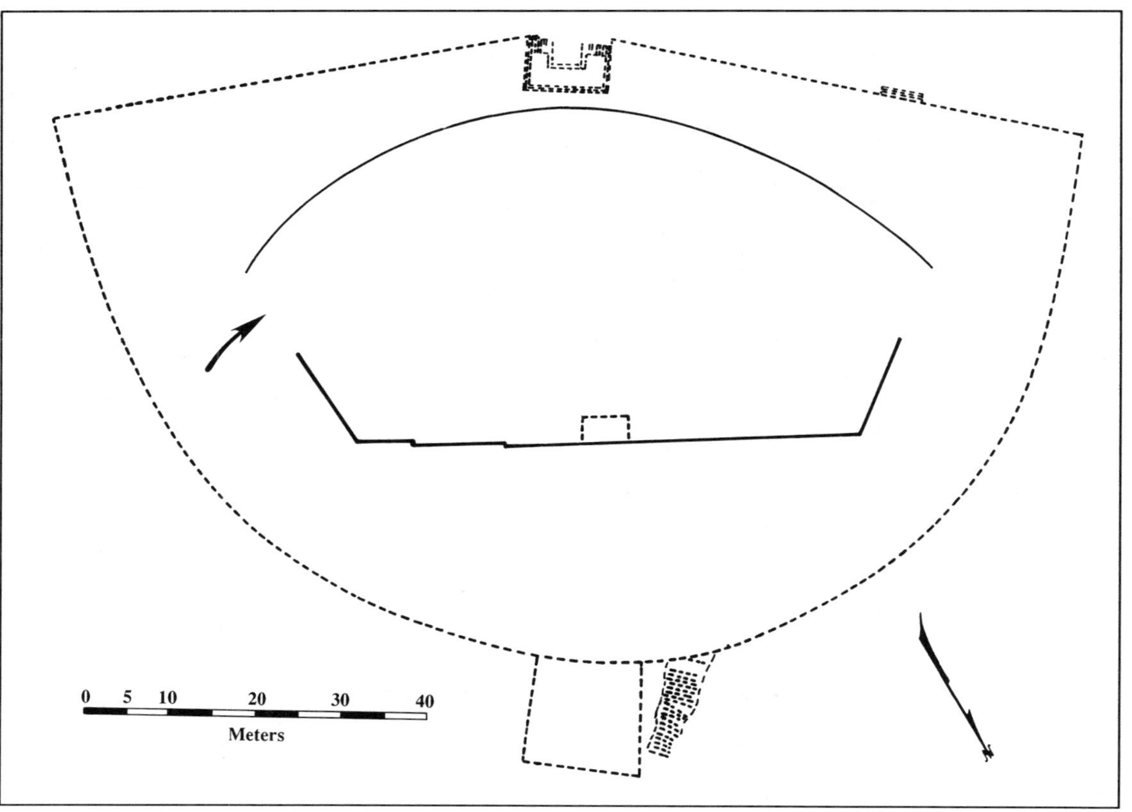

Figure 3. Sketch illustrating proposed restoration of Period I (after Kourouniotes and Thompson, Hesperia)

being heard clearly by all present would have been problematic at best. Even the strongest speakers would have been challenged to make their messages intelligible to the entire audience, and the task would have been altogether beyond those without strong voices or professional training as orators (or actors).

The general claim to be advanced here is that, in the absence of either design features or artificial devices that would amplify the human voice, the distance from the *bêma* to the furthest reaches of the seating area in the Pnyx of the fifth century precluded the satisfactory transmission of vocal sound. In order to see this we must consider what happens to the human voice when it is transmitted in the open air, and the ear's ability to perceive the voice. This is no simple matter, as it turns out. The human voice produces sound waves across a wide spectrum of frequencies and with significant variations in intensity, so the sound that travels from the speaker's lips to the listener's ear is a complex phenomenon. When sound is transmitted from a source to a listener, it diminishes in intensity as a function of the distance it travels. Moreover, such ambient conditions as air temperature and relative humidity affect the rate at which the strength of sound waves degenerates, and audience-generated noise further complicates the audibility and intelligibility of speech. Additionally, though it is sensitive to a range of frequencies and intensities, the human ear varies in its ability to hear sounds of different frequencies at a given level of intensity. Finally, the ability to hear a sound and to recognize it are two different things, so that even when a speaker can be heard, the message may not be altogether intelligible.

It is beyond the scope of the present discussion to examine each of these factors in detail. Still, a somewhat general consideration will be sufficient to establish a high probability that the Pnyx was problematic as an oratorical setting. Let us look first at the sound characteristics of the voice in speech. Speech sounds, as has been noted, are extremely complex, varying constantly in intensity and frequency. Nonetheless, the voices of adult male speakers (with whom we are concerned in the case of fifth-century Athens) exhibit some general characteristics that allow us to understand the physical dynamics of public speaking. One such characteristic is pitch, which has to do with the "highness" and "lowness" of a voice. Although the human voice can produce sounds in frequencies ranging from about 50 up to about 10,000 cycles per second (or Hertz, abbreviated Hz), the energy is greatest in the 100 to 600 Hz region and the voice has little power beyond 1,000 Hz (though this level is extremely important for the consonants of speech). Moreover, adult males have an average fundamental frequency (average pitch) of approximately 100 Hz, with an average fundamental frequency range of about 80–

151 Hz.[47] Vowel sounds are transmitted at relatively low frequencies (80–300 Hz), while consonants, as has been noted, occur closer to the 1,000 Hz level.

A second critical feature of vocal sound is its intensity—the force with which energy is given off by the vocal apparatus (and, as we shall see, the energy with which a sound wave strikes the eardrum).[48] While it is not identical to loudness, intensity is a major factor in how auditors perceive the loudness of a sound. Intensity is also the principal factor in how far sound travels before it fades out (frequency being another important element). Sound intensity is measured in decibels (dB), which in the case of human speech and hearing represent the degree of power a sound has above the threshold of hearing. Other things being equal, the higher the decibel level, the louder the sound will be to the auditor and the farther it will carry (of course, other things are never equal, so these relationships are much more complex than this account suggests). The intensity-level of normal, conversational speech is about 60–65 dB, while loud speech—such as would be employed in addressing the *ekklêsia* on the Pnyx—is around 80 dB.[49] Again, it is important

---

47. For a general account of vocal frequency, see Richard A. Hoops, *Speech Science: Acoustics in Speech*, 2nd ed. (Springfield, Ill.: Charles C. Thomas, 1969), ch. 3 ("Vocal Frequency"). He notes (p. 61) that "there are some general statements which can be made regarding pitch variability. Pitch variability tends to increase with age, females have greater pitch variability than males, emotional or dramatic material produces greater pitch variability than does factual material, trained voices exhibit greater pitch variability than untrained, habitual use of the natural pitch level or slightly above this produces greater variability than does a lower pitch, and oral reading of material produces greater pitch varibility than impromptu speaking." Characteristics of male vocal frequencies are discussed in R. J. Baken, *Clinical Measurement of Speech and Voice* (Boston: College Hill Press, 1987); and Y. Horii, "Some Statistical Characteristics of Voice Fundamental Frequency," *Journal of Speech and Hearing Science* 18 (1975): 192–201.
Everest notes that, "even though basic intelligibility does not demand it, the speech energy above 7,000 Hz contributes significantly to the naturalness of speech." See F. Alton Everest, *The Complete Handbook of Public Address Sound Systems* (Blue Ridge Summit, Penn.: Tab Books, 1978), p. 27.

48. Hoops' account is particularly informative. See *Speech Science*, ch. 5 ("Intensity and Loudness").

49. For discussion of vocal intensity levels, see Hoops, *Speech Science*, p. 95; and Willem A. Van Bergeijk, John R. Pierce, and Edward E. David Jr., *Waves and the Ear* (New York: Anchor, 1960), pp. 32–33. In comparison, the rustling of leaves or a faint whisper produces an intensity of 10 dB, the noise of a large, attentive audience at a performance produces 35 dB, a pneumatic drill ten feet away 90 dB, a loud shout at one foot 110 dB, and a nearby airplane engine 120 dB. In humans, 140 dB is the threshold of pain.

to recognize that in an actual speaking performance, sounds would be uttered with both somewhat greater and less force than this, so the range of intensity in public address might be more like 70–85 dB. Moreover, intensity varies somewhat with frequency as well, sounds at the lower and upper ranges generally being less powerful than those produced in the middle. With these two factors—namely, frequency and intensity—in mind, then, we can consider what happens to sound as it is transmitted from speaker to listener.[50]

As with the voice, this is no simple matter. However, a few key aspects of sound transmission will be adequate to the present purpose. Sound always dissipates and eventually disappears as it travels, even if the space into which it is projected is perfectly quiet. It does so partly because of an energy loss due to friction. Its energy is lost in heating the air through which it moves. Sounds of higher pitch are used up more quickly than lower-pitched sounds, but over a great enough distance virtually all the sound will have turned into heat.[51] It does so also because of the absorption and scattering of sound by water molecules, dust, and other air pollutants. Indeed, temperature and humidity can play a major role in the rate at which sound deteriorates during transmission through the air. Knudsen and Harris report that warm, dry air attenuates the intensity of a sound wave more than cooler, moister air. Indeed, the loss can be as much as 16 dB per hundred feet in hot desert air.[52] This factor becomes particularly salient when we consider the arid climate in Athens.

Finally, sound dissipates due to divergence. As sound waves spread out from a sound source in a roughly spherical (with a source radiating sound equally in all directions, such as a buzzing fly) or hemispherical (with a source from which sound radiates out one side but not the other, such as a public speaker) pattern, the wave is weakened as it travels from the source. This occurs because the sound waves diverge from one another as they move away from the source, so that they hit objects (such as the eardrum) with less intensity the farther they are from the source. The degree to which sound intensity weakens is inversely proportional to the distance from the source.

---

50. Numerous other elements complicate this process, and so the conclusions to be arrived at here must be qualified somewhat. Vocal qualities such as nasality, harshness, hoarseness, and breathiness affect sound production, as do the physical size of the speaker and the amount of training the voice has had. See Hoops, *Speech Science*, ch. 8 ("Voice Quality").

51. Hoops, *Speech Science*, p. 73.

52. See Vern O. Knudsen and Cyril M. Harris, *Acoustical Designing in Architecture* (Acoustical Society of America, 1978), pp. 59–61.

The loss due to this divergence is 6 dB for each doubling of the distance,[53] so that a sound having an intensity of 80 dB at one meter will be reduced to 74 dB at two meters, 68 dB at four meters, 62 dB at eight meters, and so on. By this calculation, then, sound (such as a speaker's voice) that starts out at 70–85 dB will fall to 40–55 dB at a distance of thirty-two meters.

The last important component of the process is the human ear's range of sensitivity and acuity—that is, the range of frequencies and degrees of intensity the ear can perceive. The average sensitivity range of young ears to pure sounds runs from 20 Hz to 20,000 Hz. The ability to hear sounds at the higher frequencies (above 2,000 Hz) diminishes somewhat with age.[54] The acuity of hearing, on the other hand, has to do with the softest sound (i.e., the lowest level of intensity) the ear can detect. This is called the threshold of hearing, and it constitutes the 0 dB reference point to which other sound intensities are compared. At the other end of the scale, the threshold of pain— the point at which sound causes severe discomfort in the hearer—is about 135–140 dB.[55] One particularly significant point about hearing sensitivity and

---

53. Knudsen and Harris (*Acoustical Designing,* p. 60) note that "the loss [in intensity] due to divergence alone is 6 dB for each doubling of the distance." This rate of decay follows from the "Inverse Square Law," which holds that sound varies in intensity inversely as the square of the distance from the source. A sound of a given intensity at a given distance (say, one meter) has one-fourth that intensity at twice the distance (two meters) and one-ninth the intensity at three times the distance (three meters). Since the decibel scale is logarithmic rather than linear, this works out to 6 dB for each doubling of the distance. See Hoops, *Speech Science*, p. 75.

54. See Knudsen and Harris, *Acoustical Designing*, pp. 21–26. Also Everest, *The Complete Handbook*, pp. 44–45. It should be noted that hearing loss as a function of age is to some extent context-bound. Since high-frequency hearing loss can be caused by repeated exposure to excessively loud noise, we might expect it to be greater among people in a modern, industrial society than among those living in a quieter environment. Consequently, generalizing about hearing loss and age in the citizens of fifth-century Athens is problematic at best.

It is also important to recognize that the "threshold of hearing" described here holds only for a small portion of the population. A survey of hearing acuity among "typical Americans" conducted by the U. S. Public Health Service found that only 1 percent of the population had this level of acuity. Though this auditory threshold represents "normal" hearing, by this measure most Americans are "hearing impaired." This suggests that the typical hearing threshold of adults—even among citizens of ancient Athens—would be somewhat higher than this. See Bergeijk et al, *Waves and the Ear*, pp. 71–72.

55. See Hoops, *Speech Science*, pp. 87–89.

acuity is that their relationship to one another is not uniform: the ear detects sound more easily—at a lower dB level—in the 1,000–6,000 Hz region than at either extreme. Indeed, at 80 Hz (a low mean fundamental frequency for the human voice) the threshold of hearing is just over 40 dB, whereas at 150 Hz it is closer to 30 dB, and at 1,000 Hz it is 0 dB. At 8,000 Hz—approximately the upper frequency range of speech—the level of audibility climbs back to about 10 dB.[56]

Now, what are the implications of all this for the hearing of public address at the Pnyx? By synthesizing the foregoing information and applying it to what we know about the dimensions and configuration of the first auditorium at this site, we can conclude that under the *best possible* conditions, perhaps one fifth of the audience could not have heard well enough to have understood more than about 85 percent of what was said. Specifically, if a strong-voiced, trained speaker addressed the *ekklêsia* on a day when the wind was calm, the temperature mild, the air damp, the audience absolutely quiet and unusally gifted in hearing ability, for those auditors beyond a distance of 32 meters from the *bêma* the lowest frequencies of speech would have fallen to an intensity level that would be barely audible: those sounds in the neighborhood of 80 Hz would have dropped to near the 40 dB range, which is the auditory threshold for that frequency. Since the sound produced by the human voice is more like a chord than a single tone (that is, since it includes waves at a wide range of frequencies simultaneously), this means that portions of the vocal signal will drop out. In a highly-inflected language such as Attic Greek, where variations in pitch convey significant differences in meaning, this suggests that many of the aural nuances of the speech would be missing for a substantial portion of the audience.

This is what would happen under the *best* circumstances. When any one of the factors mentioned above is less than optimal, the situation becomes still more problematic. If, for example, the speaker doesn't speak with sufficient force, or if his fundamental frequency is at or near the 80

---

56. Cf. Knudsen and Harris, *Acoustical Designing*, pp. 20–22. Also Everest (*The Complete Handbook,* pp. 35–36) observes that "the sensitivity of our ears is definitely not uniform for the various frequencies in the audible spectrum, being more sensitive in ability to detect lower sound pressures [dB] in the 1,000–6,000 Hz region than at either extreme. The pressure of a tone at 90 Hz must be increased 40 dB over that of a tone at 3,000 Hz to be barely perceptible. Similarly, a tone at 18,000 Hz must also be increased 40 dB more than the 3,000 Hz tone to be barely detected." Likewise Hoops, who says (*Speech Science*, p. 87) that "both low frequencies and very high frequencies must be made more intense to be detected."

Hz mark, then an even greater proportion of the audience would be left out of the speech. Likewise, if the audience itself included a substantial number of older or hearing-impaired citizens, then intelligibility would be a problem.[57] Likewise, if audience noise is a factor, then intelligibility is a greater problem.

The problem of audience noise is omnipresent and considerable. Knudsen and Harris (*Acoustical Designing*, p. 28) comment that "noise has the effect of reducing the acuity of hearing; that is, it elevates the threshold of audibility. . . . Unless the loudness of speech . . . is sufficiently above the level of the surrounding noise, the speech . . . cannot be fully recognized or appreciated." In order for speech to be intelligible above background noise, it must have an intensity level at least 30 dB stronger than the intensity of the noise serving as a background (see Hoops, *Speech Science*, p. 92). Everest (*The Complete Handbook of Public Address Systems*, p. 49) observes that "the people in the audience produce noise by such common activities as movement, coughing, rattling papers, and whispering. It is generally considered that average audience noise level is about 42 dB, going up to about 48 dB and, during periods of rapt attention, to as low as 32 dB." Thus, in even those situations where the audience listens to the orator with "rapt attention," the hearing threshold for the lowest speech frequencies rises to over 60 dB. Given the proclivity of Athenian citizens to whisper among themselves and to call out to the speaker, this fact reduces considerably the audience-area in which intelligibility occurs.

---

57. Everest (*The Complete Handbook*) discusses in some detail such obstacles as have been noted here. Of insufficient loudness he says (p. 42), "understandability increases rapidly with loudness and then reaches a flat maximum above which further increase in loudness actually decreases understandability. The maximum of understandability occurs when the sound pressure level . . . is in the general vicinity of 70 dB. There is a certain range of loudness which should prevail over the audience area to be acceptable. . . . Other studies list 66 dB as an average level at one meter distance. . . . Some level in this general region is certainly the lowest that should prevail throughout the audience area." See also Hoops, *Speech Science*, p. 92.

Of hearing impairment Everest says (pp. 44–45) that "one type of hearing deficiency . . . is related to aging. This hearing loss can be considered 'normal' in that we all experience it as we get older. . . . [It] is far more serious at the high (treble) frequencies than at the lower (bass) frequencies. . . . The greater loss at the higher frequencies creates an unbalanced sound. . . . [In] speech the sibilant sounds, which strongly affect intelligibility, are especially discriminated against."

Finally, if atmospheric conditions are not ideal, again intelligibility is problematic. During most of the year Athens enjoys a relatively warm, dry climate. As we have seen, such conditions are not the most conducive to sound-transimission. When the presence of the northeast wind is figured in (almost always a factor on the Pnyx), the difficulties confronting the orator and the audience are practically insurmountable. Speech articulation tests done in an open-air setting indicate a significant reduction in the area of intelligibility when a moderate wind (20-25 mph) is blowing. Indeed, when the results of these tests are applied to the Pnyx (see fig. 4), the proportion of the audience within the area of 75 percent "syllable articulation" (regarded as "satisfactory") falls significantly below half.[58]

What it comes to, then, is that as an auditorium for large audiences, the Pnyx of the fifth century was a most unsatisfactory oratorical setting in almost all circumstances. The various factors leading to loss of intelligibility impose limitations on the size of open-air theaters if certain standards of acoustics are to be maintained. Indeed, "a seating capacity of about 600 should be regarded as the upper limit of size when the theater, not equipped with a sound-amplification system, is to be used principally for spoken drama [and oratory], if all auditors are to hear without undue strain and if the actors

---

58. Figure 4 is adapted from Kourouniotes and Thompson and from Knudsen and Harris. The latter contribution is used with permission from the Acoustical Society of America.

Knudsen and Harris (*Acoustical Designing*) report of these tests (pp. 63–64) that under no-wind conditions, a speaker addressing an audience in a large, outdoor auditorium could be heard at a 75 percent level of syllable articulation from a distance of approximately 140 ft (42.7 m) in front and 100 ft (30.5 m) to the sides. In a wind that varied from 20 to 25 mph, the corresponding distances were 85 ft (25.9 m) and 52 ft (15.9 m). The curves described by these distances (taken from the diagram in Knudsen and Harris, p. 64) as they apply to the Pnyx are represented in fig. 4. "Articulation testing" is explained (p. 156) as a process of determining the percentage of unconnected syllables heard correctly. "For example," they write, "if a speaker calls out 1,000 speech syllables, and the observer hears 850 correctly, the percentable articulation is 85 per cent . . . [and] only approximately 3 discrete words out of 100 will be misunderstood; the conditions are very good. . . . If the syllable articulation is 75 per cent, approximately 6 words out of 100 will be incorrectly understood; the conditions are satisfactory, but attentive listening is required. If the syllable articulation is 65 per cent, approximately 10 discrete words out of 100 will be misunderstood; the hearing conditions are barely acceptable and are fatiguing to the listener. For values . . . below 65 per cent, speech is usually not heard satisfactorily."

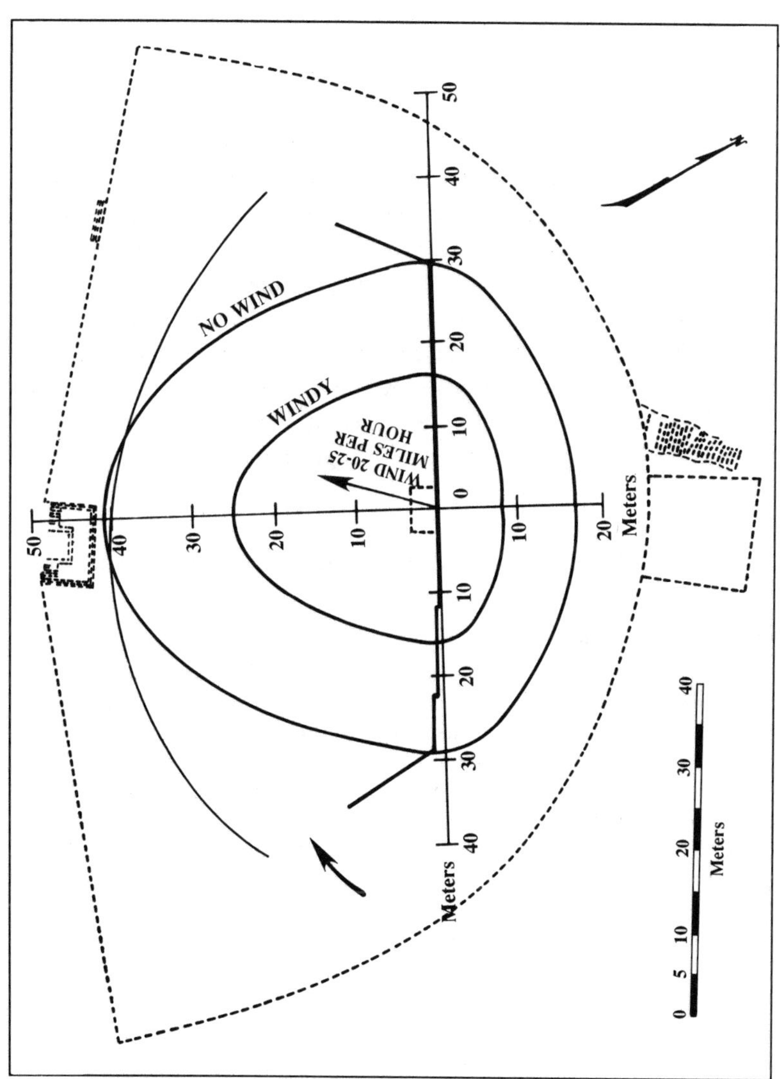

Figure 4. Illustration of 75 percent speech intelligibility at the Pnyx (after Kourouniotes and Thompson; Knudsen and Harris)

are to speak without undue effort."[59] Clearly, the Pnyx did not conform to such design specifications. When the *ekklêsia* met there during the fifth century, it is doubtful whether even half of the 5,000 present could regularly understand what speakers were saying.

III

The findings of this investigation suggest a number of adjustments in our thinking about the role of oratory in the Athenian deliberative process during the Classical Period. At the very least we are led to appreciate anew the primacy of delivery (a point not lost on Demosthenes a century later) in the efficacy of speech as political action. Such a conclusion indicates that vocal strength and formal oratorical training were significant factors in the influence a citizen-orator could exercise at meetings of the assembly. It also indicates that such influential citizens were probably relatively few in number.[60] Though many citizens might have spoken, it seems doubtful that many of them could have been particularly effective, given the obstacles presented by the acoustical defects of the Pnyx.

More significantly, these findings compel us to reassess the dynamics of the deliberative process in the Athenian assembly during the fifth century.

---

59. Knudsen and Harris, *Acoustical Designing*, pp. 67–68. They continue: "This corresponds to a maximum depth of about 75 feet [22.9 m] and a maximum width of about 85 feet [25.9 m]. If open-air theaters are designed to accommodate a larger audience than this, it is probable that auditors in an area beyond these dimensions will experience difficulty in hearing the performance unless the speakers raise their voices and speak with deliberate clarity. . . . [When] listening to speech, for good intelligibility one must be able to hear even the weakest portions of the sounds (the unvoiced consonants)." Given the dimensions of the Pnyx in Period 1, this judgment strongly suggests that the problems identified in this paper were quite real.

60. Mogens H. Hansen ("The Athenian 'Politicians,'" in *The Athenian Ecclesia II* [Copenhagen: Museum Tusculanum Press, 1989]), in considering how many Athenians took it upon themselves to act as *rhêtores* in the *ekklêsia*, remarks (p. 94) that "traditionally they are counted by the score and not by the hundred, and this narrowing down of political participation when we come to its highest level is sometimes viewed as an oligarchic element of Athenian democracy." He goes on to argue, however, that "an astonishing number of Athenian citizens must have acted as *rhêtores* and . . . active participation in the debate and in the formulation of proposals, though restricted to a minority of the attendants, must have been far more widespread than is usually assumed." The findings of the present study seem to challenge this proposition.

If many or most of those in attendance could not understand speakers adequately, when it came time to vote on competing proposals, on what did they base their decisions? Apparently it cannot have been the eloquence of the speaker himself, nor the arguments—at least not directly. Perhaps the content of speakers' addresses was passed from the front to the rear of the auditorium by those who could hear clearly. If this is so, then the noise level in the area would have been even greater than has already been suggested. And clearly, much would have been "lost in the translation." Perhaps, alternatively, those citizens who could not hear clearly voted merely on the basis of the speaker's name and reputation. If this was the case, then the primacy of public address in public decision making at Athens must again be questioned.

The results of this inquiry raise more questions than they settle, and this is just as well. One of my aims here has been to demonstrate that there are a number of such unsettled questions regarding the nature and role of oratory in ancient political life, and that these questions can only be addressed if we consider seriously and systematically the physical contexts within which oratory was performed. My hope is to have initiated such a consideration with this essay.

Six

Demosthenes: Superior Artiste and Victorious Monomachist

Donovan J. Ochs

"Form," says Kenneth Burke, "is the creation of an appetite in the mind of the auditor, and the adequate satisfying of that appetite."[1] Demosthenes' speech "On the Crown" offers an unusual variant of the form apologia in that, as I will argue, the appetites created (and satisfied) include not only the usual one of vindication or forgiveness, but also those of aesthetic superiority and symbolic death for the opponent. Such a claim raises several fascinating theoretical issues for the practice of generic criticism and, as a species of genre theory, for studies of discourse classified as apologia. To establish this claim I propose briefly to review the current theoretical state of apologetic criticism and to offer several arguments that can account for the success of Demosthenes' eloquent speech of self-defense. Then I shall outline some implications of the analysis for contemporary research.

Genre Theory and Apologia

Currently, the accepted definition of a genre is provided by Campbell and Jamieson: "A genre is a complex, an amalgam, a constellation of substantive, situational, and stylistic elements."[2] Guided by this definition one can proceed inductively and study exemplar speeches given in similar situations

---

1. Kenneth Burke, *Counter-Statement* (University of Chicago Press, 1931; rpt. 1957), p. 31.

2. Karlyn Kohrs Campbell and Kathleen Hall Jamieson, "Form and Genre in Rhetorical Criticism: An Introduction," in *Form and Genre: Shaping Rhetorical Action*, ed. Karlyn Kohrs Campbell and Kathleen Hall Jamieson, (Falls Church, Va.: Speech Communication Association, 1978), p. 18.

in order to illumine similarities and differences, or one can proceed deduc-
tively and argue that a particular speech fits a posited definition. Either course,
according to Conley, is fraught with peril. In his essay, "The Linnaean Blues:
Thoughts on the Genre Approach,"[3] he demonstrates the conceptual problems
involved in establishing any classification system based on a biological analogy of genus-species relationships. No doubt scientific precision is difficult
if not impossible to attain when dealing with discourse. Conley does offer a
particularly valuable insight to practitioners of genre criticism when he observes that "clearly rhetorical genre can better be thought of as a congeries
of expectations which the audience brings to the occasion . . . , a problem
which is solved in a new way by each successful work. . . . Audiences, while
setting the speakers those problems, expect the solutions to be novel as well
as fitting."[4] Locating these audience expectations does require a critic to
employ more than a close textual reading, but, if successful, the yield can
only enrich the theory and practice of generic criticism.

Nonetheless, similar situations do recur across time and the discourse
employed in them does tend to display, for the most part, similar forms and
stylistic strategies. Deaths call forth eulogies, installing a new president brings
forth rehearsal rhetoric, and when one's character is seriously questioned or
publicly attacked, speeches of self-justification usually occur. To each situation audiences do bring commonly-held cultural experiences and expectations—not identical, to be sure, but sufficiently held in common to constrain
a speaker's choice of forms and subject matter. Within the area of genre
studies, however, the species *apologia* is of particular interest, and it is to this
species that we now turn.

Our scholarly literature is richly endowed with studies, theoretical and
applied, that account for and critique discourse categorized as apologia.[5]

---

3. Thomas Conley, "Ancient Rhetoric and Modern Genre Criticism," *Communica-
tion Quarterly* 27 (Fall 1979): 47–53. More recently see his article, "The Linnean
Blues: Thoughts on The Genre Approach," in *Form, Genre, and The Study of
Political Discourse*, ed. Herbert W. Simons and Aram A. Aghazarian (Columbia:
The University of South Carolina Press, 1986), pp. 59–78

4. Conley, "Ancient Rhetoric," pp. 47–48.

5. A reader interested in the theory of *apologia* can consult B. L. Ware and Wil
A. Linkugel, "They Spoke in Defense of Themselves: On the Generic Criticism of
Apologia," *The Quarterly Journal of Speech* 59 (October 1973): 273–83; Wil
A. Linkugel and Jackson Harrell, "On Rhetorical Genre: An Organizing Perspec-
tive," *Philosophy and Rhetoric* 11 (1978): 262–81; Walter R. Fisher, "Genre:
Concept and Applications in Rhetorical Criticism," *The Western Journal of Speech*

Apologetic discourse occurs when an individual of some prominence is accused of an impropriety in a public or private action and justifies him- or herself in public. We know that an apologist is likely to assume one of four "postures of rhetorical self-defense": denial, bolstering, differentiation, or transcendence.[6] We have reason to expect an apologist to use language involving motives of affirmation, reaffirmation, purification, or subversion.[7] We also know that an apologist is likely to take "stances which demonstrate that their condemned attitudes or behavior were falsely alleged or reported, involuntary, unintentional, intentional but excusable, or justified."[8]

A significant shortcoming, however, exists in the theoretical work on apologetic discourse. Contemporary theoretical constructs are derived almost totally from cases wherein speakers address publics who share a Judeo-Christian ethic and, increasingly, wherein an apology is mass-mediated. Nixon, Kennedy, MacArthur, and, more recently, Oliver North, for example, had to justify their actions within an ethical system that commands one not to kill and not to bear false witness, an ethical system that privileges humane treatment of humans. Moreover, apologists whose speeches are mass-mediated

---

Communication 44 (Fall 1980): 288–99; Noreen W. Kruse, "Motivational Factors in Non-Denial Apologia," *Central States Speech Journal* 28 (Spring 1977): 13–23, and her more complete theoretical work, "The EIDE of Apologetic Discourse: An Aristotelian Rhetorical-Poetic Analysis," Unpub. Ph.D. dissertation, University of Iowa, 1979. For critical studies in the apologetic genre one can profitably consult James H. Jackson, "Plea in Defense of Himself," *Western Speech Journal* 20 (Fall 1956): 185–95; L. W. Rosenfield, "A Case Study in Speech Criticism: The Nixon-Truman Analog," *Speech Monographs* 35 (November 1968): 435–50; Wil A. Linkugel and Nancy Razak, "Sam Houston's Speech of Self-Defense in the House of Representatives," *Southern Speech Journal* 43 (Summer 1969): 263–75; Bower Aly, "The Gallows Speech: A Lost Genre," *Southern Speech Journal* 34 (Spring 1969): 204–13; David A. Ling, "A Pentadic Analysis of Senator Edward Kennedy's Address 'To the People of Massachusetts,' July 25, 1969," *Central States Speech Journal* 21 (Summer 1970): 81–86; and Sherry Devereaux Butler, "The Apologia, 1971 Genre," *Southern Speech Communication Journal* 36 (Spring 1972): 281–89. An extensive analysis can be found in John McKiernan, "Rhetorical Strategies of Charles Colson: Apologetics," Unpub. Ph.D. dissertation, University of Iowa, 1986. Of special interest is *Oratorical Encounters: Selected Studies and Sources of Twentieth-Century Political Accusations and Apologies*, ed. Halford Ross Ryan (New York: Greenwood Press, 1988).

6. Ware and Linkugel, "They Spoke," p. 275.

7. Walter R. Fisher, "A Motive View of Communication," *The Quarterly Journal of Speech* 56 (April, 1979): 131–39.

8. Kruse, "EIDE," p. 34.

confront audiences (publics) who are not physically present, who possess disparate information about the case with varying degrees of involvement, and who have diverse if not actually conflicting expectations. Print and electronics do alter the substance and style of an apologia, as Nelson's study of the Billy Jean King case clearly demonstrates.[9]

In 330 B.C.E. Demosthenes addressed his self-justification to a physically-present audience whose ethics, aesthetics, and life experiences dramatically differed from our own, and therein lie both the significant bases for much of his self-justification and the potential for expanding contemporary critical perspectives focused on apologetic discourse.

The Context for Demosthenes' Speech

In 336 B.C. Ctesiphon, an Athenian citizen, made the following proposal in the Assembly:

> Since Demosthenes, in the capacity of an inspector of fortifications, has conscientiously had ditches dug along the wall and has contributed for this work a sum of 100 minae from his own means, the people resolve to award him praise and to crown him with a gold crown. The herald will proclaim at the Athenian festival of Dionysius that the people of Athens crown Demosthenes for his virtue and good will, because he continues to act and to speak for the greatest good of the people and because he has shown himself zealous in doing all the good he can.[10]

Aeschines, a school teacher, soldier, accomplished tragic actor, ambassador and statesman, indicted Ctesiphon. Three charges were filed: that the crown was illegally proposed before Demosthenes was audited, that conferring a crown in the theatre was illegal, and that the proposal was contrary to the truth, that is, Demosthenes had not always acted for the public's good. Though Ctesiphon was named in the indictment, a trial of Demosthenes' character was inevitable.

Hatred, a mortal hatred built across time, best characterized the relationship between Aeschines and Demosthenes. Each believed the other was

---

9. Jeffrey Nelson, "The Defense of Billie Jean King," *The Western Journal of Speech Communication* 48 (1984): 92–102.

10. Victor Martin and Guy de Bude, *Discourse (par) Eschines* (Paris: Les Belles lettres, 1962), p. 9.

a traitor. Each had argued opposing positions in the complex and lengthy Athenian negotiations with Philip of Macedon and, later, with his son Alexander. The combatants had met in court in 343 B.C.E. and the verdict went against Demosthenes, while Aeschines lost much of his popular support. They opposed each other on the issue of allying with Thebes to halt Philip. Demosthenes won the votes in the assembly; Philip won the ensuing battle at Chaeronea in 338 B.C.E.; Athens was defeated by a foreign power.

In his prosecution speech at the Crown Trial, Aeschines charged Demosthenes with a battery of character defects. According to Aeschines his opponent was a traitor and an embezzler with a character best described as sacrilegious, impious, immoral, corrupt, and cowardly. This last accusation, an apparently serious one, referred to Demosthenes' running away from the battle at Chaeronea. In short, the entirety of Demosthenes' private and public life—his character, actions, and policies—were categorically displayed as devoid of any merit and emblematic of depravity personified. At the conclusion of the trial, Demosthenes won the verdict and Aeschines was exiled.

The Apologia

Not surprisingly, Demosthenes and his speech, "On the Crown," have attracted much scholarly attention. Galen O. Rowe's chapter, "Demosthenes' Use of Language," is an exhaustive analysis of the linguistic strategies utilized in the speech. Rowe concluded that "so great is the mesmeric effect of 'On the Crown' that a special effort is required to resist its charm."[11] Another classicist, Cecil W. Wooten, used the stylistic qualities in Hermogenes' *On Ideas* as the scaffolding for his analysis of Demosthenes' verbal style.[12]

However, scholarly debate continues in the effort to account for the success of Demosthenes' speech. Andrew R. Dyck encapsulates the debate in this way:

---

11. Galen O. Row, "Demosthenes' Use of Language," in *Demosthenes' "On The Crown": A Critical Case Study of a Masterpiece of Ancient Oratory*, ed. James J. Murphy (Davis, Calif.: Hermagoras Press, 1983), p. 199.

12. Cecil W. Wooten, *Cicero's Philippics and Their Demosthenic Model* (Chapel Hill: University of North Carolina Press, 1983), ch. 2. See also C. D. Adams, *Demosthenes and His Influence* (New York: Longmans, Green, 1927); Demosthenes, *The Oration of Demosthenes on the Crown*, trans. F. P. Simpson, rhetorical commentary by F. P. Donnelly (New York: Fordham University Press, 1941); and W. Jaeger, *Demosthenes, the Origin and Growth of His Policy* (New York: Octagon Books, 1963).

The orator's portrait of Aeschines has caused difficulties: it has been called inconsistent, parts of it have been wished unwritten, it has been found to be unmatched in vileness in the extant work of any Attic orator, and [it] has been regarded as several digressions. I submit that, after so many attempts, the function and technique of this portrait still call for elucidation.[13]

Rowe observes that "the terms of abuse referring to Aeschines are highly suggestive of the language of Greek comedy," and he argues that the speech was successful as a consequence.[14] Wooten locates the success of the speech in its use of form, specifically (following Burke's conception) of progressive, repetitive, conventional, and minor forms.[15] While both Rowe and Wooten present instructive accounts, neither moves his analysis sufficiently into contextual elements, namely, the audience's experiences and cultural expectations which, if used artistically in the speech, would contribute significantly to its success.[16]

I offer four lines of reasoning featuring contextual, substantive, and stylistic elements that, taken together, function to produce a distinctive spe-

---

13. Andrew R. Dyck, "The Function and Persuasive Power of Demosthenes' Portrait of Aeschines in the Speech *On The Crown*," *Greece and Rome* 32 (April, 1985): 42. Cf. Ivo Bruns, *Das literarische Portrat der Griechen in 5. and 4. Jahrhundert vor Christi Geburt* (Berlin, 1896), p. 573. Also, *Aeshines Against Ctesiphon*, ed. Rufus Richardson (Boston, 1889), p. 28 n. 4; and Edmund M. Burke, *Character Denigration in the Attic Orators with Particular Reference to Demosthenes and Aeschines*, Unpub. Ph.D. dissertation, Tufts University, 1972, p. 232.

14. Galen O. Rowe, "The Portrait of Aeschines in the Oration *On the Crown*," *Transactions of the American Philological Association* 97 (1966): 398.

15. Cecil W. Wooten, "The Nature of Form in Demosthenes' *De Corona*," *Classical World* 72 (1979): 327.

16. Dyck ("The Function") refutes Rowe by noting that an audience could view a "comic portrait" as "stereotypical and therefore [as] incredible" (p. 44). Wooten's treatment of minor forms, e.g., metaphor, paradox, bathos, etc., begins to approach a discussion of contextual elements but stops short with the observation, "through the frequent repetition of these images Demosthenes implants in the minds of his audience a persistent concept difficult to refuse" (p. 327). Cf. Rowe, "Demosthenes' Use of Language," 181–82. An exhaustive analysis can be found in Edmund M. Burke, "Character Denigration in the Attic Orators." He observes that "character denigration was something less than an honest expression of passion and emotion. It was in fact a device, influenced on every occasion by rhetorical stylization or political considerations" (p. 2).

cies of the apologetic genre, and to afford yet another explanation of Demosthenes' victory:

1. The charge of cowardice was impossible for the audience to accept.

2. Demosthenes' shift from the forensic to the deliberative genre created different audience expectations, highly compatible with those of apologia.

3. Demosthenes' portrayal of Aeschines' persona more closely matched the aesthetic tenets of the era than did that of Aeschines himself.

4. The vehemence of Demosthenes' personal assault on his opponent was sufficiently analogous to the *pankration* to create audience appetites only satisfied by symbolic surrender or death.

The Charge of Cowardice

The precise number of jurors at the Crown Trial is uncertain, as is the number of spectators who attended the dramatic event. Yet, when Aeschines accused Demosthenes of deserting his post at the Battle of Chaeronea, a large percentage of the audience would necessarily recall the events of the battle since they or their relatives also took part. A. R. Burn's recreation of the battle itself and its aftermath leaves no doubt that not only Demosthenes but several thousand of his fellow Athenians "deserted their posts," and did so wisely.

Philip and Alexander both led the Macedonian army against the allied forces of Thebes, Megara, Corinth, Achaia, and Athens. After the initial attack and subsequent flanking maneuvers, the Theban general Theagenes

was killed; the Sacred Band of Thebes fell in their ranks, as Philip saw them afterwards, lying as they stood on parade. The Greek right was shattered, and the rest of their line then helplessly "rolled up." The Achaians in the center were almost cut to pieces; and lastly the advancing Athenians were taken in flank and rear. Over 1,000 of their 7,000 or 8,000 men were killed, 2,000 taken prisoner.[17]

For Aeschines' charge of "cowardice in the face of the enemy" to be accepted, then, many in the jury and many of the spectators also would need

---

17. A. R. Burn, *Alexander the Great and the Hellenistic World* (New York: Collier Books, 1962), p. 41.

to perceive themselves as cowards because they, too, escaped a totally hopeless military engagement by "deserting their posts." In the text of the Crown Speech, no refutation, no denial, no excuses, in fact, no mention of the allegation of cowardice appears. Demosthenes' eloquent, but recognizable, silence on the charge is a mute acknowledgment of his own and his fellow Athenians' action as neither valorous nor shameful but expedient and necessary given the situation. An unfair claim, one encompassing the listeners themselves, would be impossible to accept as true. Indeed, Demosthenes offers his audience (244) an alternative perspective from which to perceive themselves and their action—pride for their attempt. Such a claim would function not simply to ingratiate, but to eradicate any self-remorse or residual shame.

Demosthenes' Genre Shift

Jurors in a court case ultimately expect to render a verdict of either guilty-as-charged or innocent. Concerned with effecting justice, these jurors expect to hear past actions discussed in terms of existing laws and narrations describing the facts of the case. Policymakers in a deliberative setting, however, expected to decide among conflicting advice offered by many speakers. Proposals would be linked to culturally-held views of the just, the lawful, the expedient, the pleasant, the possible, or the necessary. Rules and conditions of deliberative speaking in fourth-century Athens enforced brevity and proscribed invective and personal abuse.[18] Yet, precisely in a deliberative context would an audience expect to hear a plea to come to the aid of someone or some country, which coincidentally is the fundamental plea of anyone making an apologetic speech.

True, Demosthenes' speech was positioned in a legal context: he was the defendant. Two of Aeschines' charges did cite existing laws that could be used for punishment or redress. To address the issue of his reputation, however, he needed to create audience expectations used in deliberative contexts.

Demosthenes did change audience expectations in two brilliant passages at the outset of his address.[19] In section 10 he pleads:

---

18. Jonathan A. Goldstein, *The Letters of Demosthenes* (New York: Columbia University Press, 1968), p. 114.

19. For a more detailed analysis see, Donovan J. Ochs, "Demosthenes' Use of Argument," in Murphy, ed., *Demosthenes' "On the Crown"*, pp. 157–74.

If you know me to be the type of man he has accused me of being (for
I have never lived anywhere but among you), do not tolerate the sound
of my voice, not even if my statesmanship has been brilliantly successful,
but stand up and condemn me now.

In the following section (11), instead of addressing legal issues, questions of justice, or any topic associated with judicial contexts, situations, or
speeches, he boldly previews his intended procedure:

I will review my policies, the subject of your abusive falsehoods, and
will take up later your loose insults—language worthy of peasant women
at a comic festival—if these present are willing to listen to them.

How, then, do these passages function to shift an audience into the
usual expectations of deliberative contexts? The first passage amounts to a
safe dare. Expedience dictated that no one stand because doing so would
amount to a confession of guilt. Failure to prosecute malefactors was punish-
able by law and Demosthenes' language here can be read as an invitation to
remain seated "while he comes to their aid," a deliberative, not a forensic
motif. In the second passage clearly the emphasis is centered on his policies,
and policies are the sine qua non of deliberation. Policies, not past actions
and not the facts of the case, but *policies* are forecasted. Since policies are
observable indicators of an individual's character, both Demosthenes' policies and his character could be re-recommended to an audience now prepared
to consider such factors as the expedient, the honorable, the necessary, etc.
In other words, his audience would be considering the expedience and desir-
ability of "coming to his aid."

Portrayal of Aeschines' Persona

Anyone who reads the Crown Speech for the first time is immediately
aware of the repeated personal attacks on Aeschines. In this section and the
one following I develop two different but related perspectives on Demosthenes'
use of personal attack in his apologia. Here I start from the assumption that
audiences do possess, and bring to a discourse, certain generalized conceptions about what constitutes the good and the bad, the beautiful and the ugly.
These conceptions would have been present among Demosthenes' listeners.
It remains, then, to explore these aesthetic dimensions and relate them to
Demosthenes' use of the personal attack in his self-defense.

George Kennedy, in his critique of Demosthenes' speech "On the False Embassy," observes:

> Another unattractive feature of the speech, and of several speeches of Demosthenes, is the personal attack on the background, private life, or appearance of an opponent. Aeschines, of course, makes similar attacks on Demosthenes. These techniques reflect the fourth century interest in personality and are a kind of perverted ethos.[20]

To a contemporary reader the ferocity of the scurrilous attacks on Aeschines may seem perverse if not actually perverted. To a member of Demosthenes' audience, however, the expostulations and stylistically controlled portraits of one's "evil" opponent would be expected and, if artfully executed, meet with aesthetic approval. Aristotle, for example, recognized that portraiture could elicit emotions in an audience.[21] That a significant change in what was expected to be included in these portraits occurred in the mid–fourth century has been well established.[22] As Webster observes in his *Art and Literature in Fourth Century Athens*:

> The communication of opinions about a person (alive, dead, or imaginary) is the common element in all portraiture. He is to be made intelligible, and being intelligible will awaken some reaction in the audience. The orator hopes that they will praise his client and blame his client's opponent. The historian may want to place his character in a favorable or unfavorable light.[23]

In the middle of the century Athenians were most interested in the organic structure of a work of art. Later, the interest in portraits shifts "from the structure to the surface and the details of external appearance, and the individual characteristics of the original are emphasized."[24]

---

20. George Kennedy, "The Oratorical Career of Demosthenes," in Murphy, p. 46.

21. *Rhetorica*, 1389a2, 1378a7.

22. Ivo Bruns, *Das Literarische Portrat*, n.13.

23. Thomas B. L. Webster, *Art and Literature in Fourth Century Athens* (University of London: Athlone Press, 1956), p. 5.

24. Webster, p. 6. For further clarification see, B. S. Ridgway, *Fifth Century Styles in Greek Sculpture* (Princeton: Princeton University Press, 1981). He describes the basic traits as "a representational, seemingly naturalistic approach to the human figure in its most perfect form" (p. 12). For a visual illustration one can consult Martin Robertson, *A Shorter History of Greek Art* (Cambridge: Cambridge University Press, 1981). One can compare the "Doryphoros" of Polykleitos (p. 113) and the coin of Lysimachos (p. 186) to note the aesthetic shift.

Applied to the Crown Speech, the Athenian aesthetic would account for the vivid descriptions of Aeschines in which Demosthenes exhibits his superior command of portraiture. One extended illustration will suffice here. Near the end of the speech Demosthenes "sculpts and paints" his rival with these words.

You, Aeschines, a man haughty and contemptuous of others, compare your luck with mine, luck which saw you raised in deepest poverty, assisting your father in the schoolroom, grinding ink, swabbing benches, sweeping the room, doing the chores of a servant, not of a free man's son; (259) when you became a man, you read the holy books for your mother's rituals and organized the other details: at night wearing a fawn skin, mixing the wine, cleansing the initiates by wiping them with mud and bran, and, after the purification, instructing them to say, "I have escaped the bad, I have found the better," priding yourself that no one ever could howl as loudly as you (and I believe it; [260] don't think that he can speak so loudly here without being absolutely brilliant at howling); in the daytime, you led your noble bands through the streets wearing garlands of fennel and poplar, squeezing puffed-cheeked adders and waving them over your head, crying "Euoi Saboi" and dancing to the rhythm of "Hyes Attes Attes Hyes," the leader of the dance, the ivy-wreathed leader of the band, the bearer of the winnowing-fan, and addressed with these titles by the little old ladies, taking your pay in the form of sops and cakes and pastry (what glorious rewards! who would not think himself and his luck most truly blessed to receive them?).[25]

Descriptions such as this function not necessarily in the realm of fact but in an aesthetic domain. Caricature, performed with elegance, displays the character, the *ethos* if you will, of the speaker as superior to the person portrayed. No doubt the novelty of the passage (and numerous others in the speech) would amuse, entertain, and charm the audience. In doing so, however, a listener is diverted from considering guilt-innocence (forensic) or expedient-inexpedient (deliberative), and is invited to make aesthetic judgments of good-bad and beautiful-ugly. Webster goes so far as to claim that Demosthenes' mastery of portraiture "may be the decisive factor in deciding the case."[26] In the context of self-justification, dramatically enacting an implicit claim that one has the ability to produce a work of art more pleasing

---

25. *Crown*, 258–60. Keaney's translation in Murphy, pp. 59–126.

26. Webster, *Art and Literature*, p. 99.

than one's opponent's demonstrates superiority and dominance. Quite apart from the delight and pleasure Demosthenes' verbal image of Aeschines evokes, an audience is enticed into using as criteria for judgment not the rhetorical but the aesthetic. Embedding forms within his discourse, then, that both create and satisfy appetites in an aesthetic context, enriches and enhances Demosthenes' earlier shift from the forensic to the deliberative.

Personal Attack As Pankration

Barry Brummett has advanced a compelling argument that "texts may be especially rhetorically effective when the content, the medium used to convey the content, and real life experiences that make the content relevant are formally or structurally similar."[27] This proposition, termed the "homology hypothesis," holds that formal parallels exist among seemingly disparate things or experiences. Brummett explains: "most formal patterns in discourse that are similar enough to an audience's experiences to induce identification are also dissimilar enough to induce further identification with differentiated parts of the discourse."[28] These homologies are "correspondences in structure . . . not on the surface, at the level of the observed, but below or behind empirical reality."[29] As an illustration, Brummett observes: "A 'quest' legend, for instance, is homologous with my lived experience not because my experience is a quest but because it is quest-like. My experience follows the form of the quest: it struggles toward a distant goal, overcomes obstacles, and achieves, or at least hopes for, victory and transformation."[30]

Demosthenes' Crown Speech is structured in such a way as to evoke for the audience the formal parallel of the battle between the two antagonists and their real-life experience at an Olympic event known as the *pankration*. In Greek gymnastics this event combined boxing and wrestling. The event was not conducted according to any rules and the competitors engaged in a type of hand-to-hand and body-to-body combat. "Victory was not decided until one of the combatants was killed, or held up a finger in

---

27. Barry Brummett, "The Homology Hypothesis: Pornography on the VCR," *Critical Studies in Mass Communication* 5 (1988): 202.

28. Brummett, 206.

29. M. Lane, *Introduction to Structuralism* (New York: Basic Books, 1970), p. 14.

30. Brummett, "The Homology Hypothesis," p. 203.

token of defeat."[31] Such a claim of formal parallelism immediately raises a question as to whether or not the audience for the speech perceived the encounter as a "battle" in any sense of the term. Critics and commentators are in clear agreement that, indeed, they did.[32] The legality of crowning Demosthenes was, simply put, the judicial issue at stake. However, Aeschines, by adding to the charge the falsity of Ctesiphon's praise of Demosthenes, "clearly envisioned a political showdown."[33] By viewing the speech as a "rematch," the jurors would be less concerned with the case and more concerned with the contest, less concerned with false allegations and more concerned with strategy.

Granting that the jurors viewed the trial as a battle, one need next inquire what experiences the audience had that would be homologous to the rhetorical rematch, that is, experiences that would induce identification. Three possibilities present themselves: monomachistic confrontations in epic literature, military engagements, and the pankration. Each has as its objective vanquishing an opponent in some way, i.e., overpowering, securing surrender, or killing. Each, too, is significantly different from the others. However, the classic duels between Patroclus and Hector or Achilles and Hector were events at which Demosthenes' jurors were not physically present, not participant observers, and certainly not directly affected by the outcomes. In a military engagement—Chaeronea, for example—Demosthenes' audience would have been physically present, participants, and physically involved in the outcome. But a military encounter is a clash of groups, not a monomachistic duel. The pankration would be the most likely homolog, I believe, because it best fits the criteria of physical presence, lack of personal effect from the outcome, and a battle between two contestants. Significantly, in the actual trial the jurors controlled the decision.

That Demosthenes viewed his self-justification as a combative struggle is amply documented by Wooten's analysis of the metaphors used in the speech:

> Many of his metaphors, reflecting his combative nature, are dominated by the idea of struggling, and many of them are taken from warfare.

31. "Pankration," in *Harper's Dictionary of Classical Literature and Antiquities*, ed. Harry Thurston Peck (New York: American Book Company, 1923), pp. 1165–66. The best ancient source is Philostratus, *The Art of the Athletic Trainer*.

32. Demosthenes, *Rede fur Ktesiphon uber den Kranz*, erl. v. H. wankel, vol. 1 (Heidelberg, 1976), p. 59.

33. Dyck, "The Function," p. 42.

There are also metaphors from hunting, another form of combat. One sees this obsession with struggling in his metaphors taken from physical life as well, especially in metaphors concerning sickness and health. He also prefers images of the weather, a natural phenomenon against which man struggles for survival, just as, according to Demosthenes, the Athenians were struggling against Philip and just as Demosthenes himself was struggling for his own political survival. Demosthenes' similes are thematically very similar to his metaphors. They also deal primarily with struggle and combat, activity and movement, sickness and health, reflecting once again Demosthenes' own psychological makeup.[34]

In addition to the metaphors and similes of combat, the speech contains a designed sequencing of the personal attacks on Aeschines remarkably similar to that of a pankration: maneuvering for position, clinching, hitting, holding and throwing, controlling and dominating. The early sections of the speech, for example, contain numerous interspersed and short epithets. Aeschines is a "liar" (9, 11, 41), uses "abusive slander" (10, 14, 95, 111) and "insulting language" (11, 15, 28, 34, 50, 73), is "shameless" (22, 82), and is a "hireling of Philip" (33, 36, 38, 52). The density and diversity of these relatively short epithets can be read as analogous to maneuvering in a pankration. The content, pacing, and length of the personal attacks change noticeably from section 119 to section 128. Within these sections, Aeschines is labeled, in rapid succession, "all-wicked, hated of the gods, and utterly vindictive," "so imperceptive and so stupid," "a miserable man who makes malicious accusation," "a screamer like a comic reveler from a wagon," and "an idle babbler, this court back, this damned secretary." These, I submit, can be construed as

---

34. Wooten, "The Nature of Form," p. 27. See his article, "La Funzione delle metafore e delle similitudini nelle orazioni di Demostene," *Quaderni Urbinati* 29 (1978): 123–25. A compelling argument might be advanced that contemporary political oratory continues in the classical pattern of symbolic battle. See, for example, Jane Blankenship, "The Search for the 1972 Democratic Nomination: A Metaphoric Perspective," in *Rhetoric and Communication*, ed. Jane Blankenship and Herman Stelzner (Urbana: University of Illinois Press, 1976). Her analysis shows that metaphors of general violence, warfare, and sports were the most frequently used in the campaign. Also, Thomas W. Benson, "Implicit Communication Theory in Campaign Coverage," in *Television Coverage of the 1980 Presidential Campaign*, ed. William C. Adams (Norwood, N.J.: Ablex, 1983). He argues that "political communication is not 'normal discourse' but a form of combat. . . . Candidates are presented as boxers and beasts of prey" (p. 109).

analogous to clinching. The tone clearly shifts from brief insulting assertions to a more extended personalized series of claims.

To argue an exact homologous relationship between the Crown Speech and the phases of a pankration would require an unattainable precision of analysis. However, three major sections of personal invective and contempt occur in the remainder of the speech. Aeschines' life is debased and degraded (129–134); Aeschines' early life and public career are again mocked and ridiculed in a long passage (258–264) that is followed immediately by the antithetically phrased comparison of Aeschines' life to Demosthenes' (265–266); then, very near the end of the speech (310–313), Demosthenes completes his vehement denunciation and humiliation of Aeschines by charging that Aeschines had the opportunity to help Athens and utterly failed to do his civic duty. The placement, extension, and rapacity of these three devastating passages, destroying as they do Aeschines' life, career, and citizenship, can be interpreted as an annihilation, a total vitiation of the persona and the person of Aeschines. One can claim that the arrangement, development, and deployment of these character-extinguishing passages enabled the audience to see correspondences in the formal structures Demosthenes used and the forms in their real-life experience of viewing a pankration. To the extent that this audience appetite was aroused, forensic outcomes of guilt or innocence were no longer at issue. Victory and superiority become the means of satisfying the auditor's psychological appetite. An audience, perceiving the form of verbal "combat to the death" as homologous to the form of the pankration, could identify with Demosthenes' superior ability in defeating and symbolically destroying his opponent.

Conclusion

This analysis of Demosthenes' Crown Speech offers alternative explanations for its success. Positioned in both textual and contextual vantage points, I have argued that Demosthenes capitalized on Aeschines' charge of cowardice, not by direct refutation but by silence and the substitution of pride for shame. His jurors, many of whom were themselves forced to flee at Chaeronea, would be more willing to accept the substitution than to share the allegation of cowardice along with the defendant. Admittedly, the argument wherein Demosthenes shifts the trial from the forensic to the deliberative genus is not new, but the functions it serves, in context, are novel. Once the shift is accomplished, Demosthenes and his audience are enabled to "come to the aid" of each other. To his auditors Demosthenes offers pride, dignity, and a clear sense of the greatness of their heritage and civic actions. To Demosthenes the jurors can—and did—offer a satisfying verdict.

Moreover, I have argued that the verbal portrait Demosthenes presented in his several attacks on the person of Aeschines more closely corresponded to the aesthetic standards of the time than did those of Aeschines. By demonstrating the he was a superior *artiste*, a superior word-carver, if you will, Demosthenes offered a pleasurable experience to his auditors.

Finally, I have argued that Demosthenes' controlled placement, ever-increasing ferocity of attack, and choice of combat metaphors created a homologous relationship for his audience in which they could view—and control the outcome—of a monomachistic duel akin to the pankration. Taken together, these four arguments help explain the success of a speech that should not have succeeded.

What, then, are the implications of this study for critics of contemporary apologetic discourse? The singular instance of Demosthenes' Crown Speech contains much that is not generalizable to a twentieth-century apologist or to an auditor of an apologia. To cite only a few significant differences, one can note that the attack on Demosthenes' character came from a single source, not from the media, an investigating committee, or a "court of popular opinion." Too, Demosthenes' audience shared a more homogeneous conception of ethics, aesthetics, and cultural experiences than one can anticipate in modern, geographically disparate, and pluralistic societies. Finally, Demosthenes' life, accomplishments, and policies were much better known to his auditors in the small *polis* of Athens than one could expect in a contemporary situation involving an apologist addressing a national or international audience.

Nonetheless, the Crown Speech suggests that one can, with profit, focus attention on the functions of vehemently confrontational, stylistic modes of personal attack when they are used in self-justification. For example, critics might look again at Robert Emmett's, "Speech Before Judgment Pronounced," Clarence Darrow's, "They Tried To Get Me," Harry Truman's, "My Actions in the White Case," or selections from Oliver North's testimony during the Iran-Contra hearings. Such reexaminations may discover what functions vilification can serve, what audiences are being created by means of such language, what appropriate responses to such language might be required or prompted.

Further, the homology hypothesis seems to hold considerable riches for critics of apologetic discourse. On might profitably study the real-life experiences of the several audiences to which Lee Ioccoca apologized for his company's odometer practices or to which Exxon's statement about the Valdez oil spill was directed. Apologists, whether individuals or corporations, do seek out rhetorical means to repair their reputations. Audiences, acting as quasi-jurors, do bring their real-life experiences to bear in determining their judgments of guilt-innocence, honor-dishonor, desirable-undesirable, pleasurable-unpleasurable, victory-defeat.

Demosthenes' "On the Crown" remains an exemplar of an orator skilled in securing successful judgments from his audience. Perhaps from his stellar effort we can enhance our own critical practice.

Seven

Aristotle's Accounts of Persuasion through Character

William W. Fortenbaugh

Some years ago at a conference in Tatnic, Maine, I suggested that Cicero's account of winning goodwill *(benevolentiam conciliare)* is not a simple development of Aristotelian persuasion through character *(pistis dia tou êthous)*.[1] For Cicero is interested in creating favor for the orator and his client; as a result he blurs Aristotle's distinction between persuasion through character and emotional appeal. In contrast, Aristotelian persuasion through character is not intended to arouse an emotion in the audience. It provides grounds for trusting the orator and does not undermine the impartiality of the audience. This view of Aristotelian persuasion through character has been refined and developed since the Tatnic conference. I discussed it in a lecture at The Pennsylvania State University[2] and have published several articles on the subject.[3] Others, too, have taken up the topic and generally endorsed my view.[4] Normally that would be grounds for silence,

---

1. The conference was held on 2 October, 1987 and proceedings were published in *Rhetorica* 6 (1988); my contribution is *"Benevolentiam conciliare* and *animos permovere*: Some Remarks on Cicero's *De oratore* 2.178–216," on pp. 259–73.

2. The lecture was held on 23 October, 1991 as part of a lecture series organized by Christopher L. Johnstone.

3. "Persuasion through Character and the Composition of Aristotle's *Rhetoric*," *Rheinisches Museum* 134 (1991): 152–56; "Aristotle on Persuasion through Character," *Rhetorica* 10 (1992): 207–44; "Ethos," *Historisches Wörterbuch der Rhetorik*, ed. G. Ueding, vol. 2 (Tübingen: Niemeyer, 1994), col. 1517–25.

4. J. Wisse, *Ethos and Pathos* (Amsterdam: Hakkert, 1989), p. 34; L. Calboli Montefusco, "Aristotle and Cicero on the *officia oratoris*," in *Peripatetic Rhetoric after Aristotle*, ed. W. Fortenbaugh and D. Mirhady, vol. 6 of *Rutgers University Studies in Classical Humanities* (New Brunswick, N.J.: Transaction, 1994),

but it now appears to me that Aristotle's account of persuasion through character is more complex than I had realized. In particular, there are two principle accounts, not one, and the two accounts reflect two different orientations which should be clearly stated in order that the accounts can be properly understood.

In what follows, I shall (1) set forth the principle passages; (2) discuss the first account—that of *Rhetoric* 1.2—which is oriented toward judicial oratory; (3) discuss the second account—that of 2.1—whose focus is deliberative oratory; and (4) take up a parenthetical remark—one found in 1.8— which is concerned with deliberative oratory but differs in an important way from the second account. It would be foolish to think that I am now offering the "last word" on persuasion through character, but perhaps I can provide some helpful corrections as well as new perspectives.

The Principle Passages: *Rhetoric* 1.2 and 2.1

There are two passages in the *Rhetoric* that are fundamental for understanding Aristotle's thinking on the character of the orator. The first occurs in book 1, chapter 2. There Aristotle defines rhetoric (1355b26–34), draws a distinction between technical and nontechnical proofs (1355b35–1356a1), and lists three modes of technical proof.[5] He says that the first—our special concern—is "in the character of the speaker," the second is "in disposing the listener in some way" (i.e., arousing an emotional response), and the third is "in the speech itself through showing or appearing to show something"

------

pp. 67–68 (Calboli Montefusco is careful to distinguish *benevolentiam conciliare* as set forth in the *De oratore* from *delectare* as found in the *Brutus, Orator,* and *De opimo genere oratorum*); E. Schtrumpf, "Non-Logical Means of Persuasion in Aristotle's *Rhetoric* and Cicero's *De oratore*," in *Peripatetic Rhetoric after Aristotle* p. 110 n. 90.

5. The three modes are introduced as "proofs provided through the speech" (1.2.1356a1). The label "technical proof" is not repeated, but there can be no doubt that the proofs taken up for discussion are technical modes. Unlike the nontechnical modes, which pre-exist and are merely used by the speaker (1355b36), the "proofs provided through the speech" are all the product of the speaker or speech writer and therefore satisfy Aristotle's criterion for counting proofs as technical; namely, that they be constructed by the orator or invented by him (1355b38–39). The verb "to invent" *(heurein)* is Aristotle's, but its occurrence does not mean that Aristotle has a developed notion of "invention" *(heuresis)*. In particular, it does not mean that Ciceronian *inventio* is already present in Aristotle. See E. Schtrumpf, "Non-Logical Means of Persuasion," pp. 100–105.

(1356a1–4).[6] This initial list is immediately followed by brief remarks concerning each of the three modes, beginning with that which is "in the character of the speaker." Here is what Aristotle says about this mode (1356a5–13):

> Therefore [we have a case of persuasion] through the character [of the speaker] when the speech is such that it makes the speaker worthy of belief. For we believe upright men more fully and quickly, [and that is true] generally concerning all matters and absolutely [so] in matters in which there is no exact knowledge but opinions differ. It is necessary that this happen through the speech, rather than on account of a pre-existing opinion about the character of the speaker. For not as some writers on rhetoric posit in their treatises [saying] that the uprightness of the speaker contributes nothing to persuasion; rather character has almost, so to speak, the greatest authority in winning belief.[7]

The second passage is found in book 2, chapter 1. After a brief reference to the preceding discussion of materials for deliberative, epideictic, and judicial oratory (1377b16–20),[8] Aristotle tells us that it is not enough to produce persuasive arguments. The orator must also do two other things: he must present himself as a certain kind of person, and he must work an emotional effect on the audience (1377b21–24). The former is said to be more useful in deliberative situations and the latter in judicial proceedings (1377b25–1378a6). In the remainder of the chapter, Aristotle first discusses the self-presentation of the orator and then introduces the topic of emotional appeal (1378a6–30). The following is what Aristotle says concerning the first topic (1378a6–20).

> There are three reasons why speakers themselves are credible. For that is the number of reasons on account of which we are persuaded apart

---

6. It is clear that this threefold division of technical proof is based on a tripartite analysis of the oratorical situation into speaker, listener, and argument (cf. 1.3.1358a38–b2). The division governs, albeit imperfectly, the organization of *Rhetoric* 1–2.

7. The last sentence (1356a10–13) is awkward, and an emendation of the Greek text was printed by D. Ross in his Oxford Classical Text (1959). The emendation is, however, not an improvement and therefore is passed over in silence (i.e., without specific reference in the *apparatus criticus*) by R. Kassel in the Teubner edition (1976).

8. The reference is to 1.4–14. The intervening discussion of nontechnical proofs in 1.15 is not mentioned in 2.1. See below, note 23.

from demonstrative arguments. They are [1][9] wisdom and [2] virtue and [3] goodwill. For men err concerning what they say or advise, either on account of all of these or on account of some one of them. For either [1] they do not hold correct opinions on account of a lack of sense; or [2] they hold correct opinions but do not say what they think on account of wickedness; or [3] they are wise and upright but lack goodwill, on account of which it is possible for them not to advise what they know to be best, and beyond these there is no [other cause]. It is necessary, therefore, that the person who appears to possess all these attributes will be credible with his audience. How men appear wise and good is to be understood from what has been said concerning the virtues. For a person may establish his own virtue in the same way as that of someone else. Concerning goodwill and friendship we must speak in the account of emotions.

The second passage, clearly, is longer and fuller than the first. It lists three attributes that a speaker seeks to claim for himself: wisdom *(phronêsis)*, virtue *(aretê)*, and goodwill *(eunoia)*. In contrast, the first passage mentions only uprightness *(epieikeia* 1356a11–12). Since "uprightness" is almost certainly used synonymously for "virtue"[10]—in 2.1 men of virtue are called "upright" men *(epieikeis* 1378a13)[11]—it is natural to say that 1.2 is simply a first statement in which Aristotle mentions one of three attributes. In 2.1 he offers a more detailed statement, adding two attributes for a total of three. In both

---

9. The numbers in brackets are added for the sake of clarity. This contrasts with *Politics* 5.9 1309a33–39 (see note 29), where the numbers are part of the Greek text.

10. That is, "virtue" *(aretê)* in the sense of moral virtue or virtue of character. In the passage quoted from 2.1, "virtue" is first used in this narrow sense: it is distinct from practical wisdom (1378a8–9). Subsequently it is used inclusively to cover both moral virtue and practical wisdom (1378a17). Cf. *Politics* 5.9 1309b5–6, where "uprightness" is a variation on "virtue," both words being used to distinguish goodness of character from the experience and knowledge required of generals. For more on *Politics* 5.9, see the section below entitled "The Speaker's Character in Deliberative Oratory: On 2.1."

11. "Upright" men *(epieikeis)* are also referred to in 1.21356a6. It may be worth noting that Greek lacked a common adjective cognate with *aretê*, so that Aristotle necessarily used words like *epieikês* and *agathos* when he wanted to describe someone as virtuous. In 1.2, Aristotle first uses the adjective *epieikês*, "we believe upright men," and subsequently introduces the cognate noun *epiekeia* (1356a6, 11–12). In the latter passage, he might have used *aretê* but chooses not to vary his vocabulary.

passages, Aristotle is concerned with a single mode of persuasion that is distinct from both arguing the issue (proof "in the speech itself") and emotional appeal (proof "in disposing the listener is some way"). The fundamental idea is that a speaker becomes credible (*pistos* 2.1. 1378a6–16) or worthy of belief (*axiopistos* 1.2. 1356a5–6) by presenting himself as a man of wisdom, virtue, and goodwill. When arguments on different sides of an issue are equally strong, the listener has little choice but to consider the speakers and to decide in favor of the person who appears wise, virtuous, and full of goodwill. Such a decision is not an emotional response. The listener experiences no strong feeling of joy, exhilaration, or the like. Rather, he recognizes that wisdom, virtue, and good will are grounds for trust, and therefore supports the speaker who exhibits these attributes most clearly and fully.

As a composite statement concerning persuasion through character, the preceding paragraph has merit, but it also obscures some interesting differences between 1.2 and 2.1. A case in point concerns "character" *(êthos)*. In 1.2, when listing the three modes of technical proof, Aristotle uses the phrase "in the character of the speaker" (1356a2–3); and some two lines later, when introducing his comments on persuasion through character, Aristotle begins with the phrase "through the character [of the speaker]" (1356a5). That contrasts with 2.1, where the word "character" *(êthos)* does not occur, let alone the two phrases found in 1.2. Unless I misunderstand the passages, this difference is not simply verbal. It reflects a substantial difference: one of orientation. In 1.2 Aristotle is concerned with judicial oratory and therefore focuses on that attribute which carries special weight in courtroom cases. In 2.1 Aristotle has a different concern, namely, deliberative oratory and the three attributes that give politicians credibility.

The Speaker's Character in Judicial Oratory: On 1.2

In 1.2, Aristotle's remarks on self-presentation by the speaker are confined to character *(êthos)*. This character is an established moral disposition, which contrasts with deliberative capacity. The contrast is found in several of Aristotle's works, including the *Ethics*, the *Poetics,* and the *Rhetoric*. In the *Ethics*, it underlies the distinction between the moral virtues and practical wisdom *(êthikai aretai* and *phronêsis)*. The former are called virtues of character *(aretai tou êthous)*, and the latter belongs among the virtues of thought *(aretai tês dianoias,* 1138b35–1139a1). In the *Poetics*, the distinction between character and thought is found within the qualitative parts of a tragedy. Character is what makes us say that a stage figure is a certain sort of person.

Thought is shown when a stage figure demonstrates and generally argues for something (1450a5–7, b11–12). In the *Rhetoric*, Aristotle introduces the distinction within the discussion of narration in judicial oratory. We are advised to reveal choice and to avoid speaking from thought, for the former manifests character and the latter practical wisdom. We should say, for example, "I wanted that and made a choice; and if I did not profit, so much the better" (1417a15–18, 23–7).[12]

In 1.2, Aristotle uses the noun *epieikeia* and the adjective *epieikês* (1356a6, 11–12) in order to specify the character a speaker ought to exhibit. That character is moral goodness; it contrasts with *phaulotês* or "baseness" (cf. 1.15. 1376a28–9).[13] *Epieikeia* may be translated in various ways, including "goodness," "uprightness," and "fair-mindedness."[14] I have preferred "uprightness" and have translated *phaulotês* as "baseness." That seems to capture the contrast nicely; but I want to acknowledge that "fair-mindedness" is attractive in that it suits an ambiguity in Aristotle's use of *epieikeia* and *epieikês*. Sometimes the two words are not used generally in reference to moral goodness but narrowly for what is fair or equitable. This usage is found in *Rhetoric* 1.13, where Aristotle takes account of the fact that laws cannot cover all cases. He tells us that the fair *(to epieikes)* seems to be just, and the fair is what is just contrary to written law (1374a26–28). Fair individuals *(epieikeis)* are said to be forgiving: they take account of circumstances and the intention of the lawgiver (1374b3–13). Similarly in *Ethics* 5.10, Aristotle offers reflections on the fair or equitable as rectification of law (1137b26, cf. b12–13); but he also recognizes that the word *epieikês* is used more generally for what is good (1137b1). And earlier in 4.9, he himself uses the word in reference to the virtuous man. The topic is whether shame is a virtue, which Aristotle denies. He tells us that shame is not characteristic of the fair-minded or upright man (*epieikês* 1128b21). For shame is felt at voluntary actions, and

----

12. For fuller discussion of the passages mentioned in this paragraph, see my article "Aristotle's Distinction between Moral Virtue and Practical Wisdom," in *Essays in Ancient Greek Philosophy 4: Aristotle's Ethics*, ed. J. Anton and A. Preus (Albany: State University of New York Press, 1991), pp. 97–102.

13. The lines 1376a28–29 conclude the text 1.15.1376a23–29 quoted in translation later in this section. For the adjectives *epieikês* and *phaulos*, see 2.19.1392b22–24.

14. For the first two, see the translation of Rhys Roberts in *The Complete Works of Aristotle: The Revised Oxford Translation*, vol. 2, ed. J. Barnes (Princeton: Princeton University Press, 1984), p. 2155 and 2194 (1.2.1356a6, 11–12; and 2.1.1378a13); for the third, see George Kennedy's translation in *Aristotle, On Rhetoric: A Theory of Civic Discourse* (Oxford: University Press, 1991), pp. 38 and 121 (the same passages).

upright men never voluntarily do what is base (1128b28–29). Rather it is the base man (*phaulos*) who does what is shameful (1128b25–26).

The application to *Rhetoric* 1.2 is immediately intelligible: in judicial oratory, the speaker's character is important. A prosecutor improves his chances of obtaining a conviction if he can show that the defendant is *phaulos*—base or vicious—either generally so or in some relevant respect, for then the judge or jury will think the defendant likely to have committed the crime in question. Conversely, the defendant wants to present himself as *epieikês*, an upright or virtuous individual, for such a person does not commit acts of injustice. The defendant will be less interested in establishing his goodwill toward the victim, for good will may give way to vice or moral weakness. He will be even less interested in manifesting practical wisdom; indeed, he may even wish to present himself as simple minded and generally lacking in reasoning skills, for deliberative capacity may be a prerequisite for committing the alleged crime.[15]

It may be helpful to consider Aristotle's treatment of nontechnical proofs and in particular his remarks on witnesses who give testimony concerning the character of the speaker and his adversary (1.15. 137a23–29):

> There are testimonies concerning the speaker himself and others concerning the adversary, and testimonies concerning the deed and others concerning character. It is clear, therefore, that [the speaker] can never be at a loss for useful testimony. For if there is no testimony relating to the deed, either agreeing with the speaker or contradicting the adversary,[16] at least there will be testimony concerning the character either of the speaker himself with a view to his uprightness or of the adversary with a view to his baseness.

This passage concerns the testimony of witnesses in judicial proceedings. The testimony is taken in advance of the courtroom speech and is not to be

---

15. See my article "On the Composition of Aristotle's *Rhetoric*: Arguing the Issue, Emotional Appeal, Persuasion through Character, and Characters Tied to Age and Fortune," in *Festschrift Carl Werner Müller*, ed. Chr. Mueller-Goldingen and K. Sier in Beiträge zur Altertumskunde (Stuttgart: Teubner, 1996), sec. 3 with n. 53. In *On the Murder of Erathosthenes*, Lysias has the defendant rebut a charge of premeditated entrapment not only by denying planning and foreknowledge (40–42) but also by presenting himself as a naïve person who is easily deceived (10).

16. My translation of 137a26–28 differs from that of Kennedy (*Aristotle*, p. 113): "for if there is no testimony relating to the fact or supporting the speaker or contradicting the opponent. . . . " The first "or" seems to me an error. There are not three alternatives, only two: "if there is no testimony relating to the deed, *either* (testimony) supporting the speaker, or (testimony) contradicting the

confused with persuasion through character *qua* technical proof.[17] Nevertheless, Aristotle's statement concerning the testimony of witnesses shares an important feature with his remarks on persuasion through character in 1.2. In both passages, we have not only an explicit reference to character (*êthos* 1.2. 1356a2, 5; 1.15. 1376a28) but also a clear reference to the uprightness *(epieikeia)* of the speaker (1.2. 1356a11; 1.15. 1376a28–29). The reason for referring to uprightness is the same in both places: persons of good character do not commit crimes. It is true that 1.15 contains a reference to the character of the adversary, his baseness (1376a29), which is missing in 1.2, but that does not speak against comparison with 1.2. In fact it enhances the comparison. For in 1.15, in regard to both the speaker and his adversary, Aristotle is clearly concerned with moral character in a judicial context.[18] Similarly, in 1.2 Aristotle's focus is on the courtroom and the benefits of establishing moral character.

In 1.2, at the end of the discussion of persuasion through character, Aristotle criticizes certain writers of rhetorical handbooks who deny that the uprightness of the speaker contributes to persuasiveness. According to Aristotle the reverse is true: character has almost the greatest authority with regard to persuasion (1356a10–13). The writers of handbooks to whom Aristotle refers are not further identified in this passage, but from the preceding chapter (1.1) it seems clear that Aristotle is criticizing writers who emphasize emotional appeal in judicial oratory, for in that chapter Aristotle attacks the writers of handbooks who ignore arguing the issue in favor of extraneous matters. They are said to pass over enthymematic argument and to concentrate on arousing pity, anger and the like,[19] which has nothing to do with the issue but is

---

opponent ... " Each of the alternatives concerns testimony relating to the deed. Cf. the Oxford translation of Rhys Roberts (*Complete Works of Aristotle*, p. 2192): "For if we have no evidence of fact supporting our own case or telling against that of our opponent ... "

17. On Aristotle's discussion of witnesses, see D. Mirhady, "Non-technical *Pisteis* in Aristotle and Anaximenes," *American Journal of Philology* 112 (1991): 6, 13–16.

18. If the testimony shows that the adversary is of bad character, he loses his credibility. Should he be the defendant, he will be thought likely to have committed the crime. In cases where he is the plaintiff, he will appear to be the sort of person who brings false charges.

19. At 1.1.1354a17, Aristotle mentions pity and anger, because he is thinking of judicial oratory, in which the arousal of these and similar emotions can be quite effective. The immediately preceding mention of slander (a16) also reflects the courtroom, in which orators employ slander to arouse anger and hate. I am not claiming that such emotions are never usefully aroused in a deliberative situation; but their primary home is in the courtroom.

directed toward the person who is judging the case (1354a11–18). Their concern is how orators affect the condition of a decision-maker (1354b19–20).
They say nothing about deliberative oratory; instead, all try to write about
speaking in court (1354b25–27), for in judicial cases it pays to win over the
listener or judge, so that he listens with partiality and surrenders himself
rather then deciding between the disputants (1354b31–1355a1). The same
writers of handbooks are almost certainly the target of Aristotle's attack in
1.2. They are said to recognize little or no persuasive force in the uprightness
of the speaker, for they put their confidence entirely in emotional appeal.
Aristotle disagrees with these writers and calls uprightness most authoritative. He challenges them on their own ground—judicial oratory[20]—and makes
a technical proof out of that attribute, uprightness or moral goodness, which
is so important in courts of law. If Aristotle expresses himself strongly in
saying that the speaker's character has "almost, so to speak, the greatest
authority in winning belief,"[21] the strength of his expression is entirely appropriate, for he is replying to writers who have themselves overstated the importance of emotional appeal.

The Speaker's Character in Deliberative Oratory: On 2.1

In 2.1, there is a shift in focus. Aristotle is concerned with deliberative
oratory and therefore mentions wisdom and goodwill as well as virtue (1378a8–
9). All three attributes are looked for in the credible speaker, for when they
do not occur together, men fail to give the best advice (*sumbouleuein* 1378a10,
14). Aristotle explains that men who lack wisdom hold false opinions; that
men who opine correctly do not say what they think on account of wickedness; and that men who are wise and upright may lack goodwill and therefore

---

20. According to 1.1. 1354b25–26, the writers of handbooks have completely
stayed away from deliberative oratory. This may be overstatement, but it is not a
wild exaggeration. The special interest of these writers has been judicial oratory,
and Aristotle meets them head-on by advancing a notion of persuasion through
character that is oriented toward the courtroom.

21. In 1.1, Aristotle says that the enthymeme is, "so to speak, without qualification
most authoriative among the modes of proof" (1355a7–8). In 1.2 Aristotle does
not contradict this assertion and rate the character of the speaker more important
than enthymematic argument. "Almost" (1.2.1356a7–13) is weaker than "without
qualification" (1.1.1355a7), and in both passages Aristotle is careful to add "so to
speak." More important, Aristotle asserts himself strongly in 1.2 because he wishes
to counter the writers of handbooks who overrate the authority of emotional
appeal in judicial oratory.

fail to offer the advice which they know to be best (1378a10–14). Aristotle states clearly that these three explanations of bad counsel are exhaustive—"and besides these there is none" (1378a14–15)—and concludes that the speaker who appears wise, virtuous and full of goodwill is credible to the listeners (1378a15–16).

The connection with deliberative oratory is clear even before the mention of three attributes.[22] Aristotle begins with a brief reference to the preceding treatment of materials for deliberative, epideictic, and judicial oratory (1377b16–20),[23] after which Aristotle tells us that persuasion through character is more useful in deliberative oratory, while emotional appeal is of greater utility in judicial oratory. I give the passage in full (1377b21–31):

> Since the art of rhetoric exists for the sake of judgement—for men judge advice and a legal verdict is a judgement—the orator must not only consider how the argument of his speech will be most demonstrative and credible, but also make himself a certain sort of person and the hearer as well. For it is quite important, especially in giving advice but also in legal proceedings, that the speaker appear to be a certain sort of person and that [the listeners] think him to be disposed toward them in some way, and in addition that [the listeners] themselves happen to be disposed in some way. That the speaker appears to be a certain sort of person is of greater use with a view to giving advice, and that the listener be disposed in some way (is of greater use) with a view to legal procedings.

In what follows, Aristotle makes clear what he means by the listener "being disposed in some way." The reference is to the emotional condition of the audience. Aristotle first mentions emotional conditions useful in legal

---

22. I.e., before the passage that is discussed in the preceding paragraph and quoted in translation above.

23. The reference is to 1.4–14. There is no reference to the immediately preceding account of nontechnical modes of persuasion in 1.15. This omission may be an indication that Aristotle's mind is on deliberative oratory, for the nontechnical modes of persuasion concern judicial oratory (1.15.1375a23–24). Nevertheless, there are grounds for caution. First, the transitional passage at the beginning of 2.1 may have been inserted by an editor. Second, the nontechnical modes are easily passed over in silence, not only because they are nontechnical (neither constructed by the orator nor, strictly speaking, part of his speech) but also because they are treated as a kind of appendix to Aristotle's account of the materials for judicial oratory (1375a23–30).

proceedings: friendly feelings and hate, anger and gentleness. When a juror has been so affected that he has friendly feelings toward the defendant, then he will see no injustice or only a little in the deeds of the defendant. The opposite is the case if the juror has been brought to hate the defendant (1377b31–1378a3). After that, Aristotle mentions emotional conditions useful in deliberative situations. Should a member of the assembly desire something pleasant and view it with confidence, then he thinks that it will come about and be good. Should he be indifferent or annoyed, then he will think the opposite (1378a3–6). Here we have a reminder that emotional appeal can be used effectively in deliberative assemblies, but that does not contradict Aristotle's fundamental claim: emotional appeal is more useful in the courtroom, and persuasion through character has greater utility in matters of counsel.

This conclusion may seem inconsistent with persuasion through character as presented in 1.2, but there is no formal inconsistency, for Aristotle has two recommendations for two different circumstances. In 1.1, he recommends that the speaker exhibit uprightness, for his thoughts are on the courtroom; and in 2.1, he recommends three attributes that suit the assembly and other deliberative situations. Uprightness or virtue is not dropped; instead it is listed alongside wisdom and goodwill.[24] The significance of this triad is not in doubt. Aristotle is referring to three attributes whose connection with good advice had long been recognized.[25] One well-known example from the fifth century is found in book 2 of Thucydides' *Histories*. There the statesman Pericles is made to address the assembly at the end of the second year of the Peloponnesian War. The Athenians have seen their land invaded twice and are now suffering the ravages of a plague. An attempt to reach an accord with Sparta has failed and the people are angry at Pericles for advising them to undertake the war. In this context, Pericles calls a meeting of the assembly

---

24. As was mentioned earlier, men of virtue are called "upright men" *(epieikeis)* at 2.1 1378a13.

25. The connection can be found already in the first book of Homer's *Iliad*, where Nestor speaks in the assembly of princes. Agamemnon and Achilles are quarrelling over whether Agamemnon should take for himself the girl Briseis, who had been given as booty to Achilles. Nestor will urge Agamemenon not to take the girl and Achilles not to oppose Agamemnon (1.274–81); but before Nestor gives this advice, Homer describes him as well intentioned toward both Agamemnon and Achilles (1.253), after which he claims for himself superiority in battle and council (1.259–73). In Aristotelian terms, Homer describes Nestor as full of goodwill and then has Nestor claim the virtues of courage and practical wisdom. See "Aristotle on Persuasion through Character," pp. 211–214.

and addresses the people, urging them to persevere. Of especial interest is the introduction to Pericles' speech, for there the statesman engages in self-characterization (2.60.5–6):

> And yet you are angry at such a man as myself, who is, I think, [1][26] inferior to no one in knowing and setting forth what needs to be done, [2] a friend of the city, and [3] superior to money. For [1] the man who knows [what needs to be done] and does not explain [it] clearly is in the same condition as if he had not thought of [what needs to be done]; and [2] the man who has both but is full of ill will toward the city, will not present a [recommendation] with the same loyalty; and [3] if this too is present and yet conquered by money, everything will be sold for this one thing.

Here we have Aristotle's triad in only slightly altered form. Practical wisdom is divided into being able to determine a proper policy and to set it forth; goodwill corresponds to being a friend of the city; and virtue is narrowed to being superior to money, i.e., a particular moral virtue much looked for in politicians. Pericles even anticipates Aristotle by remarking on the harmful effects of the opposite condition: being unable to set forth a policy clearly, having ill will toward the city, and being unable to resist money. The first of these opposite conditions—being unable to set forth policy in a clear manner—is narrower than Aristotle's lack of sense (1378a11),[27] but the general idea is the same: an absence of practical wisdom inhibits counsel, as does an absence of goodwill and virtue.

It is clear that the three attributes of 2.1 are not an Aristotelian discovery. They are traditional and a matter of practical politics.[28] It is, therefore,

---

26. The numbers in brackets are not part of the Greek text. They have been added for the sake of clarity, just as they been added to the translation of 2.1 (see note 9).

27. In 2.1, Aristotle uses "lack of sense," *aphrosunê* (1378a11), to express the absence of "practical wisdom," *phronêsis* (a8). Practical wisdom is an excellence of thought (1.9 1366b20); and in the case of politicians, that includes not only the ability to conceive of a policy but also to state one's recommendation in an intelligible manner.

28. In regard to the tradition, see note 25 concerning Homer's *Iliad*. On the practical side, pseudo-Xenophon offers an interesting answer to the question why Athenian democrats allow the knavish individual to speak in the assembly: "They know that this man's ignorance and knavishness and goodwill are more profitable than the virtue and wisdom and ill-will of the respectable man" (*Constitution of the Athenians* 1.7).

hardly surprising that they occur in *Politics* 5.9, where Aristotle discusses the criteria for high office. Here is how Aristotle introduces them (1309a33–39):

> Those who are going to hold the controlling offices [in a city-state] ought to possess a certain three attributes: [1][29] friendship toward the established political arrangement, [2] maximum capacity for the work of the office, [3] virtue and justice: in each political arrangement the [kind of virtue and justice proper] to the political arrangement. For if what is just is not the same in all political arrangements, then there must also be different kinds of justice.

The first of the three criteria, friendship *(philia)* toward the established political arrangement *(politeia)*, recalls the second attribute claimed by the Pericles: namely, being a friend of the city *(philopolis)*. In both cases, the idea is basically the same. The reliable statesman, the man most qualified for office and most persuasive when recommending a policy, is *inter alia* favorably disposed toward the city in its present form.[30] He is not trying to replace democracy with oligarchy or vice versa. The second criterion—maximum capacity for the work of the office—differs from Pericles' first attribute, the capacity for determining and setting forth what needs to be done, in that there is no explicit reference to public speaking. The omission is understandable, for not all offices demand oratorical capacity. But allowing for this difference, it is clear that Aristotle's "maximum capacity" and Pericles' "knowing what needs to be done" are closely related. In both cases, we are to think of task-related capacity. When selecting a general, we look for capacity based on experience in battle; and when deciding whether or not to declare war, we accept the advice of that speaker who has a demonstrated knowledge of warfare. Finally, the third criterion listed by Aristotle, virtue and justice, includes Pericles' third attribute, superiority to money.[31] It excludes the vicious man who values money and

---

29. In this passage, the numbers in brackets reflect the Greek text: "first . . . then . . . third" (1309a34–36). That is not true of the numbers in brackets within the translations of *Rhetoric* 2.1 (see note 9) and the Thucydides 2.60.5 (see note 26).

30. I shall soon add a qualifier. In the case of the orator, being favorably disposed need not be a well-established disposition. Instead, it may be an occurrent emotion of no long standing.

31. In fact, Pericles was not above taking money; and if Socrates' statement in Plato's *Gorgias* is not an oligarchic exaggeration, Pericles was not only fined for embezzlement but also nearly condemned to death (516a1–2).

therefore is likely to steal from the treasury or to give bad advice because he has been bribed. It also excludes the morally weak man, who does not over-value money but may on occasion give way to temptation and steal from the treasury or offer bad advice for the sake of gain.[32]

Aristotle qualifies the third criterion, virtue and justice, by adding a reference to political arrangement. The virtue looked for in a candidate is that which suits the political arrangement (1309a36–37). The qualification is a matter of some interest, for it underlines the fact that Aristotle is not thinking of a single virtuous disposition which applies to all men in all circumstances. We may compare *Politics* 3.4, where Aristotle distinguishes the virtue of the citizen from that of the good man. The latter is said to be single and perfect (1276b33–34); it is that combination of moral and intellectual excellence which Aristotle discusses at length in his ethical treatises.[33] In contrast, the former takes various forms, for it is dependent upon the arrangement of the city-state (1276b30–32). What it is to be a good citizen in a democracy is different from what is to be a good citizen in an oligarchy, for the two political arrangements are different. In a democracy, the good citizen strives to preserve the democratic arrangement; in an oligarchy, he seeks to do the same for the oligarchic arrangement (1276b28–29). That does not mean that democrats, in their zeal to preserve a democracy, should strive to remove all oligarchs from the city; nor should oligarchs seek to destroy all democrats. In *Politics* 5.9, Aristotle touches on this matter. He says that in democracies and oligarchies alike, political leaders err when they divide a city in two. In democracies, demagogues ought to seek to speak *(legein)* on behalf of the

---

32. On moral weakness, cf. *Politics* 5.9.1309b8–14. Among politicians contempo-rary with Aristotle, Demosthenes may serve as an example of weakness in regard to money. Plutarch, citing Demetrius of Phalerum, tells us that he could not be corrupted by money coming from Macedon, but he was accessible to gold from Susa and Ecbatana and was overwhelmed by it (Plut., *Demosthenes* 14.1–2 = Dem. Ph. fr. 133 Wehrli).

33. Instead of "combination," it might be better to speak of a "unity" of moral and intellectual excellences, for in the ethical treatises Aristotle advances a conception of perfection such that moral virtue and practical wisdom do not come apart (esp. *Nicomachean Ethics* 6.12–13; *Eudemian Ethics* 5.12–13). That alone is sufficient to mark off the virtue and wisdom of the perfect man (e.g., Socrates) from the virtue and wisdom looked for in candidates for office and in credible speakers. For in the latter two cases, the attributes do come apart, so that a politician can be wise and not virtuous or virtuous and not wise. Cf. *Politics* 5.9 1309a39–b14 and *Rhetoric* 2.1 1378a9–14.

wealthy; and in oligarchies, the oligarchs should appear to speak on behalf of the people. Rather than swear to be full of ill-will *(kakonous)* toward the people, oligarchs ought both to hold and to exhibit the opposite attitude (1310a2–12). The application to rhetoric is obvious. The orator who wishes to unify his city does well to present himself as a man of goodwill toward all the citizens.

In the passage just cited, Aristotle speaks of demagogues "seeming" *(dokein* 1310a6) to speak on behalf of the wealthy, and of oligarchs "exhibiting" *(hypokrinesthai* 1310a10–11) an opposite attitude toward democrats.[34] Those words may suggest feigned concern, and undoubtedly there are moments to be disingenuous. But Aristotle also says that the oligarch ought to hold *(hypolambanein* 1313a10, without *dokein* or a similar verb expressing appearance) a positive attitude toward democrats.[35] That is not a slip.[36] Aristotle is concerned with the unity of the city, and that cannot be achieved by endless acts and words of deception. There must be genuine goodwill, at least on occasion; and that goodwill must be manifested in some, even most, political speeches.

What, then, is this goodwill? Is it a fixed disposition or an emotional response?[37] There is, I fear, no simple answer to the question. If we focus on

---

34. The verb *hypokrinesthai* is used for acting on the stage, where appearance is paramount. However, the verb is also used of an orator's delivery (*Rhetoric* 3.1 1403b23; 1413b23, 28, 30) and need not imply a feigned exhibition. It is, therefore, aptly used by Aristotle in a passage concerning how oligarchs ought to express themselves. That is not to overlook the fact that the immediate context is the oligarch's oath to hold ill-will and to plan whatever evil he can (1310a9–10, 11–12). Nevertheless, the passage as a whole is about speaking on behalf of political opponents: democrats on behalf of oligarchs and oligarchs on behalf on democrats (1310a6–7). The verb *hypokrinesthai* applies every bit as much to the public speeches of oligarchs as to their sworn oaths; or even more so.

35. The repetition of *kai* in 1310a10 separates *hypolambanein* from *hypokrinesthai*: it is necessary *both* to hold an opposite attitude (i.e., goodwill), *and* to exhibit this attitude. Goodwill is important and so is expressing it.

36. Earlier in 5.9 Aristotle cites the principle that the persons in favor of the political arrangement should be in the majority (1309b16–18), after which he is careful to say that extreme forms of democracy and oligarchy are self-destructive (1309b30–35) and that neither democracy nor oligarchy can exist and endure without the wealthy and the multitude (1309b38–39).

37. The choice here is not between a persistent emotion that may be latent and an occurrent one whose presence is manifested by the speaker (cf. Homer, *Iliad* 1.80–83 and 102–104). Rather it is between an *êthos* and a *pathos*; i.e., between an established disposition acquired through civic *paideia* and a feeling that may or may not reflect the character of the speaker.

the need to unify the city, we will think of an established disposition to wish all citizens well; but if we consider political strife in ancient Greece, then occasional, short-lived feelings of goodwill would seem to be all that can be hoped for.[38] Be that as it may, I want to *suggest* that in *Rhetoric* 2.1, goodwill *(eunoia)*, is to be thought of as an emotion. Aristotle does not repeat the phrases of 1.2 (i.e., "in the character of the speaker" [1356a2–3] and "through the character [of the speaker]" [1356a5]), because the mention of the character *(êthos)* by itself could be mis-construed. In 2.1, Aristotle is recommending a mode of persuasion in which an emotion (goodwill) and an intellectual quality (wisdom) are given equal status alongside moral character. Moreover, Aristotle refers to his discussion of emo-tions for instruction on how a speaker creates the appearance of goodwill (1378a19–20).[39] The reference is entirely sensible, for emotions motivate deliberation. Anger makes men deliberate about how to achieve revenge, and fright makes men consider ways to achieve safety.[40] Goodwill *qua* emotion is no different. The orator who feels (experiences) goodwill toward the city is motivated to offer sound advice; and if the listeners believe that the speaker is moved by goodwill, they are likely to accept his advice.

---

38. When analyzing Aristotle's notion of persuasion through character, we do well to emphasize debate within the city-state. Nevertheless, we should remember that politicians occasionally went abroad as ambassadors. Sometimes they addressed allies, but on other occasions they addressed a hostile audience, which had good reason to suspect anything that might be said. In such a situation, the orator might choose to appeal solely to the self-interest of the audience, but a show of goodwill might also have some effect. If the hostility was of long standing, the orator could hardly claim that he and his fellow countrymen had an established disposition of goodwill toward the audience, but he might claim a change of heart or new feeling, especially if he could address his audience under some convincing description. For example, an Athenian might address the Spartans as Greek allies against the Persian King, ignoring the fact that the Spartans were long-standing enemies who supported oligarchic governments over democratic ones.

39. In the immediately preceding lines (1378a16–19), Aristotle refers to the account of virtue in 1.9 for instruction on how to appear wise and good. In 1.9 Aristotle tells us that this chapter will offer materials as a result of which a speaker is believed to have a certain sort of character (1366a25–26). Aristotle then adds that this is the second mode of persuasion. At first reading that may seem confused, for in 1.2 persuasion through character is introduced first (1356a2–3, 5–13), but in fact there is no confusion. The materials for persuasion through argument are presented first (1.4–14), and when Aristotle turns to persuasion through character in 2.1 he first refers to the preceding discussion of these materials (1377b16–23) and then, second, takes up the condition of the speaker (1377b24, 1378a6–20) before, third, that of the judge or listener.

40. Cf. *Rhetoric* 2.5 1383a6–7; and on this passage, see my *Aristotle on Emotion* (London: Duckworth, 1975), pp. 79–80.

It may be helpful to state clearly that Aristotle's mode of expression throughout 2.1 is compatible with construing goodwill as an emotion. To introduce his subject, Aristotle says that the orator must not only consider the argument of the speech, "but also make himself a certain sort of person and the hearer as well" (1377b24). Here the same phrase, "a certain sort of person" *(poion tina)*, is used of both the condition of the speaker and that of the listener. The phrase itself is quite general and covers not only well-established dispositions like moral virtues but also short-lived ones like emotions. In the case of the hearer, the condition in question is undoubtedly emotional;[41] in the case of the speaker, it is a complex, of which one component (goodwill) is, I think, an emotion. That seems to be confirmed by what follows. Aristotle calls it important "that the speaker appear to be a certain sort of person and that [the listeners] think him to be disposed toward them in some way" (1377b26–28). Here again we have the words "a certain sort of person" *(poion tina)*, but this time Aristotle adds "to be disposed in some way" *(pôs diakeisthai)*. The latter phrase recurs two lines later in reference to the emotional condition of the audience (1377b30–31).[42] Unless I misunderstand Aristotle, he has expanded his description of the speaker in order to make clear that the speaker's condition, or perceived condition, is emotional as well as one of wisdom and virtue. The hearers think that the speaker feels goodwill toward them and assume that this emotion is motivating his deliberations.

There are, however, two difficulties with this analysis. First, the definition of emotion that follows in 2.1 concerns strong emotions that cause a change in judgment (1378a20–21). If the hearers think the speaker is experiencing an emotion of this kind—if they believe that his mind is now no better than a warped straightedge (cf. 1.1 1354a25–26)—they will be suspicious of his recommendations and more apt to believe another speaker who appears dispassionate. Second, the account of the individual emotions that follows in 2.2–11 does not discuss goodwill. The omission is puzzling and might indicate that Aristotle did not conceive of goodwill as an emotion. The reference to the account of individual emotions might then be the confused addition of a later editor. Concerning this second objection, it is possible to refer to the accounts of friendship *(philia* 2.4) and kindness *(charis* 2.7) and to say that the discussion of these emotions provides material which can be easily transferred to goodwill. For example, the definition of friendship—"wishing for someone things you believe to be good, for his sake and not for your own, and

---

41. Cf. 1.1 1354b20.

42. Cf. 1.2 1356a3, where emotional appeal *qua* technical mode of persuasion is first introduced as "disposing the hearer in some way," *ton akroatên diatheinai pôs.*

being ready to do these things to the extent possible" (1380b34–1381a1)—could guide the orator who wants to present himself as full of goodwill toward his audience. Similarly, the orator might draw on the account of kindness, claiming that he wants to assist the audience "in its need, not in return for anything, nor for some advantage to himself, but for some advantage to the audience" (1385a18–19). In lecture, Aristotle himself may have made the connection between these passages and goodwill. If he did, then he (not an editor) may well have introduced the reference to the account of individual emotions, making special mention of friendship (2.1 1378a19–20).[43]

This still leaves the first objection: if emotions are conceived of as strong feelings that affect sound judgment, an orator *qua* adviser should not claim them for himself. This objection is, I think, well taken, but I do not think it fatal to the claim that in 2.1 Aristotle thinks of the goodwill of the speaker as an emotional condition. Rather, it points up a lack of clarity in Aristotle's treatment of emotion. He needs to draw a clear distinction between strong emotions that are usefully aroused in the audience, precisely because they affect judgment, and weak emotions that motivate without impairing judgment. Aristotle may have thought the general idea obvious and therefore left it unstated. Alternatively, he may have discussed it at some length in a lost work like *Emotions [or On] Anger* (Diogenes Laertius, *Aristotle* 5.23). In any case, there is a passage in the *Nicomachean Ethics* where Aristotle marks off goodwill from feelings of friendship, pointing out that goodwill lacks the intensity and desire of the latter (9.5 1266b33–34). The application to rhetoric is, I think, obvious. The intensity of feelings of friendship make a person biased, and for that reason the feelings are important in emotional appeal (2.1 1377b31–1378a3). In contrast, goodwill, being milder, may motivate without disturbing judgment. In the audience, it arouses attention and encourages an open mind, so that a sound decision is reached.[44] In the speaker, it gives direction to his deliberations; and together with wisdom and virtue, it ensures that he will advise what is best for the audience.

---

43. The issue is complicated by the fact that the account of individual emotions was almost certainly written for a different context and transferred to its present position, probably but by no means unquestionably by Aristotle himself. See my "On the Composition of Aristotle's *Rhetoric*," sec. 2 with nn. 32 and 34.

44. When an orator openly asks his audience to listen with goodwill (e.g., Lysias, *In Defense of Mantitheus* 9: *met' eunoias akroasasthai*), he is calling for a fair hearing and not urging his listeners to surrender their capacity to make an informed judgment. In fact, there is nothing to prevent an audience from feeling goodwill toward all speakers, even though the speakers are opposed to each other. That is what Isocrates calls "common goodwill," *koinê eunoia* (*Antidosis* 22).

Speech Expressive of Character: On 1.8

In the preceding section, I have suggested that "goodwill" *(eunoia)*, in 2.1 should be construed as an emotion. I now want to consider a passage that calls for a different interpretation. It occurs in 1.8, where Aristotle discusses political arrangements. He tells us that being able to persuade and to deliberate well requires knowledge of all political arrangements, including their customs, legal usages, and advantages (1365b22–26). Differences in the supreme authority are spelled out (1365b26–1366a2), as are the ends of each political arrangement (1366a2–6). Differences in customs, legal usages, and advantages are referred to the ends of political arrangements, and the character of the speaker is mentioned on account of its connection with ends (1366a6–16). It is the last passage that interests me. It runs as follows:

It is clear, therefore, that the customs *[êthê]* and legal institutions and advantages relating to the end of each [political arrangement] must be distinguished, for men choose [these] by referring to this [the end of the political arrangement]. Since persuasion occurs not only through demonstrative argument but also through speech expressive of custom/ character *[êthikos logos]*—for we trust the speaker because he appears to be a certain sort of person, i.e., if he appears good or full of goodwill or both—we should know the customs *[êthê]* of each of the political arrangements. For the custom *[êthos]* of each is necessarily most persuasive with regard to each. These [customs] will be grasped in the same way [as the character of the speaker].[45] For customs/characters *[êthê]* are clear on account of choice, and choice is referred to an end.

Here Aristotle is concerned with the customs of different political arrangements. He tells us that we should know these customs, for the speaker who uses them effectively increases his persuasiveness.[46] Parenthetically,

---

45. The Greek phrase *dia tôn autôn*, "through the same thing" or "in the same way" (1366a14), is not altogether clear in this context, but given the preceding reference to the character of the speaker it seems most likely that Aristotle is saying that both the *êthê* of political arrangements and those of speakers are grasped in the same way, i.e., through the ends. In adopting this interpretation, I am following E. Cope and J. Sandys, *The Rhetoric of Aristotle* vol. 1 (Cambridge: Cambridge University Press 1877), p. 157; and departing from Kennedy, *Aristotle*, p. 77.

46. Aristotle can express himself quite briefly, for the idea is neither obscure nor new. Cf. Plato's *Gorgias* 513b–1, where Socrates is made to tell Callicles that political success requires likening one's self to the political arrangement (512e–513a, 1–2) and that whoever can make him most like the Athenian demos will

Aristotle makes reference to the character of the speaker, saying that goodness and goodwill have a persuasive effect. The reference is promoted by the fact that the same Greek word, *êthos*, is used for both *custom* and *character*.[47] In addition, the customs of political arrangements are grasped "in the same way" as the character of a speaker; that is, custom and character are made clear through reference to an end.

For our purposes, the important point is that here in 1.8 goodwill is mentioned within a discussion of *êthos*. It is part of the speaker's character and not an emotion. Like goodness, it is manifested "through speech expressive of character" (*di' êthikou [logou]* 1366a10).[48] The notion of speech expressive of character is not opaque and occurs elsewhere in the *Rhetoric*. Three passages may be mentioned. One occurs in 2.18, where Aristotle summarizes what he has already accomplished. As part of this summary, Aristotle refers to the customs of political arrangements—i.e., to 1.8—and says that the he has determined how speeches are made expressive of custom/character (1391b20–23). A few lines later, there is another reference to making speeches expressive of custom/character (b26–27), but there is no reference to speeches manifesting emotion. A second passage occurs in 2.21. Here Aristotle takes up the maxim *(gnômê)* and toward the end of the discussion says that maxims may be used to make speeches expressive of character. He explains that maxims reveal choice, and morally good maxims make the speaker appear to be of good character (1395b12–17). Again there is no reference to emotion, though earlier in the chapter there is mention of emotion. Aristotle distinguishes between using (contradicting) maxims when the speaker wants to manifest good character and when he wants to speak emotionally. The two uses are regarded as distinct; and character, not emotion, is explained in terms of choice (1395a18–32). A third passage is found in 3.17, where Aristotle discusses proof as a part of an oration. He warns against using enthymemes when one creates emotion and when one makes speech expressive of char-

---

help him become a politician and orator, for each group is delighted by speeches spoken in its own character (b6–c2). Socrates says that imitation is not good enough; there must be a genuine likeness (b3–4). This observation is intended to make clear how mistaken it is to admire political success in a city like Athens, but it also points up the fact that many people, including the teachers of rhetoric, believe that artful self-presentation, whatever the speaker's real character, can be persuasive in political oratory.

47. See E. Cope, *An Introduction to Aristotle's Rhetoric* (London: Macmillan, 1867), pp. 108–13, 181–83.

48. *Logou* is supplied from 1366a9: *di apodeiktikou logou.*

acter.[49] Again he separates emotional speech from that which expresses character. The latter is connected with choice; and as in 2.21, we are told to use maxims to express character (1418a12–21).

It seems to me that all these passages, including 1.8, work with a single notion of speech expressive of character. Since it occurs both in Aristotle's handbook-like treatment of the parts of an oration (3.17)[50] and in a summary passage that makes no mention of emotional appeal as a technical mode of persuasion (2.18),[51] it probably predates the establishment of three technical modes of persuasion. That might explain in part the oddity of recognizing two attributes in 1.8, and not three as in 2.1.[52] But whatever the truth concerning the development and composition of Aristotle's *Rhetoric*, it seems certain that goodwill in 1.8 should not be construed as an emotion. It is an attribute of character; and as such, it is presented through speech expressive of character (*di' êthikou [logou]*).

If this interpretation of 1.8 is correct, what should we say about 2.1? Should goodwill in both 1.8 and 2.1 be construed as a character trait? Or was

---

49. The Greek verb *poiein* is used with *pathos* in 1418a12 and understood with *êthikon ton logon* in a15. In translating a12 "creates emotion," I follow Kennedy (*Aristotle*, p. 274), who has "would create *pathos*." Roberts (*Complete Works of Aristotle*, p. 2265) translates "trying to rouse feeling." That seems to me misleading, for it may suggest that Aristotle's primary concern is with arousing an emotional response in the listeners. On the contrary, Aristotle's concern is with the speaker and his manifestation of emotion. That can and often does arouse emotion in the listeners (3.7 1408a23–24); but it is nevertheless distinct from their response.

50. See my "Aristotle on Persuasion through Character," pp. 235–236.

51. I am here disagreeing with Cope and Sandys (*Rhetoric of Aristotle,* 2: 175), who suggest that Aristotle intended "to include the *pathê* under the general head of *êthikoi logoi*," and with Kennedy (*Aristotle,* p. 173 n. 104), who thinks Cope's view probable, but adds the possibility that Aristotle "just overlooked" the preceding account of emotions. See my "On the Composition of Aristotle's *Rhetoric,*" sec. 2 and 3 with nn 45 and 55.

52. While I think it probable that persuasion through character as set forth in 2.1 is a comparatively late addition to Aristotle's course of lectures on rhetoric, the omission of any reference to practical wisdom in 1.8 may reflect no more than a difference in topic. In 1.8, Aristotle is discussing customs that serve the ends of political arrangement. Parenthetically he introduces the character of the speaker and mentions traits that refer to ends. The moral virtues involve choice, which is directed toward an end, and goodwill is above all a proper orientation toward the political arrangement. In contrast, practical wisdom is concerned with discovering means and takes its direction from moral virtue and goodwill. For that reason it may have been omitted in 1.8 but mentioned in 2.1, where Aristotle's topic is the attributes looked for in a fully credible speaker. He lists three attributes, including practical wisdom, and says that all are required for credibility. In 1.8, Aristotle

it correct to interpret goodwill in 2.1 as an emotion? My preference is to accept the latter alternative and to say that Aristotle works with two notions of the speaker's goodwill. In 1.8, he views it as part of the speaker's character; in 2.1 , he regards it as a weak emotion. That is potentially confusing, which may be one reason why later rhetoricians distinguished between weak and strong emotions, labeling the former *êthê*, "character-traits," and the latter *pathê*, "emotions." The distinction is most familiar to us from Quintilian, who speaks of it as an ancient tradition (*Oratorical Education* 6.2.8–9). We find it already in Dionysius of Halicarnassus (*Demosthenes* 2 and 22); and in my judgment, we should look for its origin in the early Peripatos.[53]

Whatever its origin may have been, extending the use of *êthos* to cover weak emotions will have enabled rhetoricians to sidestep difficulties concerning goodwill. They could group goodwill together with virtue and practical reason—they could call goodwill an *êthos* and say that the speaker reveals it in *êthikos logos*—without having to decide whether goodwill is a part of character or a weak emotion. From one point of view, that is replacing one ambiguity with another; but from a different point of view it is a practical way to deal with a real difficulty. Most often the deliberative orator wants to present himself as dispositionally full of goodwill; but as was pointed out in the previous section, there are occasions when the speaker cannot plausibly claim long-standing goodwill, and an audience would not believe him if he did. On these occasions, a feeling of goodwill, a positive emotion, is what the artful speaker tries to present. Rhetoricians understood that; and having widened the meaning of *êthos*, they did not need to complicate their analysis by distinguishing different kinds of goodwill. They could speak simply of *êthos* and the speaker's use of persuasion through character.

------

allows that the speaker may be persuasive if he is good or full of goodwill or both (1366a11–12). Only two attributes are listed, and one alone may be sufficient to win the trust of the listener. That may jar with the doctrine of 2.1, but there is no formal inconsistency, for it is only in the later chapter that Aristotle is concerned to list all the attributes of the fully credible speaker.

53. While no text tells us that early Peripatetics labeled weak emotions *êthê*, there is an interesting passage in Simplicius' commentary *On Aristotle's Categories* 8.8b26–27, in which Theophrastus (*Sources* no. 438 FHS&G) is said to have recognized a difference in degree between closely related emotions. The passage places goodwill among the weak emotions and friendship among the strong. For more on this passage and on the likelihood that some early Peripatetic decided to call weak emotions *êthê*, see my article "Quintilian 6.2.8–9: *Ethos* and *Pathos* and the Ancient Tradition," in *Peripatetic Rhetoric after Aristotle*, ed. W. Fortenbaugh and D. Mirhady, vol. 6 of *Rutgers University Studies in Classical Humanities* (New Brunswick, NJ: Transaction 1994); pp. 183–91.

Eight

Reworking Aristotle's *Rhetoric*

George A. Kennedy

My title, "Reworking Aristotle's *Rhetoric*," has several possible meanings. For one thing, all of us who study rhetoric are in some sense engaged in our own reworking, interpretation, and application of it. More specifically, I have recently worked through the *Rhetoric* again in the process of making a new translation of it, with introduction and notes. I would like to discuss some of the things I have noticed, but will only comment occasionally on my own translation. Finally, I will say something about the strengths and weaknesses of the *Rhetoric* and how it, as a general rhetoric, may need to be reworked for the purposes of the modern world.

Those of us interested in philosophy and rhetoric have, in the last generation, become increasingly aware of the origins of philosophical thought and human discourse generally in language and metaphor. Though the rhetoric, language, and metaphorical practice of some philosophers—Plato, Vico, Rousseau, Nietzsche, and Heidegger, for example—have been given much scrutiny, there has been little attention paid to this phenomenon in the case of Aristotle, presumably because his extant treatises, in contrast to his lost dialogues perhaps, have been perceived as nonliterary. But Aristotelian thought and language, like all thought and language, is characterized by certain dominant metaphors that are basic to the thought and may even in some sense have generated it. Plato speaks of an ancient quarrel between poetry and philosophy,[1] and the whole thrust of Aristotle's *Poetics*, with its justification of poetry as a form of learning, would seem to be an attempt to reconcile the two traditions. Aristotle thought that rhetoric and poetics dealt with knowledge, though on a more popular level than did formal philosophy, and his theory of the metaphor in particular is based on cognition. Let us, then, start

---

1. Plato, *Republic* 10.607b.

with some consideration of Aristotle's views of perception and image as inherent in language.

In the opening lines of the *Metaphysics*, and elsewhere,[2] Aristotle proclaims the superiority of sight to all the other senses, but it does not seem to have been generally appreciated that throughout his works he speaks or writes in visual terms. Sight, visualization, and a sense of the existence of phenomena in physical space are very common motifs in his work. Since the reader is perhaps well acquainted with the *Poetics*, I remind you of the importance given to visualization in that treatise. For example, in an unusually prescriptive passage at the beginning of chapter 17, Aristotle proclaims that in constructing plots and working them out in language, the poet should as much as possible put the scene before his eyes; for by thus seeing most clearly, as it were being present at the actions themselves, he will discover what is appropriate and be least likely to overlook inconsistencies. *Enargeia*, or "visual clarity," is a basic concept of the *Poetics*, as is its counterpart, *energeia*, or "actualization."

Rhetoric also is given spatial visualization and actualization by Aristotle. A striking instance occurs in his famous definition of rhetoric as an ability or faculty of *seeing* the available means of persuasion in each case.[3] The word I translate "seeing" is *theôresai*, often rendered "observing," which rather mutes the image, and of course it is related to *theôria*, English "theory," a word that occurs in Plato[4] but which Aristotle perhaps first made basic in philosophical speculation. The noun *theôros*, "the spectator or one who sees," is one of the two categories of an audience in the third chapter of the *Rhetoric*, where it is applied especially to the audience of epideictic as "spectator" rather than "judge."[5] The practitioner of rhetoric is also a *theôros*, a spectator of the available means of persuasion.

A second important concept in Aristotle's vision of rhetoric is that of *topos*, the "place" where topics are to be found that provide the strategies for persuasive reasoning.[6] The would-be orator should look into these places systematically to find what can be said on his subject. Aristotle constantly

---

2. *On Sense Perception* 437a.

3. See *Rhetoric* 1.2.1.

4. E.g., *Philebus* 38b; *Republic* 6.486a.

5. *Rhetoric* 1.3.1.

6. *Rhetoric* 2.23.1–29. Thomas Cole has sugguested that the origin of this usage may be the "place" in a handbook where the topic is found. See *The Origins of Rhetoric in Ancient Greece* (Baltimore: Johns Hopkins University Press, 1991), pp. 88–89.

speaks of "seeing" and "grasping" thought, arguments and aspects of theory, not only inventional but stylistic, even though other terms for knowing or applying were available to him and are occasionally employed.[7] It is not too much to say, I think, that for him rhetoric takes place in what might be called a "civic space," specifically the open space of the agora, just as drama, for Aristotle also a civic art, takes place in the space of the theatre, another word derived from root *thea-*.

Other basic Aristotelian words with visual imagery are *horos*, literally a "boundary stone," which is his word for definition,[8] and *methodos*, which as "method" is in English a very abstract conception, but which in Greek means going "along a road" (*meta* plus *hodos*, "road").[9] It combines the visual with the teleological, as it were "along the road of life to a predetermined goal," observing the "places" and "boundary stones" along the way: Aristotle is a "peripatetic," or "walker."

This observation of Aristotle's visual imagery leads me in two directions, which may be dismissed as fanciful digressions, though like other *supplement* they carry with them some serious implications. One was prompted by an article I read in the January 1989 issue of Piedmont Airlines' promotional magazine supplied to passengers, which sought to provide practical advice to business people seeking to make oral presentations. They should be aware, it was claimed, according to the research in neurolinguistic programming by Richard Bandler and John Grinder, that people think in three primary ways. Some are visualizers who think in terms of pictures; some are auditors who think not in pictures but in sounds; others perceive through feelings and are tactile and emotional. To convey a message, the speaker needs to be sensitive to the mode of thought of the hearer, and it was claimed that these forms of thinking could be perceived by the eye movements of a hearer. If his or her eyes move upward while thinking, thought is being visualized; if the eyes move downward or to the left the person is hearing the words but not seeing them as images; if the eyes move down to the right the message is being experienced emotively. I fear that Aristotle may have been one of those notorious professors who lecture to an upper or lower corner of the room—or in his case the portico of the gymnasium—rather than making eye contact with the students. According to the ancient biographers he also spoke

---

7. E.g., *gignôskien* and *manthanein* in *Rhetoric* 1.1.6.

8. E.g., *Rhetoric* 2.8.2.

9. As at *Rhetoric* 1.1.11: "it is evident that artistic method *[entecknos methodos]* is concerned with *pisteis*."

with a lisp, was bald, had a paunch, and wore lots of rings: probably not a spell-binding lecturer.

If there is anything to the theory of neurolinguistic programming, possibly different writers and philosophers can be characterized in one of the three groups. As dramatic representations of Socrates and others, the metaphors of the Platonic dialogues may be influenced by how historical individuals actually thought. Socrates apparently did not lecture and probably looked his interlocuter in the eye. In Plato's own letters, of which at least some are genuine, there seems to me to be a comparative absence of the visual and perhaps a greater preference for the emotive or tactile, but I haven't worked it out statistically. Yet many would perhaps agree that whereas Plato felt things that can only with difficulty be visualized, the Forms for example, Aristotle saw concrete realities and analyzed them.

A second, perhaps more fanciful, direction in which my thinking goes is one popular in current literary criticism. It involves the theory of gynesis, as advanced by Alice A. Jardine (*Diacritics* 12 [1982]), who claims that technology and time are inherently associated with the male; nature and space, with the female. Aristotle was more concerned with nature and space than with technology and time, though he has a theory of time and some interest in history. His fascination with nature and space is borne out by his imagery. Could he possibly be described as a closet feminist? As a *tour de force* one might amplify the argument thus, limiting the evidence to the *Rhetoric*. Aristotle speaks of men as physically superior to women in 1.7.4 and as morally superior to women in 1.9.22. In 1.5.6, however, seeking to define "happiness," he stresses that conditions making for happiness apply equally to men and women, and he ends by saying that in societies like the Spartan, where the condition of women is poor, happiness is only half present. Furthermore, the chapters in which the superiority of the male is asserted are laying out the conventional assumptions of Greek society in Aristotle's time, for a public speaker must work with these assumptions to be persuasive. Thus there is more emphasis here on worldly success, and especially on wealth, than is found in Aristotle's ethical writings, and the world of Greek politics was almost totally a man's world, just as it was a world of ambition and rivalry rather than of the intellectual virtue celebrated in the *Nicomachean Ethics*.

Aristotle is here being pragmatic. We might then jump to the claim that however constrained the position of women and the view of their capability, and however chauvinistic the rhetoric of the existing male-dominated society, there exists at a higher and more theoretical level a feminine principle. It can be seen, for example, in the grammatical gender of some basic qualities and institutions. Abstractions in Greek, including the conceptual vocabulary of political life and philosophy, are either feminine or neuter, depending on how they are formed. The names of all the human virtues in *Rhetoric* 1.9 are feminine, as is the vocabulary of civic life: *polis* "city"; *agora* "market"; *boulê,* "council"; *ekklesia* "assembly"; etc. How conscious of grammatical gender were the Greeks? It is clear that from time to time they thought about it, and some of the ironies are humorously played upon by Aristophanes in the *Clouds*, but Aristotle does not speculate on the subject. Other than *topos*, "place," the only important word in the Greek rhetorical vocabulary that is not feminine is the word for speech itself, *logos*. It is thus my modest proposal that Aristotle and the Greeks generally thought of masculine *logos* as working within feminine civic space, the contained and the container.

If one is familiar with the three available translations of Aristotle by Roberts, Cooper, and Freese, one may have noticed how often the word "men" appears in them. In retranslating the *Rhetoric* I have been struck by how rarely Aristotle actually uses the word "man" or "men." He rather prefers indefinites, like *tis, tines* ("some one," "some people"), and when he uses the masculine plural of other words it can be generally taken as not gender-specific. Many words in Greek have a single form for the masculine and feminine and a distinctive form only for the neuter. My new translation is thus considerably less sexist than others now in use. I don't seriously believe Aristotle was a feminist, nor did he share Socrates' and Plato's homosexual orientation, but he clearly did not believe that rhetoric was something available only to men. The whole tradition of Greek epic and drama is set against that and his citation of rhetorical examples from Sappho, from speeches of Antigone in Sophocles' play, and from other women clearly shows that.

Mention of *topos*, which with *logos* is the only masculine word in the basic rhetorical vocabulary of Aristotle, leads me to the problem of rhetorical topics as he discusses them. The problem becomes a pressing one for a translator in a number of passages. Rhys Roberts, in his translation, tried to avoid it by calling the phenomenon "general lines of argument," but one of the reasons for studying the *Rhetoric* is to learn its traditional terminology, of which *topos* is an important instance. Thus the word needs to be present, and when it might be expected and is not there this needs to be noted. Aristotle never gives a formal definition of a *topos*, even though he wrote a treatise in eight books on the subject. He does speak of that work as providing a "method," a road, and there are apparently "places" along the road where arguments are to be found. Clearly, he thinks of arguments visually and assumes that others will understand.

The word *topos* first occurs in the *Rhetoric* toward the end of chapter 2 of book 1, after Aristotle has explained the difference between inductive and deductive arguments, which are in rhetoric the use of paradigm or example, and enthymeme or rhetorical syllogism, respectively. He then says (1358a10) that dialectical and rhetorical syllogisms (that is, enthymemes) involve the use of "topics," and that these can be employed in discussing any subject—ethical, scientific, or political—for they are *koinêi*, "in common," to all. His example is "the topic of the more and the less." As illustrations I suggest something like the following, each of which involves the contrast of the more and the less: "if it is just to punish offenses, it is more just to punish great offenses"; "if a given force will move a certain body, a greater force will also move it"; "if public revenues will support a large army, they will support a smaller army." The phrase "common topics" or "commonplaces" does not occur as such in the *Rhetoric*, but subsequently he speaks again of "topics" as things "in common" to many subjects.[10]

Contrasted to topics are what he calls *idia*, using the neuter plural of the adjective derived form *eidos*, or "species."[11] Each species of subject, such as politics or ethics, has its own "specifics" or "specificities" particular to it. For example, the various kinds of constitution are "specifics" of politics and provide subject matter for the political speaker, but not for the physicist. In the following chapters of book 1, the *idia*, the specificities of the three *eidê* or species of rhetoric—deliberative, epideictic, and judicial—are then taken up in detail. Thus the fundamental *idion*, what we might want to call the "topic," of deliberative rhetoric is "the expedient," of judicial rhetoric "the just." *Eidos*, "species," and its adjective *idia* seem very abstract terms, but in fact to the Greek ear, or eye, they too are visual. *Eidos* is the noun corresponding to the verb *eidon*, which also basically means "see," and an *eidos*, a "species," is what is "seen." English "species," which we tend to think of biologically thanks in large part to Aristotle's usage, comes from Latin *species*, which is also something seen, related to *specto*, "I see." A "species" of something is thus literally the specific, visualized manifestation of the genus or class.

---

10. See *Rhetoric* 1.2.21: "dialectical and rhetorical syllogisms are those in which we state *topoi*, and these are applicable in common [*koinêi*] to questions of justice and physics and politics and many different species [of knowledge]; for example, the *topos* of the more and the less."

11. Again, at *Rhetoric* 1.2.21: "But there are 'specifics' [*idia*, n. pl. of the adj. from *eidos*] that come from the premises of each species and genus [of knowledge]; for example, in physics there are premises from which there is neither an enthymeme nor a syllogism applicable to ethics; and in ethics [there are] others not useful in physics. It is the same in all cases."

The word "topic" does not reappear in the first book of the *Rhetoric* until chapter 15 (1376a32), where it is suddenly used of the *idia* or "specificities" discussed throughout the previous eleven chapters. Aristotle is then silent about "topics" until book 2, chapter 22, when the word again appears and seems as in 1.15 to refer to the *idia*. We are twice told that "topics" are the same as *stoicheia*, "elements," another word that Aristotle has previously used without explanation. The long twenty-third chapter of book 2 then lists twenty-eight strategies of rhetoric, such as argument from the more or less, which are called "topics," though not specifically "common topics." The matter is somewhat further complicated by chapters 20–22 of book 2, which discuss what are first called *koinai pisteis*, or "common proofs," and then just *koina*, "commonalities," which include certain propositions "common" to all three species of rhetoric that had been discussed, but given no name, in chapter 3 of book 1: the possible and impossible, past and future fact, and the "greater" and "smaller," which are in Aristotle's view not the same as the "more" and the "less."

All of this not only sounds confusing, but is. We have in the Greek a series of interrelated but not clearly differentiated terms: *idion, koinon, stoicheion, topos*. Father Grimaldi, in his commentary, does much to sort out their meanings, but this does not really solve the problem for one teaching or working with Aristotle's *Rhetoric*, including a translator who, in the interests of clarity, needs to give some kind of heading to the separate discussions. Later writers—classical, medieval, and modern—often use "topic" in a general sense both of the premises of an argument drawn from the specific subject matter under discussion and of argumentative forms or strategies applicable to many subjects, and they sometimes distinguish between them as "specific" or "particular" topics on the one hand and "common" topics on the other.

Justification for this usage can indeed be found in Aristotle's text, but it is what I would call an after-the-fact justification, made possible by later passing references in the text, not by the terminology actually found in the initial discussion of each category. Even so, this leaves us with the *koina*, those arguments whose premises are "common" to all species of rhetoric— deliberative, epideictic, and judicial—but which are apparently not to be called "topics." These are, again, the possible and the impossible, past and future fact, and magnitude, as exemplified by the "greater" and the "smaller." Specifically, how does the *koinon* of the "greater" and "smaller" differ from the *topos* of the "more" and the "less"? It does not seem to have occurred to Aristotle that someone might confuse them. So far as I can see, the topic of the more and the less always involves a comparison of two things: Aristotle's first example is "if not even the gods know everything, human beings can hardly do so" (1.23.4). Of "greater and smaller" he furnishes no specific example. Indeed, he even says it would be a waste of words to do so (2.19.26), apparently because a detailed discussion of magnitude (*megethos*), a term which suddenly appears as a substitute for "greater and smaller," is really a matter for mathematics or physics. He does say, however, that one should seize opportunities for amplification of magnitude. By analogy with "possible" and "impossible," I conclude that what he means is that just as a speaker will need to consider whether an act alleged to have been done by a defendant in a court of law is possible—for if it is not the defendant is innocent—or whether a policy proposed before an assembly is possible—for if it is not there is no need to consider it—so the speaker needs to consider the magnitude of the action, whether it is of greater or lesser significance. Thus, unlike the topic of "the more and the less," "magnitude" does not necessarily involve a comparison between two actions and provides an opening for amplification of how horrendous or insignificant is the crime, how important or trivial the proposed action of the assembly.

My interest here is not so much in the resolution of Aristotle's terminology as in why these shifts in usage occur. Is it not odd that Aristotle, the inventor of logical and rhetorical terminology and the father of formal definition, can be so seemingly casual about his use of terms? Another instance of this is his shift back and forth between calling deliberative, epideictic, and judicial "genera" and "species" of rhetoric. Surely rhetoric ought to be a genus of which these are species, but that is not his consistent usage.

I think there are two approaches to this question, both of which may have some validity. The first approach is to ask for whom Aristotle writes and what he expects them to understand. There are clear signs of two different audiences envisioned in the *Rhetoric*. The most general way in which interests of these two different audiences clash is seen in the difference between those passages in which Aristotle takes an extremely austere view of rhetoric, seeming to deny that anything other than logical demonstration is appropriate, rejecting especially attempts to play upon the emotions of the audience,[12] and other passages where in great detail he explains how to do this and seems indifferent to any moral implications as he outlines the available means of persuasion.[13] There are a number of inconsistencies especially between the opening chapters of the *Rhetoric* and what follows, inconsistencies that Fr.

---

12. See, e.g., *Rhetoric* 1.1.3–5 and 1.1.9.

13. As at *Rhetoric* 1.2.2, 1.2.5, 2.1.2–3, 2.1.8, etc.

Grimaldi worked hard to resolve in his commentary (however, in conversation with him I did get him to admit that some of the problems can perhaps be explained by considering the audience addressed).

The opening chapters of the *Rhetoric*, the first two at least and possibly the third, seem to me clearly to be addressed to students of philosophy working with Aristotle in a sequence of studies that have progressed from logic to dialectic to rhetoric and will continue with ethics and politics. In the first sentence of the treatise, rhetoric is said to be the *antistrophos* or counterpart of dialectic. By "dialectic" Aristotle means his special understanding of dialectic, which the students have just finished studying. An explanation is given of the ways in which rhetoric is like dialectic, but there is no explanation of what dialectic is or in what way rhetoric differs from it. In fact the differences are considerable, and would have been worth pointing out. Dialectic takes the form of question and answer, rhetoric of a continuous speech. Dialectic deals with universals, rhetoric with particular cases. Dialectic uses only logical argument; rhetoric adds ethical and pathetical means of persuasion. Toward the end of the chapter there is an account of why rhetoric is useful. From the point of view of the typical Greek of the mid-fourth century this is a nonquestion. Of course rhetoric is useful. The real question is why anybody would bother about dialectic, whatever it is. Aristotle is still working within some of the lines of the Platonic tradition, and from that point of view, and that point of view only, there is serious doubt as to whether rhetoric is useful. In these chapters the audience is an objective, academic group focusing a cold eye on still another phenomenon of human life, not to exploit it, but to understand it. Another indication of this in chapter 1 is the digression on the framing of laws, which has most meaning for the philosophical student, least for the public speaker who in most instances must be working within the established laws.

When Aristotle is addressing students of philosophy he tends to be quite precise in his use of words. But rhetoric itself is a practical discipline that works with popular opinions and to be effective needs to avoid logical technicalities. This in fact is the difference between the enthymeme and the syllogism. There is evidence that Aristotle taught courses in public speaking to a general audience in Athens in the 350s B.C.E., before the composition of the *Rhetoric*, and the treatise that we have often reverts to that audience. When it does so, the use of terminology can be expected to become less precise, intended only to provide a general grasp of the theory. Thus, *idia* can at times be called "topics," because they are, sort of, and thus also the frequent recourse to a rather vague neuter plural adjective like *koina*, "commonalities." The general denotation is clear enough for the context and the audience, which wants to speak effectively, not necessarily to explore a theory.

The second approach to the problem, not inconsistent with the first, is to say that inconsistent usages result from the fact that different parts of the work were written at different times. My chief quarrel with Fr. Grimaldi has always been his resolute refusal to consider this. The phenomenon exists as well in other works of Aristotle, who seems to have often gone back to his manuscripts and made additions or revisions in parts but not always in the whole. The most recent edition of the Greek text, that by Rudolf Kassel, "double-brackets" numerous passages in the text that Kassel regards as late additions by Aristotle to the otherwise completed text.[14] Kassel's judgments are rather subjective and one can challenge each passage, but the basic idea is probably valid. In contrast to Aristotle's lost popular, published works, those that we have are evolving treatments of subjects on which he continued to work and lecture.

Scholars have sought to follow out various threads and to reconstruct the development of Aristotle's thought. The most recent to do so is John M. Rist of the University of Toronto in his book *The Mind of Aristotle*.[15] Rist can tell you, primarily on the basis of the philosophical argument and cross-references between the works, when Aristotle wrote what. He makes quite a plausible case and certainly evidences great familiarity with all the texts. My one general criticism is that he, like others who have worked on this matter, fail to take account of what might be called the "rhetoric" of the individual treatises, including Aristotle's conception of his audience at different times, his use of metaphor, and the different notes of objectivity or passionate concern visible in his work at different times. Particularly in the vexed question of the relationship between the *Eudemian Ethics* and the *Nicomachean Ethics,* this needs to be examined. The *Eudemian Ethics*, which Rist regards as the earlier work, reverting to the view of Jaeger and reversing that of Kenny (rightly in my view), is the objective, dispassionate treatment for the student of philosophy. The *Nicomachean Ethics* has a note of passion: we must not only understand the good, we must do it. It reflects not just a different stage in his thought, but a different audience and different historical situation, very likely back in Athens toward the end of his life.

As to the *Rhetoric*, Rist's view is that the treatise as we have it was revised into substantially its present form about 333 B.C.E., the year after Aristotle returned to Athens from Macedon and opened his school there in the

---

14. Rudolf Kassel, *Aristotelis "Ars Rhetorica"* (Berlin: De Gruyter, 1976).

15. John M. Rist, *The Mind of Aristotle: A Study in Philosophical Growth* (Toronto: University of Toronto Press, 1989).

Lyceum. Rist apparently thinks that much of the treatise was actually written at that time, but it does incorporate, in chapters 5–15 of book 1 (that is, the account of deliberative, epideictic, and judicial rhetoric and their *idia*), material that he would date about 353. The argument for this is based on three factors: first, the relationship of philosophical ideas in the treatise, especially in book 2 on ethics and politics, to those in other works that Rist has tried to show reflect Aristotle's thinking at this time, and conversely the lack of consistency with views that on other grounds Rist thinks Aristotle developed later; second, the cross-references to other works that, in the network of development, Rist sees as slightly earlier, or conversely the lack of cross-references to works that Rist regards as composed later; and third, the historical references, quite numerous in the *Rhetoric*, of which none are later than the period assigned to composition. The discussion of deliberative, epideictic, and judicial rhetoric in chapters 5–15 of book 1 accords with what Rist regards as an early stage of Aristotle's political and ethical thought. They lack cross-references to the *Topics*, and their latest historical references are to events of the 350s B.C.E.

Taking the *Rhetoric* as a whole, and thus the treatise as Aristotle finally left it, the last datable reference is usually thought to be the mention of the "Common Peace" in 2.23.18, which may well be to the Peace of 336 B.C.E., and references to events later than the 340s are all to be found in the same chapter, which I should point out is the chapter listing "topics." This suggests that the reason why Aristotle does not call *idia* "topics" in 1.5–15 and yet later does so refer to them is that he had not yet developed the concept.

We know that Aristotle taught rhetoric in some form during his first period in Athens, and apparently in the 350s. The *Rhetoric* still contains more historical references to events of that period and earlier than to later events. After 347 and Plato's death, he left Athens and went to Asia Minor and Lesbos for about five years, where he engaged in much of his scientific work in biology. If one asks when, subsequently, Aristotle's interests might have turned back to rhetoric and when he perceived an audience for such thoughts, there are two attractive possibilities. Rist opts for the second of these, soon after the return to Athens, the home of rhetoric, about 333, and he would date the completion of the *Poetics*, with its focus on Athenian drama, to the same period. An argument for this might be that Aristotle chose two rather popular subjects to work on, and thus presumably to lecture on, as he opened his new school and attracted new students. He then turned to much more difficult philosophical subjects, especially metaphysics and ethics. This is certainly a possible scenario.

The other time when Aristotle's attention was certainly drawn to rhetoric and poetics would be in the late 340s when he was the tutor in Macedon of the boy who became Alexander the Great. Alexander was then a young teenager and, given Greek ideas of education, what he would certainly have studied would have been literature and public speaking. Biographies of Alexander preserve reference to his studying rhetoric with Aristotle, even in one case (Quintus Curtius) a story that Alexander ordered Aristotle not to publish his lectures on the subject because he did not want the art known generally. This is probably part of the elaborate series of myths that were built up in later times around the association of the two men, but one person who clearly did object to the way Alexander was being taught was Isocrates. In a letter to the young Alexander, which was enclosed in a letter to his father Philip, Isocrates criticizes Alexander's teachers as likely to mislead him, and gives a brief account of the kind of study of rhetoric he would recommend. Moreover, in *Panathenaicus* (16) in 339 Isocrates complains about people who quoted his published works as models, which Aristotle did in the *Rhetoric*, but continued to say disparaging things about him. Isocrates had friends in Macedon and knew what was going on there. This suggests to me that much of the work on the *Rhetoric*, with its latest historical references (except in chapter 23 of book 2) to events of the 340s, may have been well underway some years before Aristotle returned to Athens and that the impulse for writing it up may have been his teaching of Alexander. Though the young prince would not plead in the Athenian lawcourts, he needed to understand what went on there and in other Greek states, and would have much occasion to make speeches and hear those of others. He needed to understand the art. There are even a few passages that sound as though they were especially included because of their potential interest to Alexander. When one reads the treatise, one should keep that possibility in mind.

If this is right, Aristotle wrote much of the *Rhetoric* between the late 340s and 336, which would still account for its latest historical references. We do not know very much about his activities in these years; he was perhaps living in his home town of Stagira, had a few associates working with him, but no established school, and was at greater leisure than at most other times in his career. It was a good time for him to finish off some of his projects. After 338, when the Greek cites were defeated by Macedon, his prospects for returning to Athens improved and he may have anticipated that event by preparing lectures. If he actually lectured on rhetoric in Athens after 335 it seems likely that there would be some contemporary references to that period, given his earlier custom of incorporating such references. The treatise, of course, was a part of his library and available for study by any interested student. It is through these students and not through publication that the *Rhetoric* influenced understanding of the subject for the next three hundred years. The form in which the treatise was left incorporates his more popular teaching, but it is revised for presentation to the student of philosophy.

Rist takes no account of the widely accepted view that book 3, on style and arrangement, was originally a separate work. The list of Aristotle's writings given by Diogenes Laertius (5.24) contains an *Art of Rhetoric* in two books and a separate treatise, *On Style*. The usual view has been that Andronicus, the first-century–B.C.E. editor of Aristotle, combined them into the *Rhetoric* as we know it. The latest datable reference in book 3 seems to be to phrases of Isocrates' *Philippus*, published in 346 B.C.E. (3.11.2 and 8).

There is a somewhat tantalizing passage at the end of book 2, chapter 14, that just might have something to do with the date of composition of the *Rhetoric*. Aristotle is discussing the *êthos* or character of those in the prime of life, and he says that the body is in its prime at the age of thirty to thirty-five—which, incidentally, would have been his age when he first taught rhetoric in Athens—and the mind at about age forty-nine. This probably does reflect a concept of the "ages of man," based on a life expectancy of 70 years divided into ten seven-year stages. The mind is then thought to be at its peak at the end of the sixth and beginning of the seventh stage. Since Aristotle does not specify ages for the end of youth or the onset of old age, there is no particular reason why he needs to specify the peak of maturity. The fact is, however, that when he returned to Athens in 335 he himself was 49 years old. Is he more likely to have specified the age of mental maturity as he himself approached it, or if that was in fact his age when he was writing, or as he had passed the climacteric? There are occasional touches of wry humor in Aristotle's writings. (His birthday probably fell in the first half of the year, to judge from the computation of the date of his first arrival in Athens. I do not know when the academic year was thought to begin in this period, but by Roman times it began in the fall, about the first of October.)

These matters remain hypotheses, and perhaps they are of more interest to the classicist than to the student of rhetorical theory, but the question of the audience is a factor that needs to be taken into account in interpreting the work. In a sense, the audience is a universal one, for Aristotle seeks to make definitions in universal terms. For example, the hearer is either a judge or a spectator. If he is a judge, he is judging events of the past or of the future: thus judicial, deliberative, and epideictic rhetoric. Many features of the treatise, including these, "work" when applied to rhetoric in vastly different cultures. But Aristotle naturally worked with the evidence as he knew it, and many features are specific to Greek culture. This is true, for example, of epideictic, where his definition needs expansion and restatement.

Perhaps the most conspicuous lack in the *Rhetoric*, given Aristotle's own conception of the subject, is its failure to take account of the role in rhetoric of the authority and prestige of the speaker. Aristotle, of course, allows an important role for *êthos* or character, but he limits that to the moral character of the speaker as revealed in what is said in a speech. What he is thinking about is the situation of an otherwise unknown person involved in a court trial who needs to make a favorable impression on a jury, and who could in Greece buy a speech from a logographer. The speeches that Lysias wrote for clients are particularly famous for their attractive presentation of the speaker's character, even in the case of some rather dubious characters. Aristotle does allow for what he calls nonartistic or atechnic means of persuasion, but these are restricted to matters of evidence, such as witnesses and contracts, that are not "invented" (or are not supposed to be) by the speaker, who nevertheless "uses" them. But if a speaker is a well-known person—an Aristides, a Pericles, a Socrates; or a priest, a prophet, a saint, or a seer—that person brings to the speech occasion an already existing persona that is part of the rhetorical situation. Cicero certainly knew this and exploited it, and in nonclassical rhetoric it is often the single greatest factor in the persuasion of an audience, to the extent that such a speaker can often dispense with logical argument and content himself with authoritative proclamation. In any reworking of rhetoric, this factor needs to be taken into account.

Finally, Aristotle's *Rhetoric* articulates a theory of civic discourse, and what he has to say about language is something of an afterthought, something used to attain clarity or charm in civic situations. Modern theories of rhetoric are in large part dependent on a theory of language as a system of signs. It is, in the final analysis, the energy inherent in words that creates the power in larger units of speech. Thus, a reworking of rhetoric might reasonably move in the opposite direction from Aristotle's treatise, beginning not with dialectic, but with an account of sounds and signs, moving to their composition in sentences, with consideration of metaphor and other tropes and figures, and then to the form into which speeches are cast, their civic or other contexts and occasions, and the role of the speaker and audience. In other works Aristotle sometimes does follow this pattern of moving from the smallest to the larger units,[16] and rhetoricians of the early modern period perceived the advantages of such a progression. It is already found in Bernard Lamy's seventeenth-century treatise, *The Art of Speaking,* and in eighteenth-century British successors like the lectures on rhetoric of Adam Smith. Such an ap-

----

16. E.g., in *Politics* 1 and 3 and in *On Interpretation.*

proach is especially attractive today as a way of synthesizing the diverse notions of rhetoric existing among traditional rhetoricians, linguistics, and post-structuralist literary critics. I am more optimistic than Brian Vickers, in his recent *Defence of Rhetoric*,[17] about a new synthesis of communication under the venerable arch-discipline of rhetoric.

Actually, if I were to write a new "rhetoric," I would start with something even more fundamental than the nature of language. The ultimate origins of rhetoric, it seems to me, lie in the instinct for self-preservation and survival of the genetic line.[18] Even in animals without speech there exists a form of rhetoric of intimidation or appeasement. The impulse to speak, whether to cry out a warning, to intimidate a threatening figure, or to appease a god, is extended in human society into a desire to control or at least influence the course of events in the interests of the individual, the family, or the social unit. The impulse for self-preservation is clearly present in that form of rhetoric known as judicial or forensic, for this is the speech of apology or self-defense in the law courts as well as the prosecution of others threatening the individual or society. The impulse to rhetoric is related to aggression and domination, but also to pacification and maintenance of order, which are also forms of self-preservation. Thus it finds expression in what is called "deliberative rhetoric," the debate of councils and assemblies or even of family groups. A further extension of it is found in the potentiality of words to give a limited immortality and to defeat death. Aristotle thought that the origins of literature were to be found in praise and blame; thus, epic poetry and the beginnings of historiography are concerned with ensuring the survival of knowledge of the great deeds of the past and of those who did them, or knowledge of the great sins and sinners of the past, like Tantalus, as a warning. From this comes both poetry and that form of rhetoric known as epideictic. Aristotle's distinction of three and only three species of rhetoric—judicial, epideictic, and deliberative—is universally valid, but its ultimate source lies in biological necessity.

That I have expressed some criticisms of Aristotle is no lack of respect for him. He himself argues for the evolution of the disciplines of knowledge, his own works show development over time, and the characteristic spirit of Aristotelianism, as opposed to more dogmatic philosophical movements, is

---

17. Brian Vickers, *In Defence of Rhetoric* (New York: Oxford University Press, 1988), pp. 435–79.

18. See George A. Kennedy, "A Hoot in the Dark: The Evolution of General Rhetoric," *Philosophy and Rhetoric* 25 (1992): 1–21.

one of process as facts and insights are further worked out within a network of speculation and practical applications, including the needs of different audiences. That Aristotle's *Rhetoric* shows signs of this process in its composition is thus not just a philological curiosity, but an aspect of the nature of the subject as he saw it. I thus can end with the hope that the reader too will continue the reworking of Aristotle's *Rhetoric* in the spirit in which he began it.

ABOUT THE CONTRIBUTORS

Christopher Lyle Johnstone (editor) is Associate Professor of Speech Communication at the Pennsylvania State University. His Ph.D. in Communication Arts (1976) is from the University of Wisconsin, Madison. He has served as editor of the *Pennsylvania Speech Communication Annual* (1981–83) and as Associate Editor of *Communication Quarterly* (1981–90, 1993–present), and is presently on the editorial boards of *Philosophy and Rhetoric* and *The Southern Communication Journal*. Professor Johnstone was the 1988 recipient of the Eastern Communication Association's Past Presidents Award for outstanding scholarship and has twice been appointed Senior Associate Member at the American School of Classical Studies in Athens (1987 and 1991). His articles and reviews have appeared in the *Quarterly Journal of Speech,* the *Western Journal of Speech Communication*, the *Central States Speech Journal*, the *Southern Communication Journal, Communication Quarterly*, *Philosophy and Rhetoric*, and other journals. Johnstone's research has dealt with rhetoric and ethics, the relationship between speech and wisdom, and the analysis of rhetorical texts.

William W. Fortenbaugh, Professor of Classics at Rutgers University, has A. B. degrees from Princeton University and New College, Oxford, and a Ph.D. from the University of Pennsylvania (1964). A specialist in Aristotle and in Greek rhetoric generally, Fortenbaugh has published widely on Aristotle's philosophy and its bearing on his view of rhetoric, and on such other rhetoricians as Theophrastus and Cicero. The author of two books, including *Aristotle on Emotion* (1975), he has edited four others and has published over thirty-five scholarly articles in such journals as *Classical Philology, Phronesis, Philosophy and Rhetoric*, and the *American Journal of Philology*. Professor Fortenbaugh has received numerous academic honors and awards, including Phi Beta Kappa, an American Council of Learned Societies Fellowship, and a number of grants from the National Endowment for the Humanities. He currently serves on several editorial boards, including *Rhetorica* and *Philosophy and Rhetoric*.

William M. A. Grimaldi, S. J. was Professor and then Professor Emeritus of Classics at Fordham University until his death in 1991. He received his Ph.D. from Princeton University in 1955. Father Grimaldi had an international reputation as an expert on Aristotle's *Rhetoric*. His books include *Studies in the Philosophy of Aristotle's Rhetoric* (1972), *Aristotle, Rhetoric I: A Commentary* (1980), and *Aristotle, Rhetoric II: A Commentary* (1988). His numerous scholarly essays have appeared in such journals as the *American Journal of Philology*, *Classical Philology*, and *Philosophy and Rhetoric*, and his work has been cited in the research literature of classical rhetoric in the *Quarterly Journal of Speech* and *Speech Monographs*. Among the awards Father Grimaldi received are a Fulbright Fellowship in archaeology to the American School of Classical Studies in Athens (1953–54), Visiting Fellow/ Scholar appointments in Classics at Princeton (1968–69, 1974–75, 1980–81) and Stanford (1981) Universities, and a National Endowment for the Humanities Senior Fellowship (1981).

George A. Kennedy, Paddison Professor Emeritus of Classics at the University of North Carolina, received his Ph.D. from Harvard University in 1954. Before going to Chapel Hill in 1966, Professor Kennedy taught at Harvard, Haverford College, and the University of Pittsburgh. Internationally recognized as an authority on ancient rhetoric, he is the author of several books, including *The Art of Persuasion in Greece* (1963), *The Art of Rhetoric in the Roman World* (1972), *Classical Rhetoric and Its Christian and Secular Tradition* (1980), *Greek Rhetoric Under Christian Emperors* (1983), *New Testament Interpretation through Rhetorical Criticism* (1984), *Aristotle, On Rhetoric: A Theory of Civic Discourse* (1991), and *A New History of Classical Rhetoric* (1994), as well as of numerous articles and reviews. He has been a Guggenheim Fellow, a Fulbright Fellow, and a Fellow of the American Academy of Arts and Sciences. His many honors include the Speech Communication Association's Golden Anniversary Award (twice) and the American Philological Association's Goodwin Award of Merit.

Michael C. Leff (Ph.D. University of California at Los Angeles, 1972) is Professor of Communication Studies at Northwestern University. He has taught at the University of California at Davis, Indiana University, and the University of Wisconsin, Madison. A specialist in Greek and Roman rhetorical theory and oratory, Professor Leff has published widely on Cicero, Boethius, and the legacy of rhetoric and humanism. His research interests include rhetorical criticism, writing across disciplines, and ancient and contemporary rhetorical theory. In 1983 he was the recipient of the Speech Communication Association's Award for Distinguished Scholarship in Rhetoric and Public Address, and in 1985 of the Association's Charles H. Woolbert Memorial Research Award. He has served as editor of *Rhetorica* and as an editorial board member of *Philosophy and Rhetoric*.

Donovan J. Ochs received his Ph.D. from the University of Iowa in 1966 and was Professor of Communication Studies and Rhetoric at that institution from 1967 until his retirement in 1995. Prior to that, he taught in the Department of Rhetoric at the University of California at Davis (1964–67), and he has served as Visiting Professor at the University of Illinois (1968) and at Santa Rosa Junior College (1974–75). He served for twelve years (1972–84) as the Coordinator of the Rhetoric Program at Iowa. While his research includes work in broad areas of rhetorical theory and criticism, Professor Ochs has made particularly important contributions to the literature on classical Greek and Roman public address, most especially in studies of Demosthenes, Lysias, and Cicero. He has authored, coauthored, or edited eight books, and his numerous articles have appeared in such journals as the *Speech Teacher*, *Speech Monographs*, *Rhetoric Society Quarterly*, and the *Central States Speech Journal*.

John Poulakos (Ph.D. University of Kansas, 1979) is Associate Professor in the Department of Speech Communication at the University of Pittsburgh. Prior to his arrival at Pitt in 1985, he was on the faculty of The Pennsylvania State University and held visiting faculty positions at the universities of Georgia and Arkansas. A specialist in the rhetoric of the Sophists, Professor Poulakos has published articles in such journals as the *Western Journal of Speech Communication*, *Philosophy and Rhetoric*, *Rhetorica*, the *Southern Speech Communication Journal*, and *Communication Monographs*, and he recently completed *Sophistical Rhetoric in Classical Greece* (1995). He has received numerous awards for his research and teaching, including grants from the University of Kansas, the National Endowment for the Humanities, and the American Council of Learned Societies, and he was the recipient in 1985 of the Speech Communication Association's Karl R. Wallace Award.

Edward Schiappa, who received his Ph.D. from Northwestern University in 1989, was Associate Professor of Communication at Purdue University until his 1995 move to the University of Minnesota. From 1985 to 1990 he was Director of Debate at Kansas State University, during which time he established the program as one of the top-ranked debate teams in the National

Cross-Examination Debate Association. His essays on classical and contemporary rhetoric and argumentation theory have appeared in the *American Journal of Philology, Rhetoric Review*, the *Quarterly Journal of Speech, Philosophy and Rhetoric,* and *Communication Monographs*. He is author of *Protagoras and Logos: A Study in Greek Philosophy and Rhetoric* (1991). His was a recipient in 1989 of the Speech Communication Association Outstanding Doctoral Dissertation Award.

INDEX OF AUTHORS' NAMES, TITLES OF ANCIENT WORKS, AND KEY TERMS